The Coach's Casebook

GEOFF WATTS AND KIM MORGAN

THE COACH'S CASEBOOK

Mastering the twelve traits that trap us

Published February 2015

www.thecoachscasebook.com

Edited by Xanthe Wells and Robin Bradshaw
Design by Ole H. Størksen
Printed by Printech Solutions

First edition Published 2015 by Inspect & Adapt Ltd
96 Redgrove Park, Cheltenham, Glos, GL51 6QZ
United Kingdom

ISBN 978-0-9575874-4-1

TABLE OF CONTENTS

Chapter Twelve: Dealing With Loss

FOREWORD

If you are reading this, then, like me, you are probably a coach in one guise or another. By a coach, I mean someone who:

- Has a natural desire to help others grow and develop, to become the best they can be.

- Is willing to help someone by listening to them, challenging their thinking and encouraging action.

- Sustains commitment to someone's true potential and goals, even perhaps when their own self-belief falters.

Like characters in a movie, coaches come in different guises. Perhaps you're a proper, professional, 'out there and practising' coach who makes part or all of their income from that. Or maybe you are more covert about your coaching identity, e.g. 'I'm still learning' or 'I'm wondering about it', or even 'I'm hiding in the wings.' Either way, between you and I, let's assume you're a coach, of some kind.

OK, so as you agree (or admit!) you are a coach, you also enter into a reciprocal bargain with the natural laws of our profession. It is a bargain that, if left unpaid, creates an imbalance in your coaching for others. That is, to help others grow and develop by challenging their thinking and encouraging them beyond false self-limits, these ideas must also be consistent themes within your own life. This means that before you can effectively coach anyone with integrity, you must be willing to engage in your own personal and professional development.

This book is a refreshing change in the way we might first coach our-selves, in order to better coach others. Literally the themes described, such as people pleasing, perfectionism and procrastination resonate first within our own tendencies, which is where the opportunity for self-work arises. Fortunately as well as describing these themes in entertaining ways, Kim and Geoff also provide simple ideas for making healthy progress where that is required. So as readers we are given the opportunity to learn useful, simple ideas, practice with those a little, before harnessing our learning within our work with others.

My encouragement for you as a reader, is to put aside notions of 'being a coach' and revert back to our generic title of human being. Then, as a human being, allow yourself to wander through the stories and ideas offered and see what 'sticks'. Flip forward, flip backward and notice what you notice. Try some of the routines and exercises, and encourage yourself to stay with those even when things feel uncomfortable or more difficult than you might enjoy. Harness the same sense of purpose and commitment to results that you might when coaching someone else, and employ the same encouragement, compassion and generous nature that flows naturally with those you love.

For me the true gift of this book is that as readers we first have the opportunity to receive, in the form of progressing our own development and maturity. Then in doing so, we increase our ability to coach others; literally a heightened awareness of common coaching themes and needs, plus insight and flexibility in terms of what we might do in response to those. So we read, we put in effort and we reap rewards – all of which enable us to contribute more effectively to others.

Enjoy the book, and I hope it supports the work that you do.

Julie Starr
Author of The Coaching Manual, Brilliant Coaching,
The Mentoring Manual and From Magic to Memphis.

INTRODUCTION

In this book we share stories from our coaching practice. We look at a number of presenting issues which coaches will encounter again and again. Each chapter tells the story, describes what the coach did, and discusses what tools and techniques might be most helpful in relation to each presenting issue. We look at what we learned about our clients and about ourselves as coaches; because coaches are human and susceptible to these behaviours themselves, we also describe how supervision plays a key role in enabling the coach to be a more effective helper.

The book is grounded in many years of real experience and is intended to be of practical use to anyone who is involved in or interested in coaching either as a coach or as a client, or indeed to anyone who is interested in human behaviour.

The presenting issues which we examine in this book are:

- Impostor Syndrome

- People Pleasing

- Going to Excess

- Fierce Independence

- Cynicism

- Driven by Fear

- Ostrich Syndrome

- Perfectionism

- Procrastination

- Performance Anxiety

- Searching for Fulfilment

- Coping with Loss

We believe that most people will identify with one or more of the behaviours in this list. If you are a coach, you will probably have come across them in your work with clients. This book is intended to help you understand these behaviours better and to offer suggestions as to how those behaviours may be changed in a positive way.

Traits and Traps

All of these behaviours are capable of becoming problematic and obstructive in our lives. Our clients will often seek help because these behaviours have become a 'trap' for them, a set of repeating, inhibiting and sometimes destructive behaviours from which they are struggling to escape. However, our clients' stories tell us that each of these potentially problematic behaviours may also be useful, and indeed may have contributed greatly to an individual's achieving success in the world. It appears to us that in each case there is a spectrum, that aspects of the same behaviours may be a hindrance or may be useful. We therefore use the word 'trait' to refer to such behaviours – by which we mean a characteristic behaviour which may not necessarily be inherently harmful and which, most importantly, is capable of being modified and changed. We believe that as coaches we are not seeking to eliminate such behaviours, but to enable individuals to understand and manage these behaviours better so that they can achieve a healthy balance.

Traits may be either overdone or underdone. The trait which we describe as 'people pleasing' is an example. It is potentially valuable for an individual to be able to take account of the feelings and interests of others, which can enable the building of effective and mutually rewarding relationships, professional and personal. If the trait is wholly absent and a person is incapable of recognising or taking account of the feelings of others, it is easy to see that this could be highly problematic for the individual and for society. However, if the trait is overdone and a person is always putting the feelings and needs of others before their own to the extent that they become incapable of expressing or asserting their own feelings or needs, this trait can become a trap.

In each chapter of this book the coach is working to help the client manage their traits. We use coaching to bring our clients' qualities and potential strengths into a constructive balance. In each chapter you will find a wide variety of tools and techniques which we suggest may be useful in relation to that particular trait. However, the essential elements of our approach are the same in every case. In each case the coach's objectives are:

- To understand and identify the root cause of the behaviour.

- To enable the client to acknowledge how the overuse of this trait is impacting upon the client and upon others.

- To enable the client to pay attention to other traits which are being underused.

We have included in this book a chapter on Coping with Loss. This is an issue which we all have to face as human beings and which will be a presenting issue for every coach at some stage in their career. We felt that this issue is so universal and important that it should be acknowledged within this book. It is not a presenting behaviour or trait in the same way as the others in this book. However, we believe that many of the learnings and principles regarding human behaviour set out in the book may be helpful when addressing the difficult question of how to cope with loss.

Getting the Best from This Book

You can read this book from cover to cover or you may choose to dip into a particular chapter to focus on a specific trait as it presents with your clients. Either way, we hope that you will want to add this casebook to your coaching toolkit and continue to use it to further your own development as well as that of your clients.

To provide an in-depth look at each trait, every chapter is divided into three parts:

Part One – The Coach's Casebook

The first part of each chapter presents a case study of an individual client. Although none of the case studies is based on an individual, all the case studies have a strong basis in reality and contain our own experiences of coaching combined into the singular viewpoint of 'the coach'.

Part Two - Tools and Techniques

Each case study describes the tools, techniques and approaches we used during the coaching sessions. These are embedded in the story and we hope that you will notice the many ways in which we work with the client to create some mobility in their thinking and behaviour.

Part Two builds on the techniques used in the case study and provides some additional approaches for working with this trait or trap and includes additional information with some powerful coaching questions to use. Our intention is to assist you in selecting which approach to use and when, whilst also giving you the confidence to apply them in different situations.

While we have selected three techniques for each chapter, many techniques in this book are applicable in many situations. At the end of the book is a matrix that maps which techniques can be useful for each of the traits. You can also use this matrix as a reference to locate specific techniques within the book.

We are not advocating that coaches should use the same techniques as we have used with each trait. Our approaches are merely suggested ways of working and we appreciate that every coaching client is unique and every coach will decide which approach to take depending on the client, the context and a number of other variables.

Part Three - The Interview

The final part of each chapter includes an interview with a successful and inspirational person who has generously agreed to share their story. As each of their stories unfolded, it became clear that they all have ways of managing their particular traits. We didn't seek out people who had difficult childhoods or who had been dealt a particularly bad hand in life. Almost all of the stories we heard in our interviews were a complete surprise to us (and some of them were even a surprise to our interviewees). In fact, the traits they have are so common that many of the interviewees said that they could have fitted in a number of the chapters.

Our Philosophy – 'Beware the man of one book'

We adopt an eclectic approach to coaching, employing approaches from different schools of thought across the worlds of coaching, personal development and psychology. For example, we use elements of Neuro Linguistic Programming, yet there may also be approaches that contradict or challenge some of NLP's tenets. You will notice applications of traditional Freudian or Jungian psychology alongside more modern models such as The Growth Mindset or Mindfulness. Our objective is not to align ourselves with the 'best model' or even create one ourselves, but rather to give you what we have found to be helpful in our practice.

We also strongly believe in the value of coaching supervision.

Supervision – A Coach's Greatest Tool

In each case study, we include a section referring to the coach's reflections either during or after supervision. We believe that supervision is an essential element to effective coaching, enabling both the integrity of the coaching process and the self-development of the coach.

If your role involves helping others to be more effective, whether you are a team leader who coaches, an internal coach or a freelance coach, then having a trained coaching supervisor is indispensable to your development. A supervisor is someone who can help you work through your thought processes, develop your coaching capability, challenge your limiting beliefs and assumptions, and champion you when you need it. We believe that supervision is critical to your development and its purpose is to:

- Develop your coaching skills through the engagement of an experienced practitioner.

- Work through any ethical issues on a confidential basis.

- Maintain an approach of continuous learning, development and self-reflection.

- Gain greater awareness of your own 'hot spots' – things that reduce your effectiveness as a coach.

- Explore options, new ideas and perspectives.

While there are many forms of coaching supervision, the most common format is the one-on-one, formal engagement of a qualified coaching supervisor. Qualified coaching supervisors also run small supervision groups where the same group of coaches meet regularly to review and reflect on their practice under the guidance of the supervisor. Supervision accreditation is still relatively new in the coaching industry but in other similar fields – such as therapy – it is not only well established but mandatory.

We believe that the supervision elements in the following chapters give you an insight into how we, as coaches, dealt with the situations that we faced. They also serve as examples of how coaches think, operate and gain value from the process of supervision.

Break free from your traps

Normalisation is an essential part of the process of change and one of the powerful moments in a session is when our clients realise they are not the only ones struggling with a particular issue, but that it is common. As coaches, we are in a privileged position to be invited into the inner world of our clients and to help them recognise and maximise their strengths while minimising their limiting behaviours. We hope this book is useful to you as you also work to help people master the traits that can trap them.

CHAPTER ONE

Impostor Syndrome

'Of all the judgements we pass in life,
none is more important than the judgement
we pass on ourselves.'

NATHANIEL BRANDEN

THE CASE STUDY

'Everyone else is better than me. I am not as good
as people think I am and I am going to get found out.'

'I feel like I am being left on the shelf professionally. Year after year, I'm overlooked for promotion as younger, smarter lawyers overtake me. I'm one of the longest-serving lawyers in the firm but I'm starting to think that I may never get invited to become partner.'

Jenny came to me after hearing my talk on the topic of 'Impostor Syndrome': the feeling that we are not as good as others think and that we will be found out. During the coffee break, Jenny sought me out, declaring 'I couldn't believe it – you were talking about me in your keynote address!' In fact, she initially thought I was literally talking about her and that someone had told me her story. When I assured her that many people feel this way but that the subject of my presentation was actually a composite fictional character, she experienced an immediate sense of relief. After finding out how coaching could help, Jenny engaged me as her coach on the spot.

She was aspiring to be a partner in a leading law firm and wanted coaching to help her get there. In our introductory chat, Jenny had impressed me with her career as a criminal lawyer but her Impostor Syndrome was so strong that, by the end of our first session, I was actually beginning to wonder not just how she held down the job, but how she had got the job in the first place!

In my job as coach I see part of my remit as building the confidence of my clients and helping them achieve their goals. The fact that I doubted Jenny's ability wasn't a great starting point for me and I felt uncomfortable having judgemental and uncharitable feelings towards her. This sat uneasily with one of my coaching mantras:

'Treat a man as he is and we make him less than he is.
Treat a man as though he already were what he potentially could be
and we make him what he should be'

GOETHE

However worrying this was for me professionally, I consoled myself with the assumption that how Jenny made me feel was a good barometer for how she made other people feel. In this case I noticed that I was in danger of losing respect for Jenny and believing that she was not very good at her job.

Most people have very strong 'life scripts' which determine what they say and how they behave and which elicit strong responses from people around them. As someone prone to feelings of Impostor Syndrome, Jenny was effectively telling herself:

'Everyone else is better than me. I am not as good as people think
I am and I am going to get found out'

This underlying belief led her to magnify her failings, discount her achievements, and focus a lot more on what she couldn't do than what she could do. In short, people with Impostor Syndrome tend to be harder on themselves than they deserve and more generous in their views of others.

The classic symptoms of Impostor Syndrome are:

- Having an inability to internalise your accomplishments.

- Feeling that other people have an overinflated view of you.

- Attributing any success you have to luck or just being in the right place at the right time.

- Being fearful of being 'found out'.

- Feeling like a fraud.

- Believing that the very fact that you got the job/do this work means that it can't be that difficult. Your ability to do something negates the value of it.

- Looking more at what you can't do, rather than valuing what you can do.

In all the years that I have worked as a coach, I seldom meet clients who do not experience a bit of Impostor Syndrome. Clinical psychologists Pauline Clance and Suzanne Imes *[Ref 1]* formulated the concept in 1978 to describe the set of feelings and responses they found to be particularly common in successful women (although my empirical evidence suggests that it is just as rife in men). In fact it has been claimed that up to 70% of people suffer from Impostor Syndrome at some point *[Ref 2]* and, although very difficult to prove, that statistic certainly seems to line up with my own coaching practice.

People experiencing Impostor Syndrome tend to have bouts of very high stress because they are never comfortable with their position or performance.

This syndrome is, therefore, very closely linked to perfectionism *[See Chapter 8]*. An impostor is so concerned about their imperfections that 'good enough' is never 'good enough' for them. They often push themselves further to compensate for their insecurity, which is one of the reasons that they are so successful. Of course, because their feelings inspire extreme conscientiousness and greater effort, this usually results in even more success, which in turn results in even greater feelings of being an impostor!

Over the course of our first session, as she got more into her story and the emotions became stronger, I noticed that Jenny began using more extreme language. She started catastrophising and over-dramatising her situation. Phrases such as '*everyone* is better than me' and 'I know I'm *completely* not up to the job' began creeping in. This was frustrating and a little painful for me to hear because, as an objective observer, I knew these statements to be untrue.

Jenny, however, seemed to reach a point where she truly believed them.

Jenny was so resistant to seeing any good in herself that I found myself adopting an increasingly scattergun approach as I became desperate to get some kind of breakthrough. I tried all of the following coaching interventions, which are designed to redirect a client's attention to positive aspects of themselves and see themselves from a fresh perspective:

- Inviting her to give me a list of her strengths and qualities.

- Telling her how I considered her to be a successful and competent woman and giving her positive feedback.

- Asking her to remember peak moments in her career when she had enjoyed great success and how they had come about.

- Asking her to tell me about the positive feedback she had received from others in her career.

- Inviting her to 'change places' with her boss and speak from his perspective to explain why he had hired Jenny.

I drew a blank with all these coaching interventions and, by the end of the first session, realised that I was in the presence of one of the strongest cases of Impostor Syndrome I had ever encountered. Jenny unconsciously distorted all her answers to make them fit her life script. I was completely disheartened when Jenny walked away from the session without the slightest shift in her thinking. I was looking forward to a session with my coaching supervisor before I saw her again.

Supervision

The chance to talk through my situation with my supervisor was incredibly challenging and useful. Having a strong and trusting relationship with my supervisor allows him to ask provocative questions in order to change my perspective and give me different lenses through which to look at the situation.

After I had described Jenny's session, the first question that he asked me was 'Why are you in such a hurry?' Brilliant! I regularly tell people that coaching is not a quick fix; very little change happens in the first session and it can take months, or even years, for some of our life scripts to be rewritten to the extent that we desire. In Jenny's case, she had spent 35 years developing and reinforcing her life script and associated behaviours. Why would she change after spending a couple of hours with someone she had barely met?

Why would she trust me straight away? Good relationships – like the one between my supervisor and me – take time to develop. If he had asked me provocative questions in our first session, I think I would have run a mile... or at least become very defensive. Jenny needed to trust that I was congruent and authentic before she could believe my feedback. However, I did believe that, once really good trust was established in our coaching relationship, then a provocative approach could potentially work well.

I also realised that I had fallen into two traps myself. Firstly, I had tried to rescue Jenny and 'force' her to see herself through my eyes. Secondly, I was aware that Jenny's actions were having an impact on my perceptions because I had started to believe that she might be right about herself.

We all develop a number of unconscious behaviour patterns or 'games' to support our life script.

Transactional Analysis creator, Eric Berne, suggests that these 'games' serve to maintain our life position by 'proving' that we are right about ourselves, so creating a self-fulfilling prophecy *[Ref 3]*.

As coaches, we can easily become conditioned by our client's 'game' in seemingly innocuous ways and, just as it is important to notice how you feel when you are with your clients, it is also important to notice how their actions can surreptitiously affect your perceptions and behaviour. For example, imagine seeing a beautifully presented woman at a social event and admiring her appearance and sense of style. On meeting her, she points out a small stain on her jacket and constantly touches it, apologising for it, explaining how it got there and how it has ruined the outfit for her. She has immediately taken your attention to a flaw and it is quite likely that your eyes will be drawn to that stain for the rest of the day. Jenny had constantly downplayed her achievements, drawing my attention to her failings. As a result, I had fallen into the trap of being distracted by the metaphorical stain on her jacket!

My supervisor and I talked a lot about how I seemed to be in a rush and why that might be. This was interesting for me and, I reflected, the main reason was that I seemed to be taking too much responsibility for making the change happen. As tempting as it was to believe that I was a good coach with the ability to bring about change in my clients, ultimately the only person who could make the change was Jenny herself. But this wasn't deep enough reflection for my supervisor – and this is what makes supervision so useful – so he pushed me to explore why I was taking on this responsibility.

We did some work on my drivers. One of my biggest drivers is the need for achievement and my desire for 'success' was getting in the way of my coaching work with Jenny. As a result of the supervision session, I realised that what I really needed was a more carefully thought out plan for the coaching sessions and a more sophisticated approach than I had used in the first session.

For the benefit of my client, I had to rein in my personal desire to achieve success and actually focus on what Jenny really wanted from the coaching.

To do this I probably needed to look at what else was going on in her life and where her Impostor Syndrome originated rather than trying to deal with the presenting issue.

Session Two

Jenny arrived in a state of agitation. She told me immediately that she had made a mistake in her work and been to see the senior partner in the law firm to tell him that she didn't think she was 'up to the job'. He had sent her away with reassurances that everyone else thought she was perfectly capable and that everyone makes mistakes from time to time. Jenny remained unmoved by these words of reassurance and had taken all her recent work to the partners, asking them to check if she was making more mistakes than the other lawyers.

The partners were understandably baffled by this request but reluctantly agreed to check her work. They reported back that she was performing as well as anyone else in the firm but they were more worried about her state of mind than her work. The entire incident had caused her so much stress that she had been signed off by her GP.

This was a crisis moment for Jenny. Her lack of self-belief had now led to her employers doubting her sanity and her stress levels were sky-high. She realised that she needed to address the issue once and for all.

Although moments of crisis are obviously difficult, they often have a positive flip-side as it can take a moment of crisis to bring about transformational learning. Mezirow [Ref 4] identified four situations that give rise to transformational learning:

1. Experiencing a disorienting dilemma.

2. Being in a state of puzzlement.

3. Recognising that others share our feelings.

4. The presence of an empathetic provocateur.

Jenny had experienced all these situations over the past few weeks: starting with the recognition that others shared her feelings when she attended my keynote address and culminating in a state of puzzlement and disorientation. She had also had two encounters with empathetic provocateurs – the partners in her law firm and now me.

I often think that people only change when either the pain of their current situation becomes too great, or the pleasure on offer in the alternative situation is sufficient. Jenny had arrived at the point where there was considerable pain in her current situation. Her thinking patterns had become detrimental to her life, her work and her well-being and I knew that she was now really ready to begin the work needed to change them.

Session Three

Having worked with Jenny to identify the detrimental impact which Impostor Syndrome had on her, we then looked at what pay-off or gain she might lose if she chose to believe something different about herself.

When embarking on a significant behaviour change, it is also important to acknowledge what we will be losing.

All too often we focus on the benefits of the new behaviour and underestimate how attached we are to our current behaviour. We believe that every behaviour, no matter how destructive it may seem, has a secondary purpose or gain. In Jenny's case, she identified the following:

- She regularly received lots of compliments as people tried to convince her that she was valuable and worthy.

- Setting herself up for failure meant that she and others had low expectations of her and were not disappointed in her.

I then asked Jenny to collect feedback about herself from people whose opinions she trusted and respected, and who would be scrupulously honest. She sent out the following questions to them:

- What do you most admire about me?

- What do you consider to be my greatest strength?

- What do you consider to be my greatest achievement?

- What one thing could I change for my own benefit?

- What one word sums me up for you?

When she received the responses, it was amazing for her to see their similarity. Almost all the respondents said the same positive things about her; namely that she was very bright and often thought of things that others missed. They were also consistent in stating that she needed to believe in herself more. Faced with such compelling and consistent data, it was hard for her to argue with it, especially as it had come from people that she had selected specifically for their honesty and good judgement.

Further Sessions

After several weeks, I felt that we had established enough of a trusting relationship for me to mention what came up in my supervision session and so I asked Jenny when she first remembered thinking that other people were better than her. After some time, she remembered the feeling of inadequacy when failing her 11+ exam.

Although she had subsequently done very well at school, gone on to University and achieved a first class honours degree she remained 'hypnotised' by the belief that she was not as good as others because she had failed an exam at age 11. I felt that reviewing this incident was key to Jenny changing her thinking patterns, as I wanted to enable Jenny to bring her adult wisdom and objectivity to the situation.

I invited her to imagine that, as the adult she is today, she could travel back in time and meet 11-year-old Jenny. I asked her what adult Jenny thought about the little girl, what she felt about her and what she would like to say to her. Jenny found this an emotional experience but it enabled her to revisit the incident and separate her adult responses from her 11-year-old responses.

Adult Jenny saw a little child who was doing her best in an important exam at an emotional time. Her parents were getting divorced and Jenny did not have much support or stability at home. Looking with fresh and adult eyes, she was actually amazed at how well she had coped with this situation as a young child. She also saw how resilient and determined young Jenny was because she had not let this setback stop her from getting a brilliant degree.

Adult Jenny realised that she had been negating all her achievements after the failure of her 11+ exam and she exclaimed, 'I have been letting 11-year-old Jenny rule my thinking!' I explained that when we are young and impressionable and we receive a message about ourselves from a perceived 'authority' (in this case the 11+ examination board) we tend to accept it as an unquestionable truth. For Jenny, this was: 'I am not as good as other people'.

Only by revisiting the experience and bringing to bear on it all of our adult wisdom, experience, logic, reasoning and compassion can we re-evaluate the experience and see it for what it was.

This was a revelation for Jenny and, over the next few weeks, she practiced accepting compliments, speaking positively about herself and acknowledging her strengths and weaknesses. When she received feedback, she learned to stop and consider whether the person giving feedback was someone whose opinion she trusted and respected.

I continue to see Jenny twice a year for what she calls 'an MOT'. She still falls back into old thinking patterns from time to time but usually recognises when this is happening and consciously employs the strategies we used to get her back on track.

TOOLS AND TECHNIQUES

Many people experience the feeling that they are an impostor and, just as with Jenny, the insecurity this can create is often a major factor that drives success. By constantly striving to prove herself, Jenny impressed her colleagues with her dedication and thoroughness but eventually her Impostor Syndrome spiralled into a chronic lack of confidence and almost paranoia. It was not until Jenny explored the source of her Impostor Syndrome that she could begin to bring this trait into a healthy balance.

Many people with Impostor Syndrome minimise their achievements and maximise their deficiencies. They often put their achievements down to factors outside their control. They might say, *'I was lucky'* or *'if only they knew the real me and what was going on'*. This is not through a sense of humility but simply because they struggle to internalise their achievements. The techniques that follow here are aimed at helping clients acknowledge their qualities and achievements in order to begin giving themselves more credit.

Career Timeline

The 'Impostor Syndrome Gap' is the difference between our perception of self and the perception others have of us.

When faced with a roomful of people, somebody who is trapped by their Impostor Syndrome trait immediately assumes that they know less, and are worth less, than the other people in the room. One way to help your client begin to close that gap is by having them walk you through their career timeline.

Although not essential, this technique works best when you have a good degree of floor space available. Introduce the technique by explaining that you are going to ask them to remember, and then tell you about, some of the high points in their career.

Ask your client to do the following:

1. Stand up and imagine that a timeline of your career is in front of you.

2. Position yourself somewhere in the room to represent where you are at the present moment in your career.

3. Think of about four or five key highlights of your career to date – these could be job moves, promotions, training, qualifications etc.

4. When you have had time to think through your career, walk me down your timeline to the most recent career highlight and recall that moment as vividly as possible. What did you hear, say, see, feel at that point in time? Tell me about it in as much detail as you can.

5. Consider all the strengths and skills you used as well as the achievements, positive feedback and accolades you received at that time.

6. Once you have done this, move one stage further back down your timeline and describe the next significant highlight of your career.

Repeat this process until they are back at the start of their career and ask them to talk about the experience. What did they realise? How can they take all of the positive aspects of their career to date and plan their next steps?

There is an optional, extra stage where you can ask them to walk back up their timeline, noticing any more achievements and high points, back to the present day point. Encourage them to gather up all of the realisations about their career and achievements then look back and acknowledge all that they have achieved.

It may be useful to remember that people who are struggling with Impostor Syndrome are prone to ascribe successes to luck so be sure to focus the client on **themselves** and what **they** did. At each stage of their career timeline, be prepared to ask some prompting questions if needed such as 'What does it say about you?' and 'What qualities did you need to make this happen?'

Powerful Coaching Question:
If you knew that everyone in the room had the same insecurity, how would that change your outlook?

The 5-5-5 Technique

People with Impostor Syndrome have a tendency to dilute or not accept compliments. They will put their successes down to luck or other factors rather than internalise them.

One way to begin to counter this is to ask for and, most importantly, practice accepting compliments. Imagine a compliment as a gift: you wouldn't reject a birthday present would you? So why reject a compliment?

One technique to use with 'impostors' is the '5-5-5' technique. This is a short form of 360° appraisal and, as with all the best techniques, is very simple. It usually works very well as a homework exercise i.e. something that the client does in between coaching sessions.

Give your client the following instructions:

1. Think of **five** people whose opinions you respect and trust and give them a short form with **five** questions to complete. The questions should only take **five** minutes to answer. [See template below]

2. Ask each of the five people to read out their answers to you. (Many people do this exercise over email, which is still beneficial but not as powerful as having that person in the room actually saying the words).

3. Ask them to pause after reading out each of their answers.

4. During that pause, repeat what they have said in the first person in your head. For example if the person says, 'I think your greatest strength is your creativity because you always see options that others would never even consider', you would say to yourself: 'My greatest strength is creativity because I always see options that others would never consider'.

5. Thank them unreservedly for the feedback.

Template for the 5-5-5 questionnaire

Below are five questions that I would like you to answer based on your perception of me. I have chosen you as one of five people whose opinions I trust, value and respect. I hope and expect you to be honest. This will probably take about five minutes of your time and I would like you to write down your answers first. Then, when you are ready, I would like you to tell me what you have written, one answer at a time.

Thank you

What one word or phrase describes me best?
What do you think is my greatest achievement?
What do you value most about me?
What one thing could I change for my own benefit?
What do you believe to be my greatest strength?

A note on feedback from others

People with Impostor Syndrome tend to take feedback, and especially criticism, too personally.

As coach, it can be useful to help your client consciously deconstruct feedback that they receive. The feedback should be interpreted as about the result, outcome or action rather than them as a person. Just because a child did something naughty does not make them a naughty child. Equally, they may have made a decision that didn't turn out the way they wanted it to. That doesn't make them a bad decision-maker, let alone a bad leader or a bad person.

Feedback is rarely true or false either and, because of this, coaches should encourage their clients to assess the 'credibility of the witness' and help them filter any subjectivity or bias. Finally, it is also important for coaches to help their clients see feedback as an opportunity to improve, rather than an eternal judgement upon them. This is especially important in cases of Impostor Syndrome.

Powerful Coaching Question:
Which of your assumptions about yourself would your good friends challenge?

Magazine Interview

It is easier to be fair and generous to yourself when you are looking through someone else's eyes.

Because of this, another helpful homework exercise for people with Impostor Syndrome is the magazine interview.

Ask your client to imagine that they have been interviewed by a magazine of their choice. Encourage your client to view themselves through the eyes of the interviewer, who wants to show your client in the best possible light, showcasing all of their skills, career highlights and qualities in order to inspire their readers.

Ask your client to write the interview in the third person, including some photographs, and bring it to the next session. It is even more powerful if they are prepared to read it out to you.

As this exercise is positioned to highlight our strengths in order to inspire others, we are less able to negate our achievements. In essence, this technique gives your client a legitimate device to enable them to be positive about themselves.

If they are finding it difficult, you could prompt them with questions such as:

- What is unique about this person?

- What details of their life have set them apart from others?

- What were the reasons for them taking the path they took?

- What obstacles have they overcome along the way?

- What are the key personal characteristics that have been valuable to them?

- Who would you ask for a background quote and what would they say?

Powerful Coaching Question:
How would you describe yourself if you were being as kind and generous to yourself as you are to your friends?

THE INTERVIEW

Joe Lynam

A major component of Impostor Syndrome is the inability for sufferers to own their own successes. Instead they attribute their successes to luck, fate or other people's contributions. In the following interview with Joe Lynam, a business correspondent working for the BBC in the United Kingdom, you will notice the word 'luck' comes up a lot. Joe is a presenter on the BBC's flagship Today programme – having previously been a correspondent with Newsnight, BBC Breakfast TV and Radio Five Live among others. Before becoming a journalist, Joe ran a chain of pubs in Germany in the 1990s and speaks fluent German, Dutch and Italian. Joe has broken many stories of national and international importance, especially relating to the banking and Eurozone crises of 2008-2012. Despite his successes, throughout his career Joe regularly found himself thinking, 'this is as good as it's going to get'. Thanks to a couple of key events, he managed to construct a strategy to bring his Impostor Syndrome trait into balance.

'I was being interviewed live on the BBC *Ten O'Clock News* when I suddenly froze after being asked a question. My mind went blank and I literally didn't know what to say. I had my notes below me but I felt as if I couldn't look down, as it would have underlined my ineptitude. Instead I just sat there unable to speak for what felt like a lifetime. I felt myself going white and thought to myself, 'That's it. It's all over. My dream job at the BBC has gone.' I couldn't sleep that night and I couldn't bring myself to watch it. My fiancée Riina tried to tell me that actually it was fine, that it was actually only a second and a half and that nobody thought anything of it, but in my mind I had 'died' on screen. The next day I rang my editor and apologised and his reaction was: 'Sorry for what?'

Joe Lynam is an experienced correspondent for the BBC, but he tells me that he got the job almost completely because of luck:

'I hated my previous job and, even though I had a mortgage to pay, I decided I couldn't take it any more and quit. This was in 1999 and at the height of the Dot Com boom. I knew nothing about technology but happened to know some people who did and so got them round, plied them with wine and got them to teach me. The next day I wrote an 800-word piece about technology and sent it off to Ireland's business bible, *Business & Finance* magazine, claiming to be a technology correspondent. There was so much demand for content in those days that I got a job writing about technology immediately.'

'Not long after that I bumped into a friend of a friend who was a senior producer of a show called *The Last Word* on the Irish National Radio channel Today FM, and I suggested that he should do a tech show. He told me to put my idea on paper and send it to him. I didn't actually think he would follow up but I sent him my idea anyway and *The Tech Show* was born.'

He attributes both of these events to luck rather than his efforts – a common trait of Impostor Syndrome – and then goes on to say that it was a lucky break that led to him being nominated for Journalist of the Year. He also says that it was luck that he happened to pick up the *Guardian* newspaper one day and see an advert for a job at the BBC, and how it was lucky that they were rapidly hiring at the time he applied.

'When I got the job it felt like the left-side of my body had gone numb, almost like a stroke. I was so happy that I was shaking too much to call them back. Once I had the job offer in writing and knew it wasn't a joke I called them back and asked them why they had given me the job because my interview was a disaster!'

When I call Joe out on how his success could be explained in other ways than good fortune, he says that it was a big moment when the interviewer said that it was some skills Joe wasn't aware of that caused them to offer him the job. He then tells me what he believes to be the three keys to success:

'You have to have a modicum of talent, that's true, but a lot of success is down to luck. The third factor is perseverance. I took a lot of knocks after I got my foot in the door at the BBC, but this was where I dreamed of working so I wasn't going to give it up easily. I came from a poorly regarded school and a modest university by international standards (not Eton, Harrow or Oxbridge for example). This, and the fact that I presumed that an Irish accent wasn't exactly fashionable at the time, meant that I had to work hard.'

Joe comes from a broadcasting family and despite running a chain of pubs in Germany in his early 20s, he always knew that he wanted to be in broadcasting. He describes his father as a talented presenter, but one who couldn't handle his nerves.

'He would worry all day before a three-minute slot. We wouldn't be able to talk to him because he was so stressed. And then, afterwards, to take the edge off, he would have a few beers. Eventually he quit broadcasting and focused on his more comfortable job with the Irish Tourist Board. I knew, even aged 10 or 11, that this wasn't right and I think it taught me that talent alone isn't enough to succeed in broadcasting.'

Joe and I discuss the possibility that this is where his insecurity came from: the fear that you might never be good enough and that something great might be taken away from you.

I ask him about his scariest moment and he tells me about a time in October 2010, in the midst of the financial crisis, when he had broken the story on the *Six O'Clock News* that Ireland was in negotiations with the EU about getting a bail out.

'I was due to break this story again on the *Ten O'Clock News* that night but, just before we were about to go live, the Irish government – a democratically elected and credible Western government – came out and flatly denied it. They effectively called me a liar and I knew my career was on the line. I had double-checked and triple-checked my sources and eventually decided to put my neck on the line and run with it.'

I want to know what the turning point was that changed him from the rabbit in the headlights of his early career to the person confident enough to back themselves against a government calling him a liar. He reflects that this was arguably the point where he really had to evaluate whether he was an impostor or not. Previously he had relied on perseverance to make up for when he wasn't being lucky, but now he had to look to his talent, or at least objectively evaluate his talent against other people's.

'Eventually I realised that governments are just a collection of humans too – they make mistakes and they lie just like any other humans. I was confident that I had done my due diligence and in my heart I knew I was right.'

Unwittingly, Joe had employed a common tactic for dealing with Impostor Syndrome. He had levelled the playing field by bringing others – in this case the Irish government – down from the pedestal on which he had previously placed them. A similar thing happened in 2003 when he was accidentally given an 'access all areas' pass to the World Economic Forum in Davos. He tells me about being in a room with the OPEC Secretary General, Prime Ministers and

Heads of State and, because the press weren't allowed in, they had their guard down.

'I looked at these important, powerful people without their entourage and the professional face they put on when they know they are on camera. Some of them were sitting on their own looking nervous, sheepish even, and I realised they are just human beings.'

So normalisation was a big help to him too. Was there anything else that helped him throw off his Impostor Syndrome?

He thinks about it and tells me about a time when he was being interviewed about Microsoft's row with the European Commission.

'The main presenter was Oliver Scott, who had a big and somewhat fearsome reputation. I had prepared the script with the questions he would ask me, and the answers I would give. As I was settling in, I handed him the script. Oliver took the script from me, smiled and, while looking me in the eye, dropped the script into the bin.'

Joe explains that part of Scott's fearsome reputation came from the fact that he often disregarded scripts.

'I could feel the colour drain from my cheeks and I imagined dying on air for the second time as he fired me a question that I hadn't prepared an answer for. My over-riding thought was that I HAD to get this right. And I remember my mother's voice in my head telling me that I would do it and that I would do it right. Luckily I had done a lot of research and so I could answer the question.'

I highlight to him that most people wouldn't put the fact that he had researched a topic that he was reporting on down to luck and then ask him about the significance of his mother's voice.

'My mother was where I got my inner steel from if you like. She always used to say to me that 'Shy bairns get nae sweets' and it was this that gave me the confidence to push on through the insecurities that I had. Every time I got a promotion – even when I joined the

BBC on the absolute bottom rung as a 'meet and greet' - I thought that it might prove to be the high watermark of my career; that this was as good as it would ever get, so I might as well enjoy it - but my mother always said that this wouldn't be the case.'

I ask him what else helped him deal with his self-doubt and he says how valuable it was for him to know how common self-doubt is.

'I was very lucky to have an inspirational uncle as a mentor,' he says. His uncle – Des Lynam – is a legendary UK sports presenter. 'I was amazed to find out how much self-doubt he had because, when you looked at him on screen, he seemed so calm and in control – a natural. I realised that if even he can doubt himself then it can't be that strange that I doubt myself.'

He also explains that 'Uncle Des' was one of the reasons why he was able to cope with Oliver Scott's interview.

'He (Des) told me that you can't be everything to everyone, so I should specialise in something. I used to spend hours and hours reading encyclopaedias in my grandparents' house in Donegal to pick up random facts about as many topics as I could in order to be able to join in conversations and appear intelligent, but getting a depth of knowledge in one area was the best thing I ever did and certainly gave me more confidence in myself.'

His final piece of advice is to remember that:

'I've been lucky enough to have people, such as my fiancée Riina, who will give me a cold, objective evaluation of my performance. Making sure that you are constantly getting perspective is invaluable.'

'You're never as good or never as bad as you think you are.'

CHAPTER TWO

People Pleasing

'I cannot give you the formula for success,
but I can give you the formula for failure – which is:
Try to please everybody.'

HERBERT BAYARD SWOPE

THE CASE STUDY

'I feel guilty very easily
and can't stand up for myself.'

Sophie emailed requesting an urgent appointment. She was an old client who I really liked and when she needed some emergency coaching I would try and find time for her. I moved some appointments around and told her I could see her that afternoon. She arrived at my office in a state of agitation and immediately began telling me the following story:

'For the past three months I've been power-walking with my friend, Sue. We've been going every evening after work and we can now walk five miles in an hour and have started to get really fit. I was really enjoying it and feeling good about myself, but a few weeks ago Hannah, another good friend of mine, asked me if she could join us. This threw me into a quandary as I knew that Sue wouldn't want Hannah to come along. She didn't like Hannah, plus Sue spends the time talking to me about an illicit affair she is having. So if Hannah came along, Sue wouldn't be able to confide in me. On the other hand, Hannah didn't know all this and she had a right to ask to join us, didn't she?'

I was about to respond but Sophie continued, 'I told Hannah I would ask Sue if she could join us but Hannah got really impatient and said I didn't have to ask Sue and surely I could just tell Sue she was coming along. Then, when I spoke to Sue about it later she was also annoyed and was very clear that Hannah shouldn't join us. I couldn't bring myself to say that to Hannah so I told her that Sue was still thinking about it, which annoyed Hannah even more.' Sophie paused for breath. 'Then I tried to ask Sue again and she said no again. I just didn't know what to do for the best and I didn't even really care about who I walked with!'

I was exhausted just listening to this story and was finding it hard to keep track of Sophie, Sue and Hannah. It felt like watching a game of piggy in the middle. I asked Sophie whether she had resolved this dilemma and, if so, how?

She answered sheepishly, 'I have been going for two walks every evening. First with Sue and then with Hannah and I'm exhausted. Also, my husband and children are unhappy because I'm out of the house for over two hours every night. That's why I needed to see you. My husband says I have to learn to be assertive. This isn't the first time I've got into this sort of situation because I can't say 'no' to people. I feel guilty very easily and can't stand up for myself. It's got to stop. I'm exhausted spending time trying to keep everyone happy but I am not happy and my family is also suffering.'

Looking at Sophie, she wasn't someone I would imagine having difficulty standing up for herself: an attractive young woman with a lively personality. I asked her to tell me more about her inability to stand up to people.

She gave me countless examples of her people pleasing behaviours, including always saying 'Yes' when she wanted to say 'No' and feeling as though everyone in her life wanted a piece of her, including her children, her husband, friends, colleagues and even the dog! She explained how her lack of assertiveness had also created difficulties at the nursery school where she worked. In her first year there, on 4th April the staff and children celebrated her birthday with a cake, cards and renditions of 'Happy Birthday to You'. This was lovely, except that is not her birthday. She didn't want to upset them by saying anything and nine years later her birthday is still celebrated on that day. It had gone on for so long that she felt she couldn't possibly tell them her birthday is actually in November!

'I don't like to upset people so I agree to things I don't really want to do. Then at the last minute I make excuses to try to get out of it and end up letting people down. I know I take on too much and put other people first but it is making me feel resentful: I don't have any time to myself and it feels like people take advantage of my good nature. I still don't know what to do about Sue and Hannah either.'

I explained to Sophie that everything she had told me was typical of people-pleasing behaviour. However, some of her stories were so remarkable that I hadn't known whether to laugh or cry. Sophie usually felt the same way but now mostly wanted to cry. Her behaviour was clearly impacting upon her life in a really negative way.

People-pleasing is associated with a passive behaviour style: the opposite end of the spectrum to aggressive behaviour. The balance in the middle of the spectrum is an assertive behaviour style.

Sophie and I spent some time looking at the differences between passive behaviour and aggressive behaviour.

People who demonstrate passive behaviour typically:

- Put other people's feelings and needs before their own.

- Get pushed around or taken advantage of.

- Are indecisive.

- Have a knee-jerk 'Yes' response to requests.

- Apologise excessively.

- Feel guilty for other people's feelings.

Those who demonstrate aggressive behaviour typically:

- Put their needs and feelings before others'.

- Use emotional blackmail such as sulking, silence or threats to get their own way.

- Persist until they get what they want.

- Shout, intimidate and get violent.

At this point Sophie recognised that Hannah and Sue were using indirectly aggressive behaviour to get what they wanted and she saw that neither of them were considering what she wanted. She noted that she was particularly susceptible to this type of 'blackmail'. Sophie also recognised that she occasionally used emotional blackmail or manipulation herself, especially with her husband.

This was an important realisation for Sophie. By stating this, she was also implicitly acknowledging that she had the potential to be more assertive. We all use different styles in response to the people we are with and the situations we are in. Assertive communication is generally our aim but sometimes it is necessary and appropriate to use passive or aggressive behaviour styles. For example, evacuating people from a dangerous situation may require aggressive communication. Equally, if an elderly relative is exhibiting victim-like behaviours in order to get you to help them, it is possibly best to adopt a passive stance. The important lesson is that we make a positive choice to use the appropriate behaviour, instead of reverting to our default style.

I highlighted that, compared to an assertive communication style, passive and aggressive behaviours are neither honest nor direct. Assertive communication involves knowing what we want and saying what we want in a reasonable, adult and calm way. Being assertive means that you respect both your needs and the needs of the other person but it doesn't mean that you always get what you want. Asking for what you want and being prepared to discuss options or compromises does, however, improve your self-esteem and confidence because you have been true to yourself and valued yourself in the process. Practicing assertive behaviour also means making choices about your behaviour and this sometimes means buying yourself some time, or stalling, before giving an immediate answer.

Sophie was clearly aware that the situation with Sue and Hannah couldn't continue. I suggested that she spoke to them honestly about what was going on and how it was affecting her. Sophie got really upset at the prospect of what she believed to be confronting her two friends and, even though I tried to frame it as assertive rather than confrontational, it was clear to me that this was a step too far for her.

'Would you like me to speak to them for you?' I asked impulsively.

'No. That would be a bit awkward, but thanks for the offer,' she said.

'But you can't go on like this. We need to get you to a point where you are comfortable to tell Sue and Hannah directly how you feel. In the meantime, perhaps you should alternate and walk one day with Sue and the next with Hannah.'

'That makes sense,' she agreed.

Raising awareness is the first step towards any change and, by the end of our time together, Sophie had at least developed a better ability to recognise different communication styles in herself and others. I didn't push her any further on speaking to Sue and Hannah directly. Instead we agreed that she would:

- Notice passive, aggressive and assertive behaviour in herself and others.

- Practice saying 'No' to at least three requests without trying to explain herself.

- Practice buying herself some time by saying 'I will think about it and get back to you on that' if asked to do something.

- Start thinking about what she wanted. (Before you can assert yourself you have to know what you want. Sophie spent so much time thinking about everyone else that she had lost touch with what she wanted. I encouraged her to ask herself each day 'What would I like to eat today?' and to read the newspaper and ask herself 'What do I think about this article?')

Supervision

As it happened, I was seeing my supervisor that afternoon and so my chat with Sophie was fresh in my mind and, although she wasn't an active client, I couldn't help bringing it up. His first reaction was to burst out laughing – not at the slightly ridiculous situation that Sophie had got herself into, or even her 'second birthday'. He was laughing at me.

'Can't you see what's happening here? The irony of it all?' he said.

'What do you mean?' I asked.

'You're as bad as Sophie!' he said, going on to point out that I was both offering free coaching and re-arranging my calendar to accommodate her. He also pointed out that I had offered to speak to Sue and Hannah and that, even when she didn't take me up on that offer, I still suggested a solution for her.

'You're trying to be the knight in shining armour,' he said.

This was a phrase that I was familiar with: it is another way of describing the 'rescuer' role from the Karpman Drama Triangle *[Ref 5]* – a psychological model of human interaction associated with Transactional Analysis (TA) *[Ref 6]*. Deriving from Stephen Karpman's work in the 1960s, the model presents three roles that are often taken on by people in a given situation: the victim, the persecutor and the rescuer.

The surface level of the model explains that the persecutor pressures or harasses the victim in some way and the rescuer swoops in to resolve the situation; much like the fairy-tale 'knight in shining armour'. At a deeper level, each of the people actually like their roles and thus don't want them to end: the victim doesn't really want to be rescued and the rescuer doesn't want the victim to stop needing them.

People in helping professions run the risk of becoming dependent on their rescuing tendencies. It gives them a sense of worth, self-esteem and power; in some cases it can even make them feel god-like.

It also serves as a way for the rescuer to avoid looking at themselves because the victim's needs are more apparent and important. Coaches are often classic people-pleasers!

This was both eye-opening and embarrassing for me. I was coaching someone on a behaviour that I was indulging in myself at that very moment. It was easy for me to fall into this trap as the white knight syndrome, as the 'knight in shining armour' is also known, is an extreme form of the people-pleaser driver, albeit on the more proactive end of the spectrum.

My supervisor remembered me talking about Sophie before and so identified this as a pattern – and Sophie wasn't the only example of me jumping at the chance to play rescuer. We spent my supervision session looking at where the trait came from and devising my own plan to deal with it.

We all like to be liked. Being liked ensures that we are accepted by, and remain part of, our 'tribe' and that provides security. The things we do in order to be liked by others are usually laudable acts and can be great for building relationships, progressing our career and developing society. If we all did a little more for people then the world would arguably be a better place. However, sometimes we have such an extreme desire to be liked that we define our self-worth as a human being by whether we are liked by those around us. This can be dangerous to our aspirations, happiness and – in extreme cases – mental wellbeing.

Where does it come from?

Apart from the natural, tribal element that seems to be built-in to most people, some people are more affected by the need to please others. Typically there are a few main reasons why we go out of our way to please people:

1. **It has been an over-emphasised aspect of our early life.**
   People pleasing behaviours can be the result of conditioning in our early life. People-pleasing is statistically more prevalent in women than men because, historically, women have been brought up with expectations to care for others.

   Equally, children who struggle to attain the love or attention of their parents or who have to take on responsibility for the family too young often grow up with a heightened desire to please others.

2. **Fear of being alone**
   We have an innate desire to be part of a social group and to have close relationships. If we accumulate evidence in our early years that people will reject us or leave us if we are not nice to them then this message can become deeply ingrained and magnified in our adult life. These people believe that, by being nice to others, they will not face rejection or end up alone.

3. **The hope of getting the same treatment in return**
   People with low self-esteem or confidence will hope to play on the principle of reciprocity in order to secure compliments, favours and friendship. Their plan is that by doing something nice for somebody, or saying something nice about them, they will get something nice back from that person, thus obtaining a boost to their self-esteem.

I have always been a carer and, as such, am a sucker for cries for help - often to my own detriment. By talking through this pattern with my supervisor it became apparent that I am more susceptible to victims who have similar stories to mine. I decided to look up some of my old notes from Sophie's sessions and, sure enough she had told me something that had resonated with my own life experience:

'My father left home when I was seven and my mother never really got over it. I didn't really understand what was happening but I wanted to make her feel better so I looked after her and my little sister as much as I could. I always tried not to rock the boat or make my mum more upset. She depended on me a lot. I became good at caring for others, which is why I became a nursery nurse when I left school. I still can't bear seeing other people unhappy or hurt.'

Whilst my story was completely different, the message I received in childhood was very similar. Both of my parents did a lot of volunteering and social work, so I learned from a young age that looking out for others and helping them was what you should do.

The biggest problem with the people pleaser trap is that you are compromising your integrity: because you are not acting in line with how you are feeling and thinking, you are destined to be unfulfilled, frustrated and resentful.

It is unlikely that other people will realise what the people pleaser is doing and so they are unlikely to appreciate it. This tends to lead to one of two reactions in the people pleaser: they will either feel rejected and therefore strive even harder to please them; or they will resent the other person for not appreciating their sacrifices and returning the same level of attention.

The other problem is that, in the long run, people-pleasing doesn't work. People eventually realise that you will just change your opinions to fit in with what they want/feel/say. You may be viewed as either an 'easy target' for manipulation or, perhaps even worse, false and inauthentic.

While this is an extreme, there is the potential for the people pleasing aspect of our personality to take over so much that we lose all integrity in our relationships and people start to see this.

My supervisor challenged me about what I was going to do with regard to my relationship with Sophie. It was going to be hard but I needed to return to treating her like any other client. First of all, I needed to talk to her about regular appointments, fees and the normal process that I would go through with a client. I would also bring to her attention that I too am a people pleaser and that I was falling into the trap of rescuing her. As often happens in the Karpman Drama Triangle, roles get switched – for example, the victim becomes the rescuer - and this can be both a conscious and subconscious action.

I was nervous about doing this but how could I expect Sophie to address her issues if I couldn't address mine? On the plus side this was a good opportunity to reflect Sophie's behaviour back to her. Although she found it easy to see herself as the victim and she hinted at how she used aggressive communication with her husband, it would be interesting to see how she would react to knowing that in our coaching relationship I was potentially the victim to her perpetrator.

Before we met again, I contacted Sophie and explained the situation. I told her that I was more than happy to help but that it would be within the scope of a normal coaching relationship. She would need to pay me for my time and make regular appointments. It was nowhere near as awkward as I expected it to be and she apologised profusely for crossing the line - unsurprising behaviour in many ways considering I was dealing with a chronic people pleaser.

Session Two

Two weeks later at our second meeting, and our first official coaching session, Sophie told me how she had found many opportunities to practice saying 'No' and how it had become much easier. She had started off having difficulty in overcoming the worry of what people might think of her and she told me how she actually failed a couple of times.

'Last Tuesday a friend asked me if I would look through a report she had written. I didn't want to do it and I didn't have time for it either – I had a load of stuff of my own to do – so I told her that I'm not very good at proof-reading. She told me not to worry and that just having a second pair of eyes on it would be enough. So then I told her I didn't really know enough about the project and would probably come up with some ridiculous suggestions. Again she said she would be fine with that. I didn't think I could give her a third excuse so I just did it.'

Offering excuses or reasons opens the door for people to negotiate with you and this ultimately makes it harder to say 'No'.

She had, however, experienced some notable successes. She had taken back a coffee because they had put sugar in it, whereas before she would have not said anything. She had also managed to interrupt a cold-caller trying to get her to take out an insurance product that she didn't need.

'I know these are pathetic things but they felt like massive victories for me. I really liked the feeling of standing up for myself and I liked the confidence that gave me. I still felt guilty for the barista and the salesman as they might get in trouble or not meet their targets, but it's progress isn't it?'

In our unofficial session I had tried to give Sophie some simple behavioural strategies to develop her assertiveness and I explained to her that today it would be useful to explore what values and beliefs she had that drove this behaviour.

Those with a people pleasing habit tend to have grown up in an environment where they were expected to mould to other people's

needs, were praised only for doing what others wanted or for looking after others or where their own needs were ignored.

I asked Sophie if she recognised any of these scenarios and, together, we made sense of how she had learned to base her self-worth on how much she did for other people. She was a nursery nurse, a mother, a dog-owner, a committee member on the PTA and volunteered once a week in a local charity shop. What did she do just for herself? We acknowledged that she had noble and kind intentions but she needed to show herself the same level of kindness and acknowledge her own needs.

By focusing on pleasing others all the time, Sophie was opening herself up to manipulation, emotional blackmail and abuse. People with an aggressive communication style could spot Sophie a mile off and would use her to get what they wanted, at great cost to Sophie and great benefit to themselves.

Over the last couple of weeks she was beginning to see how she put herself in other people's shoes and she had been able to identify manipulative communication and behaviour in others. Saying 'No' to simple things had also been relatively easy and she had learned that the world hadn't crashed around her feet when she did it. She reported that the most useful technique was to buy herself some time and avoid a knee jerk 'Yes' response when asked to do a favour for someone.

Sophie's perspective on the world was changing rapidly and at the end of the second session we agreed the following actions:

- To organise some activities just for her.

- To determine what was acceptable behaviour from others and what was unacceptable. Determine some boundaries for herself.

- Consider what it felt like to be treated with dignity and respect.

- Complete an audit of people in her life: Make a list of who treated her with dignity and respect and those who took advantage of her and did not respect her. Think about each of these people in turn and consider whether they were people to keep in her life.

- Seek out people who valued and respected her for who she was and not what she did for them and spend more time with them.

This was massive progress for Sophie and I felt it was time to give her a challenge. I decided to ask her to tell me what she didn't like about me or about the coaching sessions. She found this really difficult but it was essential practice for her. After telling me everything she did like, she reluctantly told me that she didn't really derive any benefit from me telling her stories from my life about my own people pleasing tendencies.

I asked her to say more. 'Well, you're not me and your experiences are not the same as mine so I don't find them very relevant. Also, I want to think that my coach has overcome their own challenges so it makes me doubt you a bit. If you can't do it, how can you help me to do it?' She hesitated for a moment and then continued, 'Also, now that I am paying you a lot of money for these sessions, I don't even want a minute of the time to be wasted on anything other than my stuff – sorry, I just had to say that! Sorry!'

I laughed out loud and told Sophie that it had made my day and that she didn't need to say 'Sorry'. I thought that was a great way to end the session, praised her for stepping so much outside of her comfort zone, and was already looking forward to our next session.

Session Three

At our next session, Sophie couldn't wait to tell me what had happened with Hannah and Sue. She had told each of them that she had been walking twice a night and they had both smiled, admitted that they had known that all along and effectively said 'More fool her'! Sophie was furious and it had been a revelation to her that her two friends could be so selfish. As a result, she had actually decided to start walking on her own at a time which better suited her and her family and she felt quite empowered by the decision.

I was amazed that Sophie decided to end both friendships when she realised that these two women were not worth having in her life and was pleased she felt liberated by this decision. Sophie commented that Hannah and Sue had already started walking together, as if nothing had happened and as if Sophie had never existed.

We met for just two more sessions. Sophie acknowledged that it was a challenge to change the habits of a lifetime but the pay-offs were so positive that she did not consider herself to be in danger of falling back.

TOOLS AND TECHNIQUES

Being amenable increases our chances of fitting in and developing bonds and rapport with others. As social animals, it is important for us to be part of the group and be liked. This is key to influencing others and everyone likes being around someone who makes them feel good. However, as we saw with Sophie, this trait can become a trap whereby she was over-committed and was being manipulated.

Ensure your client knows that careful consideration of their impact on other people is a good thing. This is what makes them a nice human being. The objective is for your client to retain their thoughtfulness and consideration without being a doormat. The following techniques are focused on helping your client to look at their situation and themselves from different perspectives and to practice developing a sense of self-worth.

Perceptual Positions

People with a strong people pleasing habit naturally spend a lot of their time seeing things from other peoples' points of view.

In this technique we utilise three positions. First position involves experiencing a situation from your own perspective, seeing it through your own eyes and accessing your own thoughts, feelings and needs. Second position involves standing in the shoes of somebody who is actively involved in the situation, often 'the other person'. The third position entails taking a detached, observer's view of the whole situation. This technique works best when there is a reasonable amount of floor space available.

1. Ask your client to imagine a situation where their people pleaser habit is overactive. Perhaps they need to:

   - Be assertive.

   - Say 'No' to somebody.

   - Tell somebody how they are feeling.

   - Give somebody some feedback.

   Ask your client to pick a place to stand in the room and label this point 'First Position'. Ask them to describe the situation as vividly as possible from their own perspective. Ask them to describe what they are experiencing, thinking and feeling. As coach, you are looking to keep the client 'associated' fully in that position, so bring them back whenever they attempt to justify their thoughts or feelings, or deviate into a narrative.

2. When the client is happy that they have exhausted the First Position, ask them to adopt the physical space and perspective of the other person in the scenario. Label this point 'Second Position' and ask the client the name of that person. Then, as coach, address your questions to that

person. Ask what they are experiencing, thinking and feeling as that person; again, keep them associated in this position.

3. When the client is happy that they have exhausted the Second Position, ask them to adopt the physical space and perspective of a detached, objective observer. Label this point 'Third Position'. Ask the name of the observer and ask them to focus on both people in First and Second Positions. Invite the client to comment on what they have seen, heard and think about the situation. Do they have any insights or advice to offer the person in First Position?

4. Now ask the client to walk back to First Position, bringing all of the new thoughts and knowledge with them and looking towards Second Position again. As coach, ask 'How is this different now?'

Because people with a strong people-pleasing trait naturally spend a lot of their time in second position seeing things from other people's points of view, you may find that standing in first position is a challenge for them. By creating three clearly defined spaces they have an opportunity to practice expressing their needs.

Powerful Coaching Question:
How would somebody who you really respect and admire deal with the same situation?

Assertiveness Practice

Developing assertiveness will enable your client to learn to take into account their own needs as well as the needs of other people.

Here are some ways you can help your client to practice asserting themselves:

- Practice saying 'No' if their basic needs are not being met. Don't encourage them to turn into a selfish, demanding egomaniac though! They should be prepared to compromise but be comfortable stating what they want. It's OK to explain why they don't want to agree to a request, but deter them from making excuses. Offering excuses opens up the opportunity for the person making the request to counter or to find a way around their excuse.

- Set some boundaries to their people pleasing. Encourage your client to experiment with applying some constraints, such as 'I can help you with that but I can only give you thirty minutes' or 'I will get back to you on that by the end of the week'. Remind them that they don't have to reply to every request straight away. Encourage your client to create an opportunity to think about whether it is a fair request and one that they *want* to go along with or one they feel they *should* go along with. It can take a lot of coaching for people to internalise that it's perfectly acceptable to say 'Let me get back to you on that'.

- Help your client to do something for themselves and only themselves. Perhaps set some time aside and watch a movie that they want to watch or eat somewhere they want to eat.

Powerful Coaching Question:
What motivates you to do things for others? Is it guilt, duty, fear or positive choice? How would you want others to be motivated to help you?

Relationships Audit

Sometimes it is important for 'people pleasers' to assess how the people with whom they surround themselves are affecting their behaviour.

As Sophie did, try asking your client to do an audit of people in their life.

1. Ask them to make a list of as many people as they can think of in their network of friends, family and colleagues. Just get them to write down on a sheet of paper as many peoples' names as they can.

2. Ask them to think about each of these people in turn and consider which of the following categories they would fall into:

Supporter	A person who is there for you and that you like to be around. A supporter is on your side and boosts your confidence.
Vampire	Someone who seems to suck the energy, confidence and life out of you when you are near them. A vampire takes much more from the relationship than they give.
Role Model	A person that you admire, look up to and respect. A person who has achieved what you want to achieve.
Consultant	Someone who has information or influence that can help you achieve your goals.
TILIS Friend	A friend who 'Tells It Like It Is' without holding back.
Enemy	A person who actively doesn't want you to succeed and undermines your efforts.

3. Once your client has done this, the first thing to look at is the balance across the categories. Does one group outweigh the others? What does that say?

4. Ask your client to consider whether they want to keep each of these people in their life. Encourage them to seek out people who value and respect them for who they are and not what they do for others and then spend more time with those people.

Powerful Coaching Question:
What advice would you give to someone you really cared about if they were scared to say what they truly felt?

THE INTERVIEW

Emily Cummins

Emily Cummins is an award-winning inventor with a passion for sustainable designs that change lives. Her latest innovation is a sustainable fridge 'powered' by dirty water and keeps the contents dry, hygienic and cool. Emily refined her fridge in African townships before giving away the plans to benefit local people. As a result of her work, Emily was named as one of the Top Ten Outstanding Young People in the World in 2010 and, in the following interview, she tells us how people pleasing can be both a strength and a weakness, and how she has tried to strike the right balance.

'I'm sorry I haven't had time to do my hair. I'm training for a 10k run at the moment and I forgot to take my hair stuff to work.'

These are the first words from Emily as we sit down to talk; a stunning 27 year old who has been named 'Woman of the Year', 'Outstanding Young Person of the World' and been awarded an Honouree of the Oslo Business for Peace Award (awards previously held by John F. Kennedy, Elvis Presley, Sir Richard Branson, Anders Dahlvig, Jackie Chan, Baroness Lawrence, Annie Lennox and Tina Turner among others). This, from someone who has dedicated her life so far to inventing products to help people in the poorest parts of the world and solving some of the biggest problems faced in the world today, such as access to clean drinking water, keeping medicine cold in Africa and tackling obesity.

'I love making things for people and helping them, almost to a fault,' she tells me. She has been like this from a young age when, for her GCSE project, she designed a toothpaste dispenser for her granddad who, because of his arthritis, was struggling with the simple day-to-day task of brushing his teeth.

'I've always had a desire to help and please others. It's a huge part of who I am and, without it, I wouldn't have done the things that I have done. However, I am regularly reminded that I can take it too far.' Emily tells me how her natural desire always to say 'Yes' has got her into trouble in the past.

'After my water carrier invention – another school project by the way - got so much attention I was thrust into the limelight and I wasn't ready for it. I was receiving hundreds of emails every day, I was given loads of awards, asked for interviews, invited to speak at conferences, schools and universities and I just kept replying to every email and saying yes to all these requests.'

I ask her why she said yes without thinking. 'I don't know really,' she replies. 'Partly because I felt like I should say yes and partly because – especially the speaking at schools – I thought it would continue my efforts to encourage more young people to solve real world problems. I didn't even realise I could charge a fee and so sometimes I was even out of pocket travelling to these places.'

'It also affected my studies and I spread myself so thin that, after I had failed a couple of exams, eventually my university tutor sat me down and told me that, the way I was going, I was going to fail my degree. This wasn't an option for me as I had made a promise to my Mum and Dad that I would come back from my gap year, go to university and get a degree.'

The fact that she describes her university degree in the context of being a promise to her parents rather than something for herself is not lost on her.

'I can't even remember who it was that asked me because I was getting so many requests for interviews and speeches, but one publication asked if I had an agent. I hadn't – and I still haven't – but the idea sparked something for me and I did something that I never thought I would do. I asked for help. I had always seen asking for help as a sign of weakness, I'm not sure why; but I swallowed hard and I got someone to help me manage my emails and to teach me how to manage my calendar.'

Emily also tells me about some little things that she did that had a profound impact for her. 'It was a source of pride for me that I answered every email that people sent to me and I didn't want to let that go, but I did put some boundaries around it for myself. I put a message on my website that said I may not be able to reply to every email which took the pressure off. Also, I agreed with myself that, sometimes, it's OK if I don't reply for three or four weeks. It's just more realistic that way.'

'Another thing I do today is that I take the counsel of people whose opinions I can trust and, when I'm asked to do something, I give myself a bit of time and ask their advice.

'I used to tell myself subconsciously that I must reply to every email straight away and that I couldn't say no to people asking me to speak at every event, because I knew these events were going to add value. However, I now know my worth, I am being kinder to myself and I can work to create win-win situations. I still want to push myself though and my ultimate mission still remains the same – to design products that help as many people as possible. Whenever I get close to saying yes to something or someone else, I ask myself whether this is helping me in the bigger picture or whether it's a distraction, something that will actually water down my impact.'

When she speaks humbly about the awards that she has won, another flag pops up. 'I am often asked when I'm going to win another award because it's been a year since I've been in the news or in the public eye. These awards are lovely but actually they bring their own kind of expectation and pressure to do even better.'

'I'm still learning and I'm still working on getting the right balance between using my drive to please people as a strength and making sure it doesn't get away from me.'

As my time with Emily comes to a close she makes a huge apology for having to leave, thanks *me* for *my* time and offers to pay for lunch. I remind her that it is she who is doing me the favour, that paying for lunch is the least that I can do and that she has already given me more of her time than she had agreed to.

'Oops. I guess I still have some work to do on that people pleaser driver don't I?' she says as she leaves.

CHAPTER THREE

Going To Excess

'Moderation is a fatal thing.
Nothing succeeds like excess.'

OSCAR WILDE

THE CASE STUDY

'Live fast, die young and leave a good-looking corpse
has always been my motto!'

The personal relationship between a coach and their client means
it is important for them to have the right 'chemistry'; they should
be able to talk to and work with one another comfortably.

It is for this reason that coach and client often have an initial meeting to get to know each other a little and to discuss the process and potential goals for the sessions. Sometimes the outcome of a chemistry meeting is that the client and coach decide not to work together. There could be several reasons for this decision including the timing or circumstances not being right or simply a lack of 'chemistry' between client and coach.

Sebastian came to a chemistry meeting when the Board of Directors of a trading company engaged me after becoming worried by the amount of burnout amongst their top staff. Sebastian himself admitted to a 'bit of a wake up call' when another of his colleagues and friend – Andrew – had 'crashed and burned' recently.

I started off by trying to find out a little about his background and he was very open for somebody in their first coaching session, especially considering that he had told me that he definitely didn't want any therapy.

'I'm a very driven and passionate person. I don't believe in half-measures – if you aren't playing to win then don't bother I say,' Sebastian began. 'I'm very good at what I do and I like to enjoy the fruits of my labour – there's nothing wrong with that is there?'

I had already been told how quickly he had climbed the corporate ladder and he had been handsomely rewarded for his successes at the company. In my brief discussion with the Board, I was told that they thought very highly of Sebastian but felt that, most of the time, he was 'unmanageable'. They feared driving him out of the company and so gave him free rein to be a bit of a maverick.

Sebastian told me how he often worked 80 hour weeks and was a 'bit of a party animal' when he switched off but that it hadn't been a problem for him so far.

'Now I'm starting to wonder how long it can all go on for. It's all fun and games until somebody loses an eye as my Mum always used to say!' He seemed to have a cliché or metaphor for everything. 'I love living life in the fast lane but, after what happened to Andrew (his colleague), I'm beginning to wonder if I need to dial it down a little.'

'What does 'dial it down a little' mean to you?' I asked.

'Well I don't know. I admit that I smoke too much and I'm probably one of those people that the media label as a 'binge drinker'. Now and again I probably work too much as well but I'm in good shape and I'm still young. I've just started this new exercise regime and I've also taken up base-jumping.'

It seemed as though his whole life was 100 m.p.h. and this was coming out in the session too. He was very fidgety and spoke very quickly, which I noticed was making me feel a little rushed. A skilled coach can sometimes influence a client's pace by initially matching it and then slowly altering their own pace, hoping to lead the client to match them. The coach may also make use of other subtle influencing cues such as tapping their foot at a slower rhythm or taking slightly more noticeable, deeper and slower breaths. For now I was just focusing on keeping myself at the pace that was comfortable for me so that I could be of best service to Sebastian.

'Have you ever tried dialling it down a little before?' I asked.

'I've tried to quit smoking a few times but it's never worked – probably because I actually enjoy smoking. And I've had periods where I haven't had any alcohol, so I know I'm not addicted, but I don't actually want to give that up. And I can take time off work – I went backpacking for six months not long ago.'

It was clear to me, and Sebastian confirmed it, that he didn't want to use coaching to find a way to stop smoking or drinking. I suspected that he didn't want to change any aspects of his behaviour.

'So what do you want from coaching?' I asked.

'I don't know,' he said, sounding a little frustrated. 'I don't know exactly what you do, but I guess if you could cure all the bad stuff that I do without making me miserable that would be great. I'm pretty sure that's not realistic though, so I think I just want to make sure that what happened to Andrew doesn't happen to me.'

We spent the rest of the session going through what coaching was and exploring whether he thought it could be of use to him.

The ultimate goal of coaching is to help the client understand themselves better so they can find ways to make the most of their potential.

This could be through a better appreciation of the client's strengths, clarification of what it is that they want to do or it could be through analysing the patterns of their behaviour or thought that are currently limiting their potential in some way.

I explained that there would almost inevitably be a 'therapeutic' angle to coaching as there is no way of delineating between our work and personal lives, just as there is no way to split our past from our present or our body from our mind. I did reassure him however that I wasn't going to ask him to lie on a couch!

I also explained that, while it could be possible for us to find a way to stop his smoking or drinking – should that turn out to be what he wanted to do, it was more likely that coaching would focus on the underlying factors that encouraged him to indulge, or over-indulge, in these things.

Sebastian listened with genuine curiosity about my approach and I finished the session by asking him to think about whether he wanted to work with me as his coach.

Session One

I was pleased that Sebastian decided to go ahead with coaching, as he seemed like an interesting person who could really benefit from the process. In our first formal session, I learned that he grew up in a big family who supported and pushed him in equal measure. As a result he had great self-belief but also believed it to be a 'dog eat dog' world.

I asked Sebastian how he would describe himself in under ten words and his response was illuminating:

'I play to win and I love to play.'

'What happens when you lose?' I asked.

'I never lose,' was his immediate reply, although with a cheeky smile on his face.

I was aware of his success at work and, given that he was still quite young, I was prepared to accept that it might actually be true that he hasn't ever 'lost' at work. But never?

'What about outside of work? What does 'winning' mean in your personal life?' I asked.

'I like pushing the boundaries there too. I agree with Neil Armstrong who said, 'I believe you've only got a finite number of heartbeats and I don't intend to waste one of them'. So I want to experience everything that I can.'

I could see a pattern becoming clear already. 'What do you think of the phrase 'everything in moderation'?' I asked.

'It's not me. Simple as that. Why would you settle for a half-measure? Live fast, die young and leave a good-looking corpse has always been my motto.'

I asked Sebastian about his tendency to go to extremes and where he thought it came from but he either didn't know or didn't want to go into it in much detail yet. My dilemma was that he seemed mostly happy with the choices he was making and the life he was living. He was only having doubts because of the burnout of his colleague. I decided to explore that a little more.

'So why do you think Andrew 'crashed and burned' but you haven't?'

He thought about this for a while before admitting he didn't really know. 'Initially I was shocked but, when I thought about it a bit more, I wasn't that surprised. He didn't stop even when he wasn't enjoying it any more, whereas I keep going because I enjoy it.'

Because he seemed to like his clichés I decided to follow this theme. 'Do you think you can ever have too much of a good thing?'

'Everybody has their limits, of course. I just think that most people don't ever get close to reaching theirs, whereas I'm always trying to find out where mine are.'

I was really interested in why he was so keen to find his limits but I didn't want my curiosity to drive the coaching. I still hadn't worked out what Sebastian wanted from our coaching relationship.

I reminded him that, in our first meeting, he said that he wanted coaching to help ensure that what happened to Andrew didn't happen to him.

'What do you think is the biggest risk of that happening?' I asked.

'I guess that I'm getting older and perhaps it will all catch up with me. Or that I reach my limits and overstep them without realising.'

'Is the risk of that happening big enough for you to want to do something about it?' I asked.

This, for me, was the crucial question.

> **If the client doesn't feel a strong need to make a change then coaching is likely to be nothing more than going through the motions since it is highly likely that any changes would either be token gestures or fail to stick.**

'If I'm honest, I would have to say that I'm not sure. Part of me thinks 'It'll never happen to me' and another part of me doesn't like the idea of letting go of things that I enjoy. I'd still like to carry on with the coaching though to see where it goes.'

I wasn't surprised by this response but couldn't help being a little disappointed.

Session Two

The next time that I saw Sebastian he was much more determined that something had to change. He had a black eye and a couple of stitches in his cheek. He explained that he'd been on a night out, got drunk and tried to chat up the prettiest girl in the club, despite the fact that she was with her boyfriend.

'It was stupid. I've been thinking about it and perhaps I'm not as 'in control' as I thought I was.'

We talked about the nightclub incident as an example of his behaviour in general and it was clear he was in a very reflective mood.

'It seems like I am only interested in doing things or going further than others would think possible. I could have easily hooked up with a number of the girls in the club but that didn't really cross my mind. I don't know why but doing what's considered normal doesn't excite me.'

He even admitted that there was a risk that he was beginning to push the boundaries too far and that, while it has been an integral part of his success so far, there was a risk that it could become his downfall.

'I want to do it. The coaching that is. I want to stop the excesses. I think it's time for me to be normal.'

The rest of the session was spent exploring what he meant by the word 'normal'. The conclusion was that he wanted to enjoy what he did without worrying about getting 'the badge' for the most, the best, the quickest or any other type of record. He also wanted to be sure that he was in control of when to stop.

My first idea was to introduce Sebastian to mindfulness as a way of helping him notice and acknowledge his thoughts and consciously decide which ones to act on. As he was also someone who seemed to operate at 100 m.p.h. all the time, it could help him to slow down a little. Slowing down could itself be a way to help him make more deliberate decisions.

He agreed to look into it before our next session.

Supervision

When I presented this case to my supervisor, he looked concerned. 'It really sounds like this guy is out of control. It immediately strikes me that he has some unmet emotional needs that he is trying to meet at any cost.'

Often when someone is doing things to excess – eating, drinking, gambling, drugs, spending, sex – they have a feeling of emotional emptiness inside them that they are trying to fill with other things.

My supervisor pointed out that, alternatively, it could be that Sebastian was rebelling against unduly lenient or unduly constrictive boundaries, which were imposed on him earlier in life. If this is coupled with success then it can become an entrenched pattern. This can be further exacerbated if the person in question also has an 'addictive personality'.

We talked about the various options available and decided that Joe Griffin and Ivan Tyrell's 'Human Givens Audit' could be a good technique for identifying Sebastian's unmet needs and exploring how he compensates for them in other ways.

At the core of the Human Givens Approach *[Ref 7]* is the idea that all human beings have a set of needs and a guidance system which ensures that they get these needs met – sometimes at any cost. Stress or failure to thrive indicates that some core needs are not being met. If people are helped to get their emotional and physical needs met in the appropriate way and in balance, they will thrive and flourish. The emotional needs include:

- Security – a safe territory and the space to unfold well.

- A sense of autonomy and control.

- Feeling part of a wider community.

- The need to both give and receive attention.

- Friendship, fun, love and intimacy.

- A sense of status within social groupings.

- A sense of achievement.

- The need for meaning – being stretched.

- The need for privacy.

My supervisor suggested that I introduce this concept to Sebastian, explaining what each of the needs means and asking Sebastian to identify how satisfied he was that each of these needs was being met. Each of us has different requirements. For example, someone with a high need for privacy would find it difficult to work in a busy, open-plan office environment and someone with a high need for attention would not be comfortable working on their own all day. Part of the discussion to have with clients is about how important each of these needs are to them. According to my supervisor, this approach should provoke a rich discussion with Sebastian about how he thought his current behaviours could meet his needs. He was unlikely to be aware of this consciously and the model could bring him some insights.

Often we choose to present this as a Wheel of Human Givens:

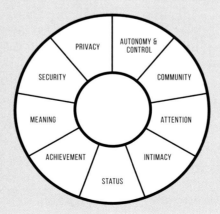

I was struck by the fact that my supervisor seemed quite concerned about this client and insisted that I take time to uncover the 'hurt' that sat behind these behaviours. I had not quite appreciated that there might be deep-seated causes for what seemed to be simply excessively hedonistic behaviour.

Session Three

Session three didn't actually happen because, on the day before we were due to meet, I received an email from Sebastian to say that he wouldn't be there. He asked for the session to be postponed because he had booked himself into an immersive, week-long mindfulness retreat in America.

Session Four

The obvious topic of conversation when we eventually saw each other was the fact that he had employed an excessive tactic in an attempt to rid himself of his excessive trait.

'I think it's great that you found the mindfulness concept useful and interesting, but do you see the irony in what you did?' I asked.

'Yeah, I thought about that as I was booking my flight but I thought an immersive retreat has to be much better than reading a book or listening to a CD. I thought about telling you but I knew you would try to talk me out of it.'

'How do you know that's what I would have done?' I asked.

'Because you're normal.'

'Maybe that's what you told yourself to justify doing it. What do you think you would have done if I had said, 'Great idea! Go for it'?' I asked.

I could tell that this question resonated with him because he almost squirmed in his chair and looked away. His eyes darted from side to side as he processed the question. Eventually, he said, 'I think it would have made it less attractive.'

I thought that perhaps we had stumbled on a way for Sebastian to limit his impulsive, excessive behaviour – to imagine asking someone who wouldn't be impressed by the excessive nature of it but rather would think it to be a normal thing to do. Before I could suggest that, however, Sebastian added, 'So I would have probably booked in for two weeks instead.'

The last thing Sebastian needed was a strategy that pushed his excessive behaviour even further, so I decided to change the subject.

'Putting all that to one side for a minute, how was the retreat itself?'

'It was really cool, although it was really hard to be around some of those people. I don't know how they ever get anything done!'

'But what if what they are doing is what they want and need to be doing?'

Sebastian didn't seem to understand this question and went on to say that they were wasting their lives, missing out on the experiences that life has to offer and that they would look back one day and regret not living life while they were young.

'That's certainly possible,' I said. 'Is that what worries you? That you will look back and regret not having done everything you possibly could have done?'

Sebastian agreed that this was certainly the case to a degree. I asked him what he thought when he looked at his social media feeds and saw pictures of the cool things his friends were doing. He admitted to feeling compelled to make sure he was doing something better or at least equally cool.

'It's a constant reminder of all the opportunities there are, and I don't want to miss out.'

Fear of Missing Out, or *FOMO* as it is often labelled, is where someone experiences anxiety as a result of comparing their current lifestyle to what they believe or perceive others are doing.

If people with FOMO see a Facebook post of a great party or an Instagram picture of a beautiful beach holiday, their immediate reaction is to reflect on how pathetic their current situation is by comparison.

Even as a child, Sebastian was constantly in a competitive environment; in the sports he played, the expectations his family placed on him at school and in terms of his sibling rivalries. The fact that he was always looking at what others were doing and trying to get one over on them had undoubtedly helped him become successful, but he was in a constant state of dissatisfaction because as soon as he achieved something then he would set a new target. He realised at an intellectual level that this was one game he was destined to lose no matter how successful he was. He used another metaphor of being on a speeding train that was just getting faster and he needed to find a way to get off.

This seemed a good moment to introduce the Human Givens Approach as Sebastian was already identifying his unfulfilled state. The technique had a profound impact on him. He scored himself really low on the following needs:

- The need for attention.

- The need for security.

- The need to feel part of a wider community.

He actually broke down in tears as he was completing this exercise. He told me that he had been adopted as a young baby and his adoptive parents had told him about it when he was five. He hadn't really understood what it meant at the time but he did know that he had never felt important or significant or secure as to his identity. He was the only adopted child in his family and he had always felt that he had not had as much attention as his siblings. This had been compounded a few years previously when he found his natural mother and, after their first meeting, she had decided not to see him again. She had a family of her own and he wasn't part of that either. He realised that he was trying to have more and more experiences that he hoped would give him the feeling of significance and belonging that was missing from his life. Sebastian was really distressed by this realisation and asked if we could end the session. We agreed that I would call him the next day to check in with him and see how he was feeling.

The day after the session

I called Sebastian as agreed and found that he had taken the day off work. He said he was still very disoriented about what he had realised in the session but reassured me that he felt that the realisations were valuable. I checked that Sebastian was still happy to wait a week until our next session to discuss this further and he agreed. I also offered a line of support and encouraged him to contact me in the meantime if he felt it necessary.

Supervision

I requested a short-notice supervision session as I was feeling out of my depth and needed guidance. As a coach, I am very used to clients expressing both positive and negative emotions but Sebastian's catharsis had been of a different dimension. During the session he appeared to be in real crisis and extreme distress.

I outlined what had happened to my supervisor and he felt that I should refer Sebastian to a therapist to work on the feelings of hurt and emptiness that stemmed from his early sense of deprivation. The supervisor felt that this needed addressing by a qualified psychotherapist but there was no reason that Sebastian could not return to me for coaching after he had finished his therapy, although this could be a longer-term piece of work.

It is a generally accepted approach to differentiate coaching and therapy by reference to the relative psychological health of a person. Therapy is generally seen as dealing with healing pain, dysfunction or conflict within an individual.

My supervisor reminded me that a coach should have:

1. An understanding that being unable to help is no reflection on their competence as a coach. Some people will have temporary or more permanent mental health issues that will prove to be barriers to effective coaching.

2. The capacity to recognise and explore the signs of possible mental health issues with the client.

3. The ability to make informed judgements in the light of the coach's own level of training and experience and ethical considerations.

4. An acceptance that coaching is not always an appropriate solution and a knowledge of alternative options.

Session Five

When I met Sebastian again I recommended therapy as the most appropriate solution for him at the moment. He accepted and agreed with my suggestion, saying that deep down he had always felt that he needed some therapy. He also said that he probably wouldn't have sought it out, so he was pleased that the coaching had led him to this point. On a personal note, while I felt slightly disappointed not to have been able to continue helping Sebastian through coaching, I was satisfied that this was the right decision for the client.

TOOLS AND TECHNIQUES

Living life to the full clearly has its positive sides although as we saw with Sebastian a potential downside to this behaviour can be burnout.

As coaches, our aim is to try to help our clients channel this drive and energy towards helpful goals rather than channelling it in a random or unhelpful direction. As with Sebastian, looking at what else is going on in their lives, perhaps from a Human Givens perspective, can be an effective complementary long-term strategy.

In this case study we felt the need to refer Sebastian to a specialist therapist and we recommend that as a coach you should continually re-assess whether coaching is the appropriate intervention for your client. *We have a link in the references section with more information on how to know when to refer somebody to therapy [Ref 8].* Not all clients will require therapeutic intervention, however, and below are a selection of techniques aimed at helping your clients become more aware and in control of their thought processes.

Attribute Shopping

Sometimes being presented with an abstract, hypothetical scenario can shift the client's thinking and allow them to rationally evaluate their behaviour from a new perspective.

Attribute Shopping is a visualisation exercise so ensure your client is comfortable – both physically and emotionally – and ask them to close their eyes. Then read them the following script:

Imagine that you are standing outside a shop. Picture the shop and, as you move towards the front door, it automatically opens. You step inside and feel a nice, warm rush of air and it's very well lit. In front of you there are a number of shelves with different things for sale. As you look closer you will start to notice that the items on the shelves are personal attributes that you can buy.

If you want to become more creative, you can buy that attribute. If you want to become more determined, you can pick up that characteristic, take it to the till and buy it. Once you have bought it, you will immediately add that trait to your skillset.

Now look along the shelf of attributes until you find the one that says 'does things to extremes'. When you find it, pick it up and look at the packaging where it describes what it does for you. What are its selling points? Why should you buy this for yourself?

(Here your client should be allowed to think and answer).

Take your time to have a more detailed look at the packaging; probably on the back there is a warning label. Here are the side effects or risks that come with this attribute. What does it say there?

(Here your client should be allowed to think and answer).

Notice how you feel about the prospect of buying this attribute for yourself.

Put it back on the shelf. Next to it on the shelf is another attribute that says 'does things in moderation'. Pick that attribute up and study the packaging. What does this one claim it would do for you?

(Here your client should be allowed to think and answer).

And what are the warnings or side-effects of this one?

(Here your client should be allowed to think and answer).

Notice how you feel about the prospect of buying this attribute.

You can only buy one of these attributes. Which one is most compelling to you? What is compelling about it?

Powerful Coaching Question:
If a child were to ask you 'What is life all about?' how would you answer them?

Mindfulness

One of the aims of coaching is to promote a greater sense of awareness within the client, to help them know themselves better and be able to manage themselves more effectively.

Prepare your client with a brief explanation of mindfulness: that they can expect to be guided through a form of meditation focused on developing a greater awareness of what we are thinking, feeling and experiencing, without judgement *[Ref 9]*.

There are many scripts, mp3 files and apps available online and the one provided here is merely one example.

Adopt a soft voice and speak slowly:

Begin by getting comfortable in your chair with your feet flat on the ground and your hands resting in your lap. Close your eyes and just breathe normally.

Focus on your breathing. Just notice how you are breathing, as if you were noticing it for the first time. Feel the air coming in and your chest expanding, maybe your belly, maybe your shoulders are rising. Then feel the air going out. Do you make a noise when you breathe? Just notice, don't try to change anything, just notice.

I am going to be quiet for a minute while you just focus on your breathing, in and out.

(Remain quiet for a minute.)

Continue breathing normally. Start to notice your thoughts. When a thought comes into your head just acknowledge it, don't evaluate it or judge it or think any more deeply about it. Just notice it and let it go.

If it helps, imagine your thoughts as balloons floating by and away, or cars going past you on a road, or leaves floating on a stream.

I am going to be quiet for a couple of minutes while you just notice your thoughts and keep on letting them go.

(Remain quiet for two minutes.)

If at any time you realise you have been judging the thoughts, or investigating them, don't worry about it, just acknowledge that and carry on with the exercise.

(Remain quiet for two minutes)

Don't go looking for thoughts, just go back to breathing and eventually another one will come along. Just notice it and let it go.

(Remain quiet for two minutes then gently bring them back)

This feeling of calm and control over your thoughts is a skill that you are developing and one that you will be able to recreate when necessary in the future.

When you are ready, take a deeper breath, slowly open your eyes and reorientate yourself.

* * *

The ultimate aim of this exercise is for the client to be able to reproduce this when they feel in danger of going to excess. By practicing a mindfulness exercise, they should be in greater control of their thoughts and be able to let go of any unhelpful or destructive thoughts they may be having.

Powerful Coaching Question:
What do you want your legacy to be?

Modelling Internal Strategies

Modelling is the process of determining the internal and external processes required to exhibit a particular behaviour.

Modelling is one of the techniques associated with Neuro Linguistic Programming *[Ref 10]*. As coach you can walk your client through the explanation of something that your client does particularly well and then help them to consciously apply that strategy to another behaviour – in this case their excessive behaviour.

Ask your client to think of a specific situation where they don't go to excess. Ask them to talk you through it as if you were someone completely new to human behaviour. They should spell it out, leaving nothing to assumption. This basic level of explanation will help them to clarify exactly what they are thinking, feeling, doing or not doing.

As coach, you may prompt or guide with the odd question to tease out exactly what is going on for them when they avoid going to excess. Some questions that might be useful are:

- What goes through your mind before you do this?

- Why do you do this?

- What do you say to yourself?

- What do you feel?

- What thoughts do you have about this situation?

- Do you have any pictures or images in your mind?

- If so – where are they? How big are they? Are they colour or black and white?

- What keeps you motivated to do this?

- What is the trigger to you doing this?

Once your client has explained in detail how they manage to avoid going to excess in this particular circumstance, ask them to repeat their strategy to enable them to bring it to mind when needed.

Powerful Coaching Question:
If you knew that what you were striving for would leave you dissatisfied, what would you do differently?

THE INTERVIEW

Pen Hadow

There is a fine line between dedication and obsession. Most successful people at some stage become aware of walking that fine line, often only after they have crossed it. We interviewed Pen Hadow who paid no heed to the old adage of 'all good things in moderation' and, as such, was the first person to walk solo to the North Pole without resupply by the hardest route (and, nine months later, without resupply to the South Pole with a sledging partner).

Pen's exploration and entrepreneurial interests combined in 1995 when he founded a specialist polar guide service, The Polar Travel Company, which organises expeditions to the Poles. In 2009 he formed Geo Mission, a pioneering environmental sponsorship organisation that has delivered the multi-award winning series of Catlin Arctic Surveys (2009-2011) investigating the rates, causes and global impact of the fast-disappearing Arctic sea ice.

In the interview that follows, Pen talks about what drove him to such feats and how this driver has been a double-edged sword for him.

'What sort of demons drive a man to choose to walk totally alone for 75 days to the most isolated place on Earth? They have to be extreme because you didn't get anything simply for arriving at the Pole; there was no band playing, nobody giving you a medal.'

Pen Hadow rose to international fame in 2003 when he achieved his extraordinary goal to become the first person to trek solo, without resupply by third parties, from Canada to the North Geographic Pole – a feat which has not been repeated and is thought comparable in difficulty to making the first solo ascent of Mount Everest without oxygen by the hardest route. It had taken him 15 years and three attempts of ever more focused effort. He had even set up the world's first guide service to the Poles so that he could build up the necessary hours of experience on the sea ice to meet the challenge that had beaten so many of the big names in polar exploration. Within months he went on to repeat the expedition to the South Geographic Pole, this time with a sledging partner, becoming the only Briton to have trekked, without resupply, to both Poles.

When I interviewed Pen it was quickly apparent that he has great self-awareness, self-knowledge and is charmingly self-effacing. Having outlined to him the theme of the book, he immediately began the interview by telling me that his core driver is 'I'll show you'.

He explained that, without this driver, he would not have been likely to do all the things he has done, but he is now fully aware that this driver comes with an array of by-products that have not always been helpful.

Pen went on to paint me a picture of a scared seven-year-old boy, crying every night at bedtime following his arrival at a boarding school, which he found to be a very frightening place. As an adult he has come to realise that his parents were doing what they considered to be the very best thing for him – sending him to a really good school that would develop key life-skills, such as self-reliance, to stand him in good stead for later life. At the time, of course, he didn't know this. He explains his three weeks of non-stop night-time crying as the outward manifestation of being 'weaned' … weaned off parental dependency and emotional attachment. Meanwhile, internally, a necessary major re-wiring of his approach to people, activities, events and life in general, was taking place.

The result of this weaning was that he closed down emotionally on all fronts. By the age of eight Pen had developed a coping strategy to protect himself from experiencing painful feelings again. As well as attempting to turn off his emotions, he adopted a subconscious motto of 'I'll show you that I'm worth loving' and the way that he outwardly responded to that motto was to be a high achiever.

There followed years of high achievement at school. Pen acknowledges that, as an adult, he now realises he has been 'reputationally' driven.

'I will keep going until you appreciate who I am,' he told me. 'So much of what I have achieved has been about seeking to influence how people perceive me, and avoiding nourishing my own deeper needs. I have turned myself inside out to do what I intuitively felt others wanted. I have been externally referenced in the extreme.'

On reflection, Pen says that his solo North Pole endeavour was a combination of self-mortification and self-discovery. It was an attempt to purge himself of his psychological baggage and to relocate his 'essential spirit' - his original self before his perceived abandonment at school.

'Hauling that almost impossibly heavy sledge across hundreds of miles of frozen ocean was dangerous every minute of every day and the fear of failure was chronically frightening. It was a kind of self-punishment for feeling I was not good enough to date. This interpretation of myself in the world was so severe that it could only be dispelled by my achieving something of an equivalent, counterbalancing scale. Not even national achievement was enough; I needed global acknowledgment.'

After the expedition Pen rose to international fame for his achievement, with *The Times* making him its lead front-page story on four separate occasions. Around the world the effort required to achieve this was written and talked about online, in newspapers and magazines, as well as on radio and television. Pen admits to a 'Ready Brek glow' around him for several months afterwards. But the glow was on the outside - not within.

In a valuable way, however, it served to clarify that the answer to 'Who he was' lay not in activity and the reactions of others, but in guided, deep introspection – a process which no achievement can substitute and requires a totally different approach. Pen was profoundly shocked to discover that this was far harder, more frightening and even more hazardous than any expedition he could ever have undertaken.

'I knew just how much of me it had taken to reach the Pole, but surprise, surprise – it didn't seem to solve the stuff inside. I was to spend the next ten years giving motivational talks about 'How I did it' but on stage I was thinking, 'It's just me, I'm nobody special'. You can separate the feat from the man, and simply by doing a feat like this doesn't mean you become the person you want to be. Having people looking up to me only amplified in my mind the disparity between who I felt I was and what they thought I was. It made me even more aware of my own fallibilities, flaws and insecurities.'

I was full of both sadness and admiration listening to Pen. He had been prepared to be utterly self-disclosing in this interview and to reveal the generous, intelligent, brave and thoughtful man he is. I really couldn't understand how he could not have known he was all these things and more? It was so obvious to me and other outside observers but Pen had not been able to see this in himself.

I was aware that he was telling me all this in the past tense and being with him in person, I was struggling to recognise the man he was telling me about. The man I was interviewing seemed calm, considered and comfortable with himself. I asked what he had done to achieve this.

Pen explained that there was a difficult period when things started to 'fall apart' in several aspects of his life and all of a sudden he started to experience emotions again. This was a huge shock to his system having had 45 years without any practice at allowing emotions to come through, and he needed to develop the ability to accept and manage them.

'There came a point, at my lowest ebb, when I decided that I had to finally address my 'demons'.'

Pen told me that he had some great 'informal therapy', which involved him spending a lot of time with an old friend who listened to him intently, and who caringly dispensed wisdom. He went in search of personal development programmes, qualified as a professional coach, and he also consciously minimised his engagement with others in his extensive friendship group. He took eighteen months out of his life – a kind of emotional sabbatical - and created a lot of space and quiet around himself. In explorer terms, he set off on the ultimate journey of discovery, heading deep into the unknown landscape of his subconscious, to locate, understand and resolve the hitherto unidentified forces that had made him who he was. Pen now looks back at this time in his personal life as 'the best thing that could have happened and the best thing I ever did', despite it having been far more frightening than any solo trek to the North Pole:

'When I started to acquire self-knowledge I thought, 'Why didn't anyone teach us about such things when we were young? That we had choices about how we interpret and react to events? ' I didn't know I had any choices back then, but now I have worked out how I function, what my default settings are, and how I can deliberately choose different responses. I have a degree of control I had never imagined possible. Once you know why things are driving you, you have choices. Only counselling, coaching and coaching-related activities helped me to understand this. Going to the North Pole didn't provide the solution, but it did reveal where to focus my attention.'

Pen was not evangelical about coaching, but thankful and realistic. He told me that there has been a big shift for him now and his relationship with people and events is essentially, subtly and significantly different. His spirit is now quietened. I asked him to tell me more about his different behaviours and he listed them as follows:

- I realise that most of us struggle, wittingly or unwittingly, with issues, irrespective of our circumstances.

- I am more accepting that I am good enough – and that the human condition involves flaws, fallibilities and insecurities.

- Any need to prove my worth is now better controlled.

- I know that it is ok to be just ok at some things, and I can choose which things I give maximum effort to.

- I have a sense of quiet and calm that I haven't known before.

- The combined effects of my changing outlook and approach to life may make me easier to be around.

I thanked Pen for his generosity and openness and congratulated him on an even more challenging feat than walking solo to the North and South Poles – dealing with his demons.

'*How am I going to show you?*' used to be my silent question,' he said as we came to the end of our interview. Then, after a pause, he added, 'But now, at last, I feel free.'

CHAPTER FOUR

Fierce Independence

'Don't go where the path may follow.
Go instead where there is no path and leave a trail.'

RALPH WALDO EMERSON

THE CASE STUDY

'I have never followed the crowd and never will.'

I met Roxy at the media company where she was a newly appointed Sales Director. I was one of several coaches she was seeing for chemistry meetings that day. The company had organised the coaching and had explained that Roxy had worked there for a couple of years, was 'pure talent' and that now she had been appointed to the board, she needed to 'fit in' and tame some of her maverick tendencies. Some senior board members had expressed concern about the image of the company that she would portray to the outside world.

'However,' said the HR Director, 'We can't deny that her sales ability is outstanding!'

I knew who she was from the moment she entered reception. She looked like she had stepped off a Vivienne Westwood catwalk. Her appearance was dramatic and non-conformist even for a media company. She made me smile as she strode across the lobby to greet me in silver Doc Marten boots.

Within five minutes of meeting me she announced, 'I'm going to work with you. It just feels right. The others bored me with their models and approaches. I like the fact that you haven't got a system.'

I wasn't sure that this was an entirely accurate assessment of my coaching approach but I was delighted to have been 'chosen' and felt sure that we would have fun working together. In the rest of the time we had together I found out that she was: 'well up' for coaching; had grown up in a commune in a hippy family; had been expelled from three schools; was named after the band Roxy Music; and liked to push the boundaries and break rules.

She had been told by the board that she would need to learn to fit into the corporate culture and she said that, although she was interested in exploring that with me, she didn't think there was a chance that it was going to happen!

I was intrigued by her ability to fly in the face of convention and wondered how the coaching sessions would unfold. We made a date to meet the following week as Roxy was keen to get started.

Session One

I was slightly apprehensive meeting Roxy for the second time. I didn't know if I was going to be able to keep her interested and I knew that I needed to stay away from any coaching models or systems if I was going to keep her happy.

I began the session by asking what she wanted to focus on. Roxy told me that she was already feeling constrained by the organisation and the new role. She felt they were trying to clip her wings and make her 'just like the rest of them'. She was bored by the 'bored meetings' as she called them and refused to wear the corporate 'uniform', which included having an expensive watch and fountain pen. She told me that she delighted in making her colleagues uncomfortable by challenging their assumptions and behaviours. She ignored company policy if she didn't agree with it and told me that she did her own thing.

'They didn't care about the way I dressed or behaved when I was Head of Sales. They left me alone and quite liked me being a bit of a character. It's all changed since I got appointed Sales Director. Who says that Directors have to look and behave a certain way? I'm just not having it. They should be the ones to change, not me.'

'Why did you go for the job?' I asked.

'Good question! Firstly, I wanted to see if I could get it; but I also wanted more money and more success. I have always known that I was going to do something amazing with my life and be really successful. I have always taken risks and gone after what I wanted and got it – against all the odds.'

'And now you have got it?'

'Now I have got it I am unhappy. I don't think they are taking me seriously. I feel that all that matters to them is my 'fitting in' when actually I am really talented at what I do. If they would just leave me alone to do my own thing I could make them lots more money. I didn't realise that things change so much when you are a Director. Things shouldn't have to change though, should they?'

Roxy was very persuasive. I couldn't disagree with her ideals but I knew that her employers didn't share those ideals.

'What options do you have then?' I asked her.

'I could leave. Or I could get them to loosen up a bit. But I just can't bring myself to toe the corporate line.'

I asked Roxy if she had ever heard of the PIE model, devised by Harvey Coleman *[Ref 11]*. She hadn't. Coleman's research suggests that there are three elements we need to focus on if we are to achieve success and get to the top of the ladder:

- Performance (how good a job we do, what results we deliver).

- Image (not merely how we are seen but how we are experienced by others, our personal 'brand').

- Exposure (ensuring that the right people know us – inside and outside our organisation).

In his 1996 book *Empowering Yourself: The Organizational Game Revealed*, Coleman shared some shocking statistics:

- **Performance counts for 10% of our success.**

- **Image 30%.**

- **Exposure 60%.**

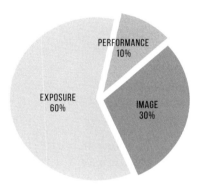

Roxy was outraged at this: 'That's just not fair!'

I told her that, interestingly, Coleman's first rule of organisational culture is, 'Nobody said it was going to be fair'. He identified that, for those who want to get to the top, no sacrifice is too great.

I had the feeling that losing her uniqueness would be too great a sacrifice for Roxy. The statistics seemed to have enraged her. We had a long discussion about whether they were true and reluctantly we both agreed that there was certainly a lot of truth in them if we looked around us.

For the rest of the session we explored how Roxy described herself in each of the three areas.

She knew she was an outstanding performer with sales results which knocked spots off anyone else in the organisation. She was also a good manager of people: inspirational, a hard-working role model and a manager who offered a good mix of support and challenge. She was conscientious and always met targets and deadlines, although she didn't always abide by company rules to get there.

'What's not to like?' she said.

I asked her to describe her personal 'brand'.

'Individual, self-reliant, edgy, fun, dynamic, maverick, risk-taking, challenging, warm, creative, energetic, memorable, feisty.' Her words came tumbling out with passion and pride.

'Exposure?' I said.

'I don't schmooze enough for 'them'. I hate all those corporate away-days. Can you imagine me on a golf day? Honestly – that was the Exec away-day this summer! Of course, I didn't go. I have a huge network of contacts in the industry and I know lots of people in TV and on the stand-up comedy circuit. At work I prefer to hang out with my sales teams than spend time with my peers.'

There was a pause, then she looked directly at me, 'You think I should change, don't you?'

'I am here because your organisation would like you to make some changes,' I replied. 'They have said that to both of us. My role is to help you think through whether you are going to do that and, if so, how. My personal perspective does not come into it. I do think, however, that your organisation has given a clear message about their expectations of you and we need to give it some serious attention in our coaching sessions.'

'Why the hell did they promote me in the first place? They know who I am!'

Roxy's question hung in the air at the end of the session. It was a good question and one which I had been asking myself.

She agreed to read Harvey Coleman's book and give some thought to playing the 'organisational game' before our next session.

Session Two

'I can't do it! I tried it and I have decided I just can't do it!'

'What do you mean you tried it?' I asked. Roxy told me that she had gone to work for a day in 'normal clothes' and tried to behave like her fellow board members. To Roxy this meant being an 'inauthentic yes-man'.

'I wanted to see what it was like to run with the pack and I hated it.' Roxy paced up and down the coaching room in a state of agitation. 'It brought out the worst in me. I just don't want to be one of their gang. It makes me go to the other extreme. I had a look at the book you recommended and I just don't see why the world should be like this. I have been thinking about successful people who are mavericks to disprove the point made in that book.'

Roxy presented me with a list of various names including Sir Bob Geldof, Grayson Perry, Oprah Winfrey and Steve Jobs.

People with a strong, fierce independence trait rarely work for long in conventional corporate environments.

We briefly discussed the implications of what this might mean for Roxy and I then learned that she had got into trouble that week for calling the Chief Executive 'mate' at a board meeting. She was feeling increasingly like a 'misfit.'

'What price do you pay for being so fiercely independent?' I asked.

'No price,' she immediately replied. 'Sometimes I upset people but I can live with that.'

I remembered that she told me she had been expelled from three schools and I thought it was worth exploring whether this was a repeating pattern in Roxy's life.

'When have you felt like this before?' I asked her.

'Most of my life, actually. Although I really don't care. I am very comfortable with the way I am and the way I do things. I don't like being pigeon-holed or told what to do. My parents encouraged me to live a fearless life of adventure and to challenge the status quo. Working with you as a coach has made me realise that I am not doing that anymore. I am compromising myself being here because I just don't fit with the company culture.'

I silently agreed with Roxy; this was the message that both she and I had received from the company. It seemed to me that they had not promoted Roxy to bring about a change in the culture of their organisation. Sometimes if organisations want to create cultural change they recruit independent thinkers who will bring in new values, beliefs and behaviours to assist this change. However, in Roxy's case they had promoted her because of her sales ability and had hoped to bring about a change in her beliefs and behaviours. It was becoming clear to all parties that this was not going to happen and both Roxy and the company were now spending more time negotiating and discussing behaviours, values and standards with one another and less time focusing on the performance of the business.

Roxy spent a long time listing all the cultural differences between herself and the organisation. I just listened as she talked herself out of being there. I pushed Roxy to explore what the costs of her current behaviours might be but she was not prepared to pursue this with me. She said she wanted to use the rest of the session to explore what else she could do with her life if she left this job.

I felt conflicted because the company was paying for the coaching. Were they paying for me to coach her to leave the company and find a new career? I couldn't help thinking that maybe they were; that maybe they knew that this was exactly what would happen. So I worked with Roxy for the rest of the session on exploring career options.

Knowing that Roxy was such a spontaneous and creative person, I thought she would respond well to The Miracle Question [Ref 12].

The Miracle Question was developed by Steve de Shazer and Insoo Kim Berg who established Solution Focused Therapy in the 1980s. The approach focuses on what the client wants to achieve and works by making conscious all the ways in which the client is already creating their ideal future. It begins with the simple question:

'Suppose tonight, while you slept, a miracle occurred. When you awake tomorrow, what would be some of the things you would notice that would tell you that your life had suddenly become better?'

Roxy loved the question and words tumbled out of her as she envisaged her 'miracle' future. She would notice that she was in South America in a hammock, that she was practising yoga every day, speaking Spanish fluently and dancing Salsa at night. She was a successful blogger, blogging about travel and culture. She was doing voluntary work with street children in Brazil.

Roxy's eyes were shining as the session came to an end. We agreed to meet again soon for our next coaching session.

Session Three

There was no session three. I received a phone call from the HR Director advising me that the coaching sessions had come to an end because Roxy had left the company. The HR Director suggested that we meet face to face so we could have a review meeting.

When we met I found out that Roxy had just 'walked out' without working her notice. She was technically in breach of contract for this but the company was not going to take any action. In fact the HR Director told me 'off the record' that it was the best outcome they could have hoped for as they had been about to offer her an exit package. Apparently Roxy was taking a 'gap year' in South America. I had the distinct feeling that the coaching sessions had accelerated what was going to happen anyway and that all parties were happy with the outcome.

Supervision

I had not seen my supervisor while I was coaching Roxy, but I wanted the opportunity to reflect on what had happened and to process the sudden ending of the sessions. I told my supervisor how guilty I was feeling. The company had paid me a lot of money to coach Roxy and I felt as though I had highlighted the lack of cultural fit and then gone on to help her plan an alternative life. I really had not wanted her to stay in her current job. I could see that it was only going to come to a sticky end but had I allowed my feelings to influence the direction of the coaching sessions?

'How much do you think anyone could influence Roxy to do something she didn't want to do?' my supervisor asked me. It was a great question because the answer was clear – not at all. She was fiercely independent and had a really strong self-concept.

The second question my supervisor asked was, 'What is the purpose of your guilt about this situation? You did what you did. You made an adult choice to work in this way with your client. I wonder if you are now looking to me to make you feel better and to tell you that you were right?'

My supervisor reminded me of the responsibility pie chart. This entails listing all of the people involved and assigning proportions of responsibility on a pie chart, marking out one's own portion of the pie last. The exercise challenged me to acknowledge my own responsibility as well as that of the other parties.

This technique relieved some of my guilt about having worked with Roxy on an alternative life and career plan.

My supervisor suggested that the organisation almost certainly knew that Roxy leaving the business was a possible outcome of the coaching sessions and that they had saved themselves a considerable amount of time, trouble and money by not having to offer her an exit package.

'Should I have recommended that she seek the advice of an employment lawyer?' I wondered.

'Possibly. If you had worked with Roxy for longer I think that might have been a good idea. However, she appears to be such a feisty and impulsive character that she took matters into her own hands before you had the opportunity to do this. As coaches, we have a responsibility to our clients to direct them towards other professionals where appropriate. These referrals may be for counselling, legal advice, financial advice or any other support outside our expertise which could help the client understand their situation more fully. If she hadn't taken matters into her own hands so quickly there are other things you might have been able to do, such as offering team-coaching sessions for the board. In some cases where there is a cultural clash with one person, team coaching can be a powerful intervention which enables members of the team to have a greater understanding of their differences and learn to work with one another, embracing and celebrating the opportunities which the diversity within the team can bring.'

'That did cross my mind' I said, 'and maybe if Roxy had been willing to stay with the coaching process for longer I may have suggested that. Mind you, I didn't ever have the impression that the board members were willing to change either.'

I reflected long and hard on this case with my supervisor. With hindsight, it appeared that there was no complex root cause for Roxy's fierce independence, just the fact that she was brought up this way by her parents with the intention of making her a unique individual who would challenge the status quo and make a difference in the world.

To outside observers it appeared that Roxy's fierce independence led to difficulty in her life: expulsion from school, losing jobs and a trail of unsatisfactory relationships. For some people these things would be good reasons to attempt to bring about a change in their behaviour. Roxy's employers wanted her to change and as her coach I had attempted to get her to see the disruptive impact of her behaviours in her life. Roxy did not see it this way at all. Impact and disruption were what she wanted. She did not experience rejection nor have a great need to be liked. She was fine feeling like a 'misfit'. She had a remarkably strong sense of herself. She did not do any real harm to others or herself and in many ways her fierce independence meant that she pushed the boundaries to do good for others and to challenge injustice.

A coach's role is to follow the client's agenda and not to impose solutions on the client.

My supervisor reminded me that there can be a number of different outcomes in coaching:

- The client can change their behaviours to adjust to their situation or to get a different outcome in their life.

- The client can change their situation to bring it in line with their values, attitudes and beliefs.

- The client can change their values, attitudes and beliefs to fit their current situation.

- The client and coach can work together with third parties to share responsibility for changing the situation.

In Roxy's case she had definitely opted to change her situation to bring it into line with her values, attitudes and beliefs. This appeared to be a good outcome for both Roxy and her ex-employers. My coach encouraged me to think of it as a good outcome from my perspective too.

Post script

About a year later I received an email from Roxy with a link to her travel blog and news of a charity she had set up working with street children in South America. She told me that she was now 'living the dream'.

TOOLS AND TECHNIQUES

Roxy is a good example of someone with a strong sense of self and a desire to leave their own individual impression on the world. Being successful was not enough for Roxy; she wanted to do it 'her way' and she cited examples of other successful people who were similar. People with this trait often achieve great success very quickly.

Many people believe seeking independence to be a basic driver of human nature. One of our driving forces from a young age is to adopt more and more responsibility – just look at any young child, they will ask 'Can I do that?' or 'Can I have a go?' and then go about doing it in their own unique way.

Fierce independence is what breaks the mould and creates new ways of doing things, thinking and being. Without fierce independence we would all follow the crowd and little or nothing would change.

Doing things 'our way' gives us energy, leaves us with a sense of personal achievement and helps us maintain our enthusiasm for tasks that otherwise would be meaningless and unenjoyable.

Obviously, too much fierce independence can cause us to push people away, sometimes upsetting others with our forcefulness. It may even cause us to do things in a different way just for the sake of it. People for whom fierce independence has become a trap can find it difficult to build team harmony and bring others along with them. They may stifle creativity and participation, as others may not see much opportunity to be heard.

As with all of the other habits in this book, a coach's role is to help their clients to take the best aspects of the habit and mitigate the unhelpful aspects.

Walk a Mile

**Many coaching techniques involve changing the clients'
perspectives and enabling them to see the world from another
viewpoint.**

This technique enables your client to experience being someone
different for a day. Instead of adopting their usual behaviours,
attitudes and dress they can choose to be someone completely
different for 24 hours of their life. If they are shy and retiring, they
could have a day of being an extrovert.

It takes courage to do this and your client may feel strange, but
the fact that it is time-limited means that most people can tolerate
the behaviour change knowing it is for a short time. After a day in
someone else's shoes, they will have gained lots of insights about
their ability to choose their behaviours and the knowledge that they
have access to a wider range of behaviours than they think. This
technique enables your client to experience another viewpoint fully.
It is particularly powerful for those who are fiercely independent
to test out being more vulnerable and relying on others for support
and ideas.

The client can do this exercise by themselves by going somewhere
where they are not known or it can be done with the support of
friends and colleagues.

One possible outcome of this technique is that your client may
decide to keep doing things as they previously were. Alternatively,
the technique may encourage your client to change some of their
habitual behaviours. Both of these outcomes are fine.

Powerful Coaching Question:
How might other people (with a different personality from
you) approach your situation?

Coach the System

Sometimes coaches have a wider brief to work with teams as well as individuals. Coaching a team might help those who have become trapped by their fierce independence to understand their rights and responsibilities.

A fairly common outcome of coaching with fiercely independent people is that they end up leaving their organisation. Sometimes this is inevitable as they are almost destined to be entrepreneurial free spirits. However, often these people leave because they feel they have no choice.

We have found that by focussing on the environment in which the client is operating – including the team of which they are a part – it is possible for fiercely independent people to not only stay in their organisation but to thrive.

In Roxy's case, she was a highly valuable employee in her original role. It was only when she was promoted that there was a clash. If we had coached the board on this issue we might have looked at other alternatives such as:

- Re-visiting the cultural norms of board members.

- Adjusting their expectations of Roxy.

- Keeping Roxy in her current role but rewarding her in a different way.

These would, ideally, have been looked at in conjunction with coaching Roxy towards a mutually agreeable arrangement in which everyone benefitted from the continued relationship. While this is not always possible, we encourage coaches to look at the possibility of expanding the coaching remit and focus in order to increase the chances of overall success.

Powerful Coaching Question:
What would be the most traditional approach to your
situation? What would be the most unconventional
approach to your situation? How many other alternative
approaches can you dream up? Which is the most attractive
approach to you?

Dependency Check

Fierce independence usually means that we do not like to rely on others at all. At its most extreme, this can lead to mistrust of others and avoidance of intimacy.

It is worth looking at the reasons behind your client's fierce independence and looking at the number of times they have shied away from any kind of dependent position. The following questions can be useful to explore together in a session or to be given as homework to be reflected upon and worked through later.

- In what situations have you shied away from any kind of dependent position?

- In what situations have you allowed yourself to depend on someone?

- What do you fear from dependency?

- What do you gain from being fiercely independent?

- What price do you pay for being fiercely independent?

Other useful techniques to bring into this analysis could include:

- Perceptual positions – to encourage your client to consider others viewpoints. *(see page 53)*

- Human Givens Audit – to look at what needs might not be being met for which their fierce independence is compensating. *(see page 71)*

- Inner Boardroom – to provide a practical tool for creating more rounded decisions. *(see page 237)*

- Know How – to consider a potential future where their fierce independence goes unchecked compared to a future where they bring it into balance. *(see page 168)*

- Stretch Zone – to create a plan for steadily reducing their fierce independence. *(see page 286)*

Powerful Coaching Question:
How do you feel when you depend on someone else? How do you feel when someone depends on you?

THE INTERVIEW

Jackie Daniel

People with a strong fierce independence trait have high levels of determination, ambition and curiosity. They push boundaries, achieve great things quickly and blaze a trail for others to follow. A great example of someone with this trait is Jackie Daniel who, at the age of 29, was one of the youngest executive directors ever to be appointed in the National Health Service (NHS).

In the following interview Jackie, who is currently Chief Executive of University Hospitals of Morecambe Bay NHS Trust, tells how this trait can become a trap and how learning from others is key to keeping this trait working for you.

'I was a working class girl from a regular family but I had an extraordinary role model in my grandmother. She was a successful businesswoman who owned a fashion shop, had money and was completely different from anything or anyone else in my life at that time. She took me places, taught me things and believed in me. She talked to me about fashion, the seasons and the business. She ran the business single-handedly, even doing her own accounts and bookkeeping. I knew from an early age that I was going to do what most others around me hadn't done (including my parents). My Gran encouraged, supported and showed me the way while everyone else around me expected me to settle down in a safe job for life, get married, have children and think myself lucky.'

Listening to Jackie I can almost feel the excitement and sense of possibility to which she was introduced by her Gran. Looking at her, I can see that her Gran's passion for fashion has also certainly rubbed off on her. Jackie's sense of style would not look out of place in a couture fashion house in London, Paris or Milan. It is certainly not the norm for a Chief Executive of an NHS Trust and, I suspect, neither are some of her other brave and bold behaviours.

Jackie describes her young self as 'a rebel without a cause', leaving home at 17 with no savings and a handful of O Levels. This didn't stop her finding her way into nursing and within five years she had also completed both an undergraduate and a Masters degree. Both of these degrees had been sponsored and championed by people in the NHS who had seen her potential and this early lesson taught Jackie that it is good to ask for help when you need it.

As Jackie tells me about her early days as a nurse, I become aware that she had demonstrated extraordinary self-belief, force of character and a passion for improvement in the NHS even when she was a relatively junior member of staff. This became a theme of the interview as Jackie revealed that she often managed to exert more influence than her position or technical ability should have afforded her and it was this that helped her bring about significant changes. I wondered where this came from.

'I have always had a sense of curiosity and I keep pushing the boundaries,' she says. 'The boundaries are always a million miles from where you think they are. I wanted to earn more, have more, influence more and be important. I think my Gran showed me that life could be better and more exciting than you might think at first. She was such a powerful role model for me and I believe she contributed greatly to my ambition, love of learning and fierce independence.'

Despite family and friends urging Jackie to celebrate her success at being appointed Ward Sister and to be content with that role for life, Jackie says she, 'Flew off the edge and went for it'. She took a corporate project role for the NHS despite describing being 'really uncomfortable at that time, mainly because I was totally out of my comfort zone. I didn't even know how to use a computer. My answer was that I worked hard, learned quickly, and was in a permanently adrenaline-fuelled state, experiencing excitement and discomfort in equal measures.'

The role took her into the boardroom for the first time in her career and she describes the first time she saw it as being 'magnetic'. She knew that this was where she wanted to be and it served to reinforce her independent drive.

In her early days as Director of Nursing, Jackie was aware of being both young and female in a mostly middle-aged, mostly male team. She was also aware of the stereotyping which came with being a corporate 'nurse'.

'I kept asking myself, *'How am I going to influence these people?'* Jackie says.

This was the one time that Jackie remembers toning down her independence as she quickly realised that she would need to tune into more masculine communication styles. For a while she even began wearing pin-striped suits for work. The situation was confusing for her until she realised that they had appointed her for her difference. Eventually, she realised that not being authentic and true to herself was damaging to her self-esteem. She had tried to stop being a nurse, stop being a woman and start speaking 'posh' in order to succeed. She had tried all these things but she found that they weren't working; they weren't the things that got her the breakthroughs.

So what were the things that got her the breakthroughs?

'Daring to be different,' she says immediately. 'I became a Champion for Improving Working Lives and took on more corporate responsibility. I took on bigger change programmes such as closing Accident and Emergency Centres, which is a highly sensitive and political issue. I began working with politicians.'

At the age of 29, Jackie was one of the youngest Executive Directors to be appointed in the NHS. For a time, she forgot all the lessons she had learned which had got her there.

'For the first time I felt completely exposed and the enormity of what I had taken on began to hit me,' she admits. 'I had no big buffalo to look up to and I didn't seek enough help. I carried the pain alone and gave myself unnecessary anguish.'

'People were saying that I was too young. I was even more conscious of being a woman and a nurse. I was responsible for the financial management of the trust and I only had a Maths O Level! For the first time I began to doubt whether I was ready for this. I worked silly hours. I thought that if I worked long enough or hard enough it would be enough, but it wasn't!'

I ask Jackie how she had managed to get out of this thinking pattern.

'I thought back to being a ward leader and reminded myself about the generalist leadership role and how the success of the ward was the sum of the parts. I sought out mentors and reached out to others for help.' Jackie acknowledged that being championed by people who she respected and trusted was affirming to her. They helped restore her self-belief and several of her champions have remained mentors or reference points for her throughout her career.

After eight years in the role of Executive Director, Jackie continued to further the breadth of her knowledge by moving into a role as Chief Executive of a Provider Strategy Board. She found herself making change on an industrial scale and once again questioned 'whether little old me could sit alongside these people?'

I marvel at how Jackie had kept moving herself into ever more challenging roles and how she kept learning from them. In this role she tells me that she learned that perhaps there were limits to how far her fierce independence could, or should, take her:

'You don't have to know it all – just know someone who does. Get the best people, the best tools and create a different blend of skills and knowledge. Look to create a perfect team. Look for diversity and difference. Find people who can influence in different ways and who have different networks. They don't have to be like you.'

She is still incredibly passionate about making improvements in the NHS; her work there isn't done yet but perhaps she has a more controlled level of independence these days.

'I am not collecting badges anymore. I am bringing all my skills to bear and leading really differently. Now I find myself being a role model to young people in my life in the same way that my Gran was to me, letting them see that there are other ways to be and to live your life.'

Jackie offers the following advice to anyone starting out:

'Trust in who you are and what you want to do and don't stop. Ask for what you need and seek it out. In the times of most doubt it is important to have someone there for you. Actively seek out self-development and a 'guided tour' by a wiser person.'

CHAPTER FIVE

Cynicism

'Life is divided into the horrible and the miserable.'

WOODY ALLEN

THE CASE STUDY

'Don't expect anything good to happen.
Prepare yourself for the worst so you won't be disappointed.'

John, one of my early coaching clients, had an unexpectedly profound impact upon me. He was a team leader in his fifties and had been in the same company for many years. In his words he had 'seen people, processes, brands and fads come and go' and was the epitome of the 'grumpy old man'. He openly acknowledged that others thought of him as cynical, although he referred to himself as 'a realist' and 'a devil's advocate'.

He came to coaching because his boss had decided that all managers at John's level would be given access to some leadership coaching. I genuinely believed in the remit to offer individual support for each of the managers, but John was sceptical about the reason for coaching and assumed that it was all part of a plan to get him managed out of the company.

'Well, either way, it's something I've got to go through so let's get on with it and tick the box,' he said.

I decided to take it slowly to begin with and just gather a little data first.

'So what can you tell me about work?' I asked.

'These guys? Well they're an argumentative bunch really. It's all I can do to keep them in line most days. They never seem to agree on anything, like a bunch of kids. God help me when we have this darned social event at the end of the week.'

'What social event?' I asked.

'Some god-awful ten-pin bowling thing followed by a meal that management have decided we should do as a team-building thing,' he replied.

'I sense that a company-funded night out with your colleagues isn't something that you look forward to.'

'You could say that. I don't know why they need to stick their noses in. It's the same with this coaching. It'll do more harm than good and it's just wasting money,' he said, quickly adding, 'No offence.'

This theme continued throughout the session. John showed no real interest in digging into anything in particular, he just seemed to want to get through the session as quickly as possible and its only value to him seemed to be the opportunity to complain about things.

John was my first client who didn't really show much interest in the process and I felt I had a lot of work to do to win him over. The guidance from the manager sponsoring the coaching was that they didn't want to know what went on in the sessions and that they could be used for whatever purpose the client wanted. The company believed that coaching was more beneficial to the individual if there was no feedback from the coach to the company. This would ensure that trust could be built between coach and client.

Session Two

We began in a pretty similar fashion and my attempts to get John to think of alternative interpretations to his pessimistic perceptions of events were fruitless. Despite claiming he was 'a devil's advocate' he was unable to use that role to put a positive spin on anything.

It was incredible how he was able to identify the gaps in any suggestion, the downside to any offer, and to ascribe a malevolent intention to anyone's activity. In desperation I found myself offering my own positive interpretations, which was not in line with our view of coaching.

The response I got to every suggestion began with, 'Yes, but...'

I had never before achieved so little rapport or progress with some-one in two sessions as I had with John and it felt disappointing, unfulfilling and, almost as John had predicted, a waste of time.

Supervision

I actually started my supervision session in a very similar fashion to how John had started with me. I needed to complain about him and even let it slip to my supervisor that I had found myself thinking that the company should get rid of John. In doing so, I discovered that I much preferred to coach optimists than pessimists. I also realised that I didn't have much experience of coaching clients who didn't want to be there and I didn't have many strategies for dealing with this.

My supervisor confirmed that John was certainly having an effect on me. In fact he commented that I had internalised John's cynicism and was now showing up for my supervision session displaying the same characteristics that John had displayed in his coaching sessions with me. My supervisor reminded me that a 'parallel process' can occur when a coach comes for supervision.

'Parallel processing' is where the coach unconsciously acts out their client's behaviours. This enables the coach to see from their client's perspective as well as enabling the supervisor to see from the perspective of the coach.

I was also reminded that coaching is an emotional and intimate occupation and that moods can be contagious, especially when we are seeking to understand a client, employing techniques such as mirroring and matching their body language, gestures, energy levels, tone of voice and words. It is therefore an occupational hazard that we may become contaminated by our client's thoughts and feelings. Supervision is a perfect and necessary repository or 'dumping ground' for such contamination.

Cynicism can be defined as an attitude of negativity and a general mistrust in others and their motives. University researcher Salvatore Maddi suggests that most cynics are made, rather than born. He contends that cynicism develops when people put in effort to achieve something and then have their hopes dashed. The gap between their expectations and the reality leaves them feeling helpless. This may result in a set of beliefs and behaviours, which might be characterised as a cynical life position: 'no good will come of this and it's not worth any of us trying'.

There have been a number of studies that suggest cynicism is not only detrimental to performance but also contagious. For example Felps, Mitchell & Byington found (using their terminology) that having just one 'deadbeat' (those who withhold effort), 'downer' (those who express pessimism, anxiety, insecurity and irritation) or 'jerk' (those who violate 'interpersonal norms of respect') in a group could bring down performance by 30% to 40% *[Ref 13]*.

Although I did not believe that John was consciously trying to sap my energy, my time with him was certainly less than enjoyable or fulfilling. My supervisor had an interesting twist on my interpretation: he wondered whether the cynicism or pessimism that others described John as displaying was in fact the result of a lack of resilience.

Resilience

Resilience is our ability to recover from setbacks or disappointments. The more resilient we are, the quicker our recovery will be. However, if we have low resilience we will actively avoid things that might feel like a setback. By developing our resilience, we give ourselves the ability to deal with disappointments. We can then 'fail' earlier, learn more quickly and through such learning may avoid more serious failures.

Developing resilience is one way to avoid a trait of cynicism trapping us into a defeatist outlook. If we are unable to accept disappointment and roll with the punches, we can easily slip into a negative spiral. For some suggestions as to how resilience may be developed, check out Jane McGonigal's great *TED talk: 'The game that can give you ten extra years of life' [Ref 14]*.

Carol S. Dweck found that students with what she termed a *'growth mindset' [Ref 15]*,who believe that their traits, skills and characteristics are not fixed but can be developed, are more likely to continue working hard despite setbacks. They are more resilient because they have a less pessimistic perspective.

Resilience is an important quality from both a professional and personal standpoint. We are less likely to be resilient if we are cynical.

Having discussed John's possible lack of resilience, my supervisor then questioned why either John or I were persisting with the coaching sessions. Neither of us seemed to feel they were worthwhile, so surely the best thing for a coach to do would be to raise this with John. John had already suggested the company was wasting its money, so why not offer him the option of stopping?

I had a powerful reaction to this suggestion and realised that I had a strong personal need to succeed. Ending the sessions without having 'converted' John so that he appreciated the benefits of coaching would feel like a failure to me. My supervisor suggested that these reactions and feelings on my part would be worth further exploration in future supervision sessions.

Session Three

I had gained some useful insights from supervision and felt that I had a decision to make on which approach to take with John. I decided I was not yet prepared to give him a way out of the coaching sessions and I felt that it would be interesting and potentially enlightening to explore where John's pessimism stemmed from - was there perhaps an originating event? However, I didn't think we had enough rapport to pursue this just yet so I opted firstly to explore the effects that John's current perspective was having on his life.

'I want to explore the trait that you call realism but that others might call cynicism,' I said. 'I certainly got the impression from our first two sessions that you are generally more of a 'glass half empty' kind of person. Would you agree?'

'Is that a bad thing?' he replied defensively, avoiding answering my question.

'Good question,' I said. 'I would think that it's helpful to be aware of downsides to a situation - the risk of reckless decisions is significantly reduced with that outlook - but I'm interested in your perspective. How would you say your approach works for you?'

John pointed out the obvious benefits that his outlook brought, namely fewer mistakes, managed expectations and fewer nasty surprises. This was the story that John had been 'selling' about his mindset for years.

'These are all fair points.' I replied. 'And how do you feel when you see someone with an optimistic outlook on things?'

'Sometimes I think to myself 'You fool', but then sometimes I'm a little jealous. A lot of the things that I guard against don't actually happen, so I've worried about them and prepared myself for them for no reason. An optimist wouldn't waste time worrying about them in the first place.'

'In an ideal world, would you like to be more like those optimists?' I asked.

'Maybe there's a small part of me that would,' he admitted. 'They certainly seem to stress about things a whole lot less, which doesn't really seem fair.'

'Why do you think they don't worry so much about things going wrong?'

'Maybe they know there is always someone like me to think about the stuff that they just ignore,' he said flippantly, although I felt that this might be something which John really believed.

'That could play a part in it. Might there be anything else do you think?'

I was really hoping that John would make some connection here because I suspected that his cynicism was really a means by which he sought to avoid disappointment. Clients can create coping mechanisms in an endeavour to avoid pain and I was inclined to believe that this was John's way of seeking to avoid having his hopes dashed. I wasn't sure, however, whether John would see this.

'Maybe they just haven't seen as many things go wrong as I have. Perhaps they are still naïve enough to believe that everything will work out OK.'

'This strategy clearly has a lot of upsides for you and it has helped you be successful. What do you think are the benefits to your 'realism'?' I asked.

John seemed to think about that question for a while before answering, 'I am prepared for any eventuality, I see problems before they present themselves and I don't get taken advantage of. I'm rarely disappointed because if you expect things to go wrong then you can only be pleasantly surprised, can't you?'

I was pleased as I saw this as a potential turning point for John. I followed this up by asking:

'And what price do you pay for it?'

'Well, as I told you when we first met, people see me as a grumpy old man and I could probably have been promoted a bit higher,' he admitted.

I waited.

'And I suppose it means that I only really see the downsides and, as a result, I don't enjoy much.'

Frustratingly for me, the session was coming to an end. I really felt we had made a breakthrough but we had to leave it at this point. John was clearly in a reflective mood so I gave him a question to ponder for homework: 'When did you decide to see the world this way?'

Supervision

Although I felt that I was now making some progress with John, I told my supervisor that I was feeling disproportionately angry and frustrated with this coaching assignment and indeed with John himself. He brought out the worst in me. I either wanted to give up on him or give him a good shaking. I really didn't like being around negative people.

My supervisor was alarmed at the strength of my outburst and wanted to explore why I was indulging myself in such negative responses to this client instead of getting on with the business of coaching him. He reminded me of the importance of 'transference' and 'countertransference' in the coaching relationship *[Ref 16]*.

'Transference' refers to the feelings and responses the client transfers onto the coach and is sometimes explained in terms of old issues from past relationships emerging in the client's new relationship with the coach.

'Countertransference' refers to the feelings and responses which the coach transfers onto the client. In 1912, Sigmund Freud identified the phenomenon and suggested it takes one of two forms: positive, loving transference or hostile, negative transference. Whether positive or negative, however, until it is brought into conscious awareness, transference can interfere with coaching.

In this case my supervisor suggested that I needed to acknowledge my transferential feelings towards John and examine the responses he evoked in me. Only if I was able to do so would the coaching be successful.

'So – who does John remind you of?' asked my supervisor.

'I just hadn't made the connection before', I said. 'He is exactly like my old boss. I left a job I loved because of him. He was a toxic person and although I love the fact that I am now a self-employed coach, I still regret the fact that I left a fantastic job because my boss created an intolerable working environment. He once told our team that he didn't just see the glass as half empty, he also thought there was something toxic in the glass. '

My supervisor reminded me that becoming aware of my counter-transference was an important step to increasing my self-aware-ness and enabling me to better manage my responses to John. My supervisor enabled me to see clearly that, of course, John was not my previous boss and deserved to be afforded the same open-minded curiosity and unconditional positive regard with which I sought to approach my other clients. I was now aware that being with John was churning up all sorts of 'emotional sediment' which I thought I had dealt with.

'Something else is happening here too,' my supervisor continued. 'John will be responding to your response to him. All this happens at an unconscious level, but by changing your response to him you may find that his behaviour changes a little too.'

My supervisor suspected that perhaps I was attempting to move John too quickly from pessimism to optimism. I recalled that coerced, externally-imposed change rarely lasts, whereas change that is self-generated and internally 'felt' by the client has a much better chance of sustainability.

My supervisor wondered how John's negative energy could be harnessed to more useful effect and suggested that I might use the Energy Investment Model next time I saw John.

The Energy Investment Model

Claude Lineberry developed this model in the 1980s *[Ref 17]*. It is designed to enable us to identify levels of motivation in relation to a task in terms of attitude and willingness to expend energy on the task. Our attitudes and levels of energy are often shaped by our past experiences, particularly in an organisational context.

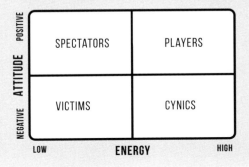

Some individuals score low on both axes of the model as they have not only a negative attitude but also low energy. The model originally categorised such people as 'victims' but later versions of the model have used the terms 'walking dead' or 'deadwood' as such individuals may add very little value to an organisation. They tend to be disengaged and powerless to take action or to exert any influence on events or circumstances. They tend to keep a low profile and can be very difficult to coach.

There are two types of individual who score strongly in relation to one factor but poorly in relation to another – the model characterises such individuals as 'spectators' or cynics. Spectators have a positive attitude but low energy, while cynics have a negative attitude but high energy. Spectators tend to be 'right behind you' and may be great supporters but do not tend to put themselves forward or put themselves on the line. Cynics, on the other hand, may be very willing to expend energy openly criticising the organisation. They are often very competent in their own work and their negativity about the organisation might often be seen as arising from frustration.

The ideal employee in this model is categorised as a 'player'. The 'player' has a positive attitude and demonstrates this through their energy and behaviours at work. It may be helpful in coaching to seek to raise our client's awareness of where they currently sit within this model and to help the client towards becoming a 'player'.

My supervisor suggested that the fact that John appeared to sit in the 'cynics' box meant that there was some hope for him to develop. He was not a 'victim' because, although he had a negative attitude, he also had high energy. My supervisor suggested that it would be worth exploring how this energy could be used to more positive effect within the organisation and in John's life.

By the time my supervision session had finished I felt a renewed energy for the work with John and was looking forward to the next session.

Session Four

John arrived sweating and flustered and complaining about the sudden heatwave, despite the fact that he had recently been grumbling about how we had had such a disappointingly wet summer. I pointed this out to him and he immediately looked sheepish. For me, this was a good way to start the session as it gave us an opportunity for him to practice changing his perspective.

'How could you have looked at this situation in a more positive light John?' I challenged him.

'Well of course I could have been grateful that it wasn't chucking it down with rain, but I hate being sweaty and I'm all stressed now because of that,' he said.

'That's a start,' I said. 'One of the things I want to work on with you is the concept of the locus of control. By claiming that the weather made you stressed, you are giving up control of your emotions to an external force, when actually it was you who chose whether you were stressed or not.'

While we may have a lot less control over the world than we would like, we actually have a lot more control over ourselves and our responses than we appreciate.

I wanted John to practice accepting responsibility for what he was feeling. I explained that the weather couldn't have made him stressed because there would be many people that day who experienced the same weather and were not stressed. I suggested that it was up to John how he chose to interpret things.

While John found it difficult to accept that he could find being hot and sweaty anything other than uncomfortable and stressful, he couldn't help but agree to the logic that I put forward. Changing beliefs is a big undertaking, but it is possible. One route is to bring into conscious awareness our habitual responses to situations and make a concerted effort to change them to something that will give us a better outcome.

At this point John reminded me that I had asked him a question for 'homework'. He said he had given a lot of thought to the question of when he had first started thinking like this and he had been able to pinpoint the exact time and place.

'I feel quite embarrassed telling you this because it was such a trivial incident but it was very important to me at the time. I was eight years old and I really wanted a dog. One of my uncles showed me some pictures of a litter of puppies and asked me to choose the one I wanted. I was so excited when I picked out my puppy. I even gave it a name. My uncle said he would get the puppy for me. After several weeks there was no sign of the puppy and I asked my parents when I would get it. They said they had thought it a stupid idea and told my uncle not to pursue it. Nobody had bothered to tell me. I was devastated. I think I decided then that it was not a good idea to believe or trust people or to expect that good things would happen.'

John shrugged his shoulders, looked at me and asked:

'Could something that happened all those years ago have started this behaviour?'

This was a powerful question for John to ask himself and my answer to it was a resounding 'Yes'. In many coaching conversations limiting beliefs and assumptions about life will emerge that stem from the client's early childhood experiences. [For more on this, see Chapter One on Impostor Syndrome.]

John and I talked through his childhood disappointment. John could see how the situation had been badly managed by his family. He could also see that at that point in his life he made a rule for himself: 'Don't expect anything good to happen. Prepare yourself for the worst so you won't be disappointed.'

We realised that this strategy had served the disappointed eight-year-old John well but that it was time for the adult John to revisit the strategy as it was no longer serving him well, particularly at work.

I suggested to John that when we have a deep-seated view of the world or a set of assumptions, we may unconsciously seek out examples to reinforce and support those beliefs. This process of selection is governed by what has been termed the Reticular Activating System (RAS) in the brain, which is a powerful remnant of our more primitive selves. The job of this part of our brain is to regulate arousal *[Ref 18]*. The RAS will focus exclusively upon anything relevant to what we currently deem important. For example, if we have formed the general view that people are lazy and untrustworthy then our RAS will gather information which backs up that belief, ignoring everything else.

Our minds are capable of deleting anything that does not conform to our view of the world and can even distort events to make them fit our view.

One way to counter this tendency is for the coach to invite the client to change their focus and look for different things. I asked John to give me examples from his life of positive events which did not conform to his cynical beliefs. John was able to tell me about a number of good things in his life, the birth of his children and grandchildren, promotions and his long-lasting and happy marriage.

I asked John to formulate a more realistic, rounded view of the world and put it into a statement that felt comfortable for him. He decided on:

'Sometimes things work out as you hope they will and other times they don't. Life is full of ups and downs and it's how you respond to them that matters. You can't change what happens but you can change your response.'

This seemed a good point at which to introduce the Energy Investment Model. John quickly identified himself as a cynic. I asked John how he could harness his energy and his critical view of his team and organisation to have some positive influence. After all, if John wasn't prepared to walk away from the company and he had so many criticisms of the way they did things, shouldn't he be offering to do something about it? John expressed the view that he had been in the company for so many years and knew so much about the business that he didn't know why they were not using him to train new members of staff, instead of bringing in external training companies.

At this point I felt able to ask John a challenging question. 'If you were the Managing Director of the company and had a cynical employee like you, what would you do about it?'

'I wouldn't tolerate it actually. I know my cynicism affects the whole team - one bad apple and all that. I would probably sack me - or I would give me a trouble-shooting role within the company. That's what I am good at.'

I knew we were getting somewhere and we ended the session with John agreeing to speak to his MD about what he felt he could bring to the business in terms of experience, understanding and his trouble-shooting mentality.

Session Five

With some clients more progress happens in between coaching sessions than in the sessions themselves.

John had done a lot of thinking since I last saw him and this proved to be our final session. Whilst it could not be said that John had suddenly transformed into a 'ray of sunshine', he had experienced some profound insights about himself and had made a conscious decision to change his attitude.

John took control of this session by telling me what changes he was making:

- Keeping a journal of good things and things he was grateful for in his life.

- Consciously changing his responses to things – particularly in the workplace.

- Sharing these changes with his friends and family so that they would support him in continuing to make changes.

John had met with his MD and talked to him about how he felt that his experience was under-used within the business and how this feeling of being undervalued had led John to become negative and disruptive. John had told his MD how much he wanted to be of value and they had had a fruitful conversation, resulting in John being given responsibility for staff training on a trial basis. What really made me smile was that John was going to include the Energy Investment Model and some other coaching techniques in his training programme. He knew that he was going to have to work hard to change the established perceptions which his colleagues had about him but he was up for the challenge.

Supervision

When I saw my supervisor after my final session with John, I was feeling pretty self-congratulatory: I felt that I had managed to 'convert' a hard-nosed cynic into something closer to an optimist. I told my supervisor that John was now a real advocate of coaching and that John regretted not having met me earlier in his life and was telling everyone about me.'

My supervisor, however, was less interested in celebrating my 'transformational powers' than in what had happened in the coaching relationship. He wanted to explore the transference and countertransference which had occurred between John and myself, and felt that I had maybe missed an opportunity to learn more about myself and also to work with John on his core beliefs. My supervisor felt that failure to address the transference adequately within the coaching relationship inhibits the effectiveness of the work.

Coaches should always be attentive to transference from the very first session.

I now found myself experiencing transferential feelings towards my supervisor. I felt that he had 'burst my bubble' and was telling me off like a naughty child for being too 'full of myself'. I noticed what was happening, however, and reminded myself to stay in an adult mindset instead of reverting to the behaviours that belonged to my childhood. Together we picked apart the transference aspects of my relationship with John:

John came to coaching with the cynicism that he brought to life in general. This had provoked in me two transferential responses: firstly, the desire to get John to see the world (and coaching) more positively and, secondly, an anger and irritation with the negativity which I subsequently learned arose from my own feelings towards my former boss. My supervisor challenged me about my need to be liked and admired and to have others share my philosophy of having a positive outlook on life. My supervisor suggested that this had led me to push for a 'quick win' with John. In his opinion I could have worked more on John's revelation about the root cause of his cynicism – the 'puppy' incident – and that this might have brought about more transformational change in John at a core belief level.

Change can be brought about at a behavioural level or at a belief level.

Sometimes behavioural change may be enough, particularly if someone lacks skill or knowledge; in this case the client may merely learn some new things and may put them into practice. However, in many cases a client's presenting behaviour is the result of the client's core beliefs about themselves, the world around them and about other people. If the client has a bedrock belief that 'you can't trust people' then their behaviours are likely to be predicated on this belief. In such cases it is necessary for the coach to challenge and modify the belief that drives the behaviours to enable the client to make lasting change. John's acknowledgement of his early life experience and his feelings about it was a really significant moment. John had demonstrated real trust in me, showing his vulnerability, putting aside his cynicism and identifying the root cause of his life position. I knew deep down that I had not grasped this opportunity for John as well as I could have done.

Supervision enabled me to see that coaches should consider carefully the question of transference in a coaching relationship. A coach might ask themselves a number of questions:

- Are my responses to my client the same as the responses of others?

- Are my client's responses to me the same as the responses of others to me?

- Is what is happening in the coaching relationship a reflection of what happens in other areas of the client's life?

- If I am feeling unaccountable feelings, for example boredom, anger or confusion, am I in fact picking up what my client is feeling at that moment?

- What can I learn about myself from the feelings I have towards my client and from my responses to the feelings my client appears to have towards me?

I noted that I left the supervision session still feeling as though my wrists had been slapped. That, in itself, was food for thought for me. I had learned that I needed to continue to be aware of and work on my need for approval from my clients and from my supervisor.

TOOLS AND TECHNIQUES

Cynicism can be a protective trait against disappointment and setbacks. Edward de Bono's famous 'six thinking hats' contains the black hat of discernment, which focuses on identifying reasons to be cautious and conservative. Those who have a cynical trait will rarely be reckless or take unnecessary risks and are also less likely to be manipulated. There is also very little chance of being disappointed by bad luck or poor performance if one is already resigned to the worst possible outcome.

However, if we are to believe Henry Ford, who is noted as saying, 'Whether you think you can, or think you can't – you're right', having an overly cynical view could be a self-fulfilling prophecy. When cynicism is overdone, as John found, there can come a time when that begins to have a negative effect on you and those around you. Cynics only see the downsides to decisions and run the risk of not taking positive action because they fear disappointment.

The following techniques may be useful to enable a client to temper a cynical trait and stop it becoming a trap.

Emotional Positions

It may be helpful to invite a client whose habitual viewpoint is a cynical one to view things from a different perspective.

This exercise is similar to the Perceptual Positions exercise in Chapter Two. You will be asking your client to stand in different places in the room to adopt different perspectives. However, instead of your client looking 'through the eyes' of different people, they will be looking at situations through the lenses of different emotions.

Ask your client to do the following:

1. Pick a scenario and visualise it in the middle of the room. For example, the situation could be the prospect of John's social, team-building event.

2. Find a space in the room where they are looking at the scenario and describe that situation from an overly cynical perspective. Invite them to really go for it and be as cynical as they can possibly be.

3. When they are ready, find another space in the room and describe the scenario from an overly optimistic perspective. Again, encourage them to be outrageously optimistic.

4. Two perspectives might be enough but feel free to suggest more positions and perspectives, for example: excited, nervous, relaxed, confused, inquisitive, surprised.

5. Invite reflection with some questions, for example:

   • Weighing up these perspectives, what do you think is a balanced perspective?

   • Which of these perspectives feels most familiar to you?

- Which of these perspectives did you enjoy the most?

- Which of these perspectives do you think would serve you best in reality?

This is a technique that you could use repeatedly with your client in order to help them practice using different 'emotional lenses', consciously choosing the most appropriate lens or lenses for them.

Powerful Coaching Question:
If you could approach this situation with a completely fresh and clear mind, what would you do?

Good Boss, Bad Boss

In a Gallup poll of over a million workers, the number one reason cited for people leaving their current job was not pay or the work itself but their direct supervisor.

It is unlikely that many people would classify a 'good boss' as having many of the characteristics associated with cynicism. This exercise can help a cynical client realise the impact of their behaviours on those around them.

Ask your client to:

1. Draw a line down the middle of a piece of paper or flipchart.

2. Label one half of the paper 'Good Boss' and the other 'Bad Boss'.

3. Think back to all of the bosses they have ever had or seen in action and write down what those bosses did that made them good or effective bosses.

4. Then list all of the things those bosses did that made them bad or ineffective.

5. For each of the actions consider the impact it had upon them.

6. Reflect on those lists in relation to their own leadership behaviours and the impact they may be having on others.

7. Identify two or three changes they could make to their behaviours that would have a more positive impact on their colleagues.

Powerful Coaching Question:
If your colleagues or friends were to write an honest reference about you, what would they say? What would you like them to say?

Positive Psychology Exercises

Increasing feelings of positivity can help to reduce cynicism and anxiety while simultaneously increasing wellbeing and resilience, giving a more balanced view of life.

While a coach must use their judgement as to whether and at what points such techniques might be appropriate, here is a selection of exercises, drawn from the research of Positive Psychologists Dr. Ilona Boniwell [Ref 19] and Martin Seligman [Ref 20]:

Three Good Things
Every night for one week (or once a week for six weeks) find three things that went well, write them down and reflect on your role in these events. The simple act of routinely focusing on positive events and your role within them has been shown to increase a sense of wellbeing and reduce anxiety.

A Gratitude Visit
In his book *Flourish*, Martin Seligman states that this exercise can be 'genuinely life changing'. The client is asked to think of somebody that they have a reason to be grateful towards and to write a letter to that person describing what that person did and how it affected the client's life. Once the client has written the letter, the client is then to call the 'gratitude recipient' and arrange to meet them in a place where the client can read the letter aloud to them.

Seligman states: 'Gratitude can make your life happier and more satisfying. When we feel gratitude, we benefit from the pleasant memory of a positive event in our life. Also, when we express our gratitude to others, we strengthen our relationship with them.'

Random Acts Of Kindness
Just something as small as handing out a bar of chocolate to a passing motorist or buying a 'suspended coffee' (paying for an extra coffee that can be claimed by someone who can't afford one) can have a significantly positive impact on your mood and general wellbeing.

Exercise

Research has suggested that physical exercise and activity is probably the most effective short-term booster for mood and outlook due to the release of brain chemicals associated with easing depression.

> **Powerful Coaching Question:**
> To what extent do you believe that you have lost before you have started?

THE INTERVIEW

Greg Dyke

Nobody we have interviewed for this book has got to the top of their field or achieved any real success without having to get through a number of disappointments along the way, and we would suggest that none would have got through those disappointments with an overly cynical mindset. Our interviewee for this chapter, Greg Dyke, is no exception. Successful people develop a healthy balance between optimism and cynicism and Greg seems to personify that balance.

Greg has enjoyed a long and distinguished career in journalism and broadcasting, most notably rising to become Director General of the BBC. He is also Chairman of the Football Association, the British Film Institute and of the Ambassador Theatre Group. Despite setbacks along the way, Greg has consistently seen the glass as half full. As you will see, this was largely a deliberate and conscious strategy.

'People with ideas are worth their weight in gold in business. I was told once that a man can go about 48 days without food, 24 hours without water and about five minutes without oxygen, but some people amazingly go through their whole life without a good idea. In any successful business, it's the ideas people who are the ones to keep. But of course many ideas don't work out and you've got to be OK with that.'

'I was in Barbados once and I was walking along the coast and noticed two types of buses - the blue buses that followed a pre-defined route, going from stop to stop - and the yellow-coloured Rasta buses which didn't follow a route but, instead looked for passengers and went where they could find them. I'm a big believer in being like the Rasta buses. Some might say I've spent too long on them but that's another story. The point is, I'm always looking for people who are prepared to think differently.'

Greg Dyke has worked in and been a successful and popular leader in a range of industries. He believes that creativity is the second most important thing he looks for in himself and others. So what's the first thing? Resilience.

'I believe someone's ability to cope with adversity is the true test of a person. I want to know if you can still have your passion after you've been kicked in the teeth. In order to be creative, you need to prepare yourself for rejection, for things not to work out sometimes.'

During the interview, his optimistic approach to life clearly shines through. 'I was investing in a movie company many years ago and I was told some statistic that only 1 in 16 films ever comes off and is successful and I might as well be throwing my money away. These people were shocked when I responded, 'Yes, but after the 14th time that it doesn't work, the odds are 1 in 2'.'

I sense he would keep going when others would give up. He tells me that, 'If you have ten ideas in business, eight of them probably won't work and certainly in TV the trick is to be able to turn the disaster into something bearable.'

He illustrates this with the example of a pilot for a show that he made in the early 1980s. 'It was an absolute nightmare. I'd even got a monkey in for one of the sketches. Anyway, needless to say it went horribly wrong and the monkey even escaped and was climbing all over the lighting rigging. The director didn't know whether to follow the monkey or the rest of the show - utter disaster.'

'The executive producer sat me down and we talked it through. Not once did I think that I shouldn't have done it but I think the key was that I learned to keep my nerve and listen to others' advice. The criticism of the production or the content was not a criticism of me, I knew that, and so we could turn that disaster into something bearable.'

In fact, bearable is far from an adequate word. Within three weeks the 'disaster' became *The Six O'Clock Show*, one of the most impactful TV shows in 80s Britain. From listening to Greg, I get the impression that many people would have been so personally attached to or invested in the idea that they wouldn't have been able to rebound from the initial disappointment of the pilot. Yet he doesn't see this as anything special, just a natural way of working.

Greg has a number of mottos that he lives by and which have served him well. One that he is passionate about and in which he clearly believes is that 'In the end, everything will be OK'.

'I can't remember when I started believing this but I know it didn't come from my parents. It's just always been with me and even in my darkest days, such as the hostile takeover of London Weekend Television (a company I helped build and viewed as my own), the break-up of my first marriage, or having to resign from the BBC, I've always believed it.'

I ask Greg how he managed to keep hold of this belief that everything would be ok when things got so tough.

'I keep things in perspective. At the end of the day, you have to ask yourself 'Who am I anyway?' And I know that I am separate from the situation, things will move on and the next question is, 'So what next? What am I going to do next?"

He tells me that it is the desire to 'keep doing stuff' that is the key to his resilience and his unshakable belief that everything will be OK. 'The only other alternative is to give up and that sounds really boring.'

'Another thing about boredom is that it kills good ideas. You have to action them quickly otherwise you over-analyse them or someone will find a reason to shoot them down. Do something quickly, then learn from it. Don't ever get possessive over an idea. The best creative sessions we had when I was at the BBC were at something called the watering hole where people would come from all over the building, from different departments, to hear, critique and build on other peoples' ideas at the same time as sharing their own. It meant you had to have the nerve to throw your ideas out there and see what happened to them.'

But how does he stop 'failures' from dragging him down and puncturing his ebullient nature? And why don't more people find this as normal and as natural and easy as he does? He explains with his favourite quote, which he has on his desk at home, by Roosevelt from his 'Man In The Arena' speech:

'It is not the critic who counts; not the man who points out how the strong man stumbles, or where the doer of deeds could have done them better. The credit belongs to the man who is actually in the arena, whose face is marred by dust and sweat and blood; who strives valiantly; who errs, who comes short again and again, because there is no effort without error and shortcoming; but who does actually strive to do the deeds; who knows great enthusiasms, the great devotions; who spends himself in a worthy cause; who at the best knows in the end the triumph of high achievement, and who at the worst, if he fails, at least fails while daring greatly, so

that his place shall never be with those cold and timid souls who neither know victory nor defeat.'

Greg is also Chancellor of York University and was shortly to be giving out degrees to that year's graduates. He says that every year he gives these young people three pieces of advice which he thinks are absolutely vital.

'Firstly you must remember to keep things simple. Most things in business are simple. They might not seem like it sometimes but they are; even the highly technical stuff is simple really when you boil it down. And, if it isn't, you need to have the confidence to ask for it to be made simple. Don't be afraid to say 'I don't understand'.'

The second piece of advice is to treat people properly.

'I've lost count of the number of people who have been mentally scarred by a manager who hasn't treated them well and that's sad. You must treat people well - you have a duty as a leader to do that, and it's good business sense too.'

And the third piece of advice, which appears to mean the most to him, is to be yourself. It seemed to me that Greg Dyke is very happy being Greg Dyke and that he views being yourself, as well as choosing not to be cynical but to see the glass as half full, as key parts of his philosophy of life.

'Success leads to confidence which leads to more success but your definition of success changes as you get older. I was never bothered about money and was so grateful that my wife never was either. It gave me the great confidence to just be me. Many people, especially when they get promoted, often forget who they are and what got them there. They stop being themselves and instead try and be what they think someone in that role should be. That's a huge mistake. If you're funny, be funny, if you're smart then be smart. If you think off the wall, then keep doing that.'

CHAPTER SIX

Driven By Fear

'May your choices reflect your hopes not your fears'

NELSON MANDELA

THE CASE STUDY

'I took a deep breath and asked again.
'What DO you want?''

I had known of Tony for a number of years. He was a businessman of some repute who had quite a high profile in the press, not least because of the highs and lows of his various business ventures. When we met for the first time he told me that he had recently had to wind up his company because his retail business had failed. I listened to him for a long time as he told me the story of his business, taking me from the initial business idea, through what Tony called his 'heyday'. He spent a long time talking about all of the famous people he had met, the parties he had gone to and how much he had earned (and spent) over the years. He told me of the awards he had won, the share options and the interviews with magazines.

He had very interesting stories to tell and, if he had been a little less self-aggrandising, he would have made a fantastic storyteller or after-dinner speaker. Before I knew it we were half an hour into the session and I had hardly said anything.

Eventually I got Tony to speak about the decline and demise of the business, but he shrugged it off with a number of clichés such as, 'Well all good things come to an end' and 'We had a really good run of it'.

'Was it inevitable or, with hindsight, was there anything that you could have done to avoid the business failing?' I asked.

'What? Of course it was inevitable. It was just an economics thing. I had a couple of managers who didn't really step up to the plate, but it was largely down to the recession. I wasn't very hands on at this stage so it certainly wasn't something that could be laid at my doorstep.'

He was adamant that the failure of the business was nothing to do with him – perhaps a little too adamant - and there was something about his demeanour that told me now wasn't the time to push him on this.

I asked him what his plans were and he told me that he wanted to set up a new business but that, this time, he intended to make sure that when he stepped away from the day to day running of the business the management didn't 'screw it up again'.

'And what's made you come to see me?'

'Well, to be honest I'm not quite sure just yet. I can't talk to any of my colleagues about what happened. I also know that you can't speak to the press about any of this.'

He then broke into another story about another celebrity friend of his who had some coaching when his restaurant failed. I thought he was going to tell me how it had been really useful to him and that's why Tony had decided to get some coaching, but instead he got caught up in the fact that the restaurant failed because his friend had too many drink- and drug-fuelled parties at his restaurant. Tony was in the middle of giving me a graphic recollection of one of these parties when I realised that we were coming to the end of the session. I hastily brought Tony back on task and we did a little work on what kind of business he wanted to set up next and where he was going to find some better people for his new management team. Despite the lack of time, we were surprisingly successful at coming to a resolution on these points and Tony was going to do some homework on them before our next session.

Supervision

At my supervision session I was keen to discuss my first session with Tony. I explained how Tony was my highest profile client for some time and also that my coaching session with Tony had probably been one of the least successful and satisfying sessions I had had for some time. I was pretty sure that Tony didn't get anything out of it and I hadn't enjoyed it either.

'Why do you think that was?' my supervisor asked me. He had an uncanny ability to ask a direct yet artfully vague question. He could have meant, 'Why you do think Tony didn't get anything out of it?' or alternatively 'Why do you think you didn't enjoy it?' or perhaps even something else. In the past we had talked about how asking an open question of this kind can open a door for the person being coached or supervised to answer the particular question that they themselves think is the most important question. Which question the client chooses to answer can in itself can be illuminating.

I chose to answer the question which most interested me, why I thought that Tony had not got anything from the coaching session. 'Well all Tony did was tell me a load of stories and anecdotes about his businesses, celebrity parties and business trips. They were very interesting but not really relevant, and when I attempted to bring things back to the business he was evasive and defensive. He soon launched into another anecdote.'

'Why do you think he told so many anecdotes?'

'I think he likes the sound of his own voice. And I don't think he was ready to be vulnerable.'

'And did you like the sound of his voice?'

'Sure. He was very easy to listen to and I am a sucker for a good story.'

'It's not uncommon for a client to have a need to 'tell their story' in the first session. Sometimes it continues for a few more sessions. Was this just a classic case of that?'

'No. With hindsight, I'm sure that the stories were a distraction to avoid talking about anything deeper. But at the time I was wondering if there were any hidden messages in the stories.'

Often a client's storytelling may be a defence or a smokescreen to avoid the 'real' conversation that is needed. At other times it may be a sign of entrenched or 'stuck' thinking.

The coach needs to be able to discern whether or not the storytelling is likely to be of value to the client, know when to move the client on, and how to do this. The coach should seek to avoid getting lost in the client's 'story' but may ask themselves: 'Does this apparently irrelevant story in fact reflect or shed some light upon some aspect of my client's situation? Might there be an unconscious message here?'

Sigmund Freud was of the belief that we cannot help unconscious thoughts and worries slipping into conscious behaviour *[Ref 21]*. The term 'unconscious leakage' eventually evolved to describe this concept. While there is a risk that coaches may try to read too much into what is being said, it is useful for the coach to consider whether such 'unconscious leakage' may be occurring.

'And what would you say the messages were?' my supervisor prompted.

'That Tony is feeling very vulnerable. I think that Tony has used his charisma and position to his advantage over the years to avoid vulnerability and I think he is quite used to getting people to listen to him. He's almost hypnotic in his storytelling.'

'Could you have fallen under his spell a little?'

'It's certainly strange for me to allow a client to dictate the session that much.'

My supervisor then took a risk himself - he suggested that I had become 'star–struck'.

'The way that you talk about the effect Tony's storytelling had upon you and how you were not your usual, challenging self, tells me that you might potentially be treating this client differently to the way in which you would usually treat a new client. How does it sound when I say that?'

One potential function of supervision is to increase the quality of the coach's reflection on how they are working as a coach.

Even though my natural reaction would have been to defend myself, I paused and replayed the session in my head in the light of what my supervisor had just said. I realised that my supervisor had a point.

Session Two

As I approached the next session with Tony, I reflected on my supervisor's view that I may have been 'star-struck'. My supervisor and I had decided together that a more dynamic and provocative coaching approach might bring about some change in Tony's thinking. It appeared that nobody in Tony's life really challenged him and his modus operandi was to be so overpowering that nobody could get close enough to him to offer either challenge or support.

When Tony arrived he launched straight into an anecdote about a famous sports personality who was a colleague on the board of a local children's charity. The story went on for a long time. I was again feeling overwhelmed by the force of Tony's personality and indeed was beginning to wonder whether I would get an opportunity to say anything.

I remembered my supervision session. Was Tony's story potentially relevant? Could there be any unconscious leakage in this story which might provide some helpful insight? It was always a possibility and the temptation was just to let Tony continue. However, in Tony's case, these stories seemed to me to be merely a series of name-dropping opportunities. I took a deep breath and decided to challenge Tony:

'I am wondering why you have taken 15 minutes of valuable time, which you have paid for, to tell me that story. I also wonder whether you are trying to avoid talking about the real issues here, namely the failure of your business and your anxiety about the future? I am a little confused about what you want from coaching and why you are here. I think we need to go back to basics. Perhaps you could answer the question, 'What do you want?''

Tony looked annoyed.

'I don't want to be analysed. I don't want to rake through my past. I don't want to waste time talking about things which have already happened.'

'What do you **want**?' I asked, this time with a slightly different emphasis.

Tony looked a bit stumped by my question.

'I don't want to find myself in this situation again. I need to make sure that doesn't happen.'

I took a deep breath and asked.

'What **do** you want?'

I had seen a successful coach demonstrate the repeated use of this question at a conference I had attended. It had worked really well and the client had identified a clear goal, along with their core values and purpose. However, it did not appear to work so well with Tony.

'I want you to stop asking me dumb-ass questions and tell me how to set about finding the right management team for my next business. I thought you were meant to be a business advisor, not a psychiatrist.'

I waited because I knew Tony was about to say more.

'I don't know if this coaching is going to help. It's not what I thought it was going to be. I think I wanted more of a mentor actually.'

I found myself trying to explain that while coaching is about moving forwards it often requires an analysis of what has brought the client to this point - for better or for worse.

Coaching is a reflective learning process in which the client may be enabled to take lessons from their previous experiences into their future.

I heard myself saying that coaching may also involve the client having a moment of truth or a cold hard look in the mirror because they would not be able to change what they were not prepared or able to acknowledge.

I suggested, politely, that Tony would need to be prepared to seek to increase his self-awareness if the coaching were to have any chance of helping him. I could see that Tony was angry with me and that he was only half-listening. The session came to an awkward and premature end as we agreed that Tony would give some thought to whether he wanted to continue being coached. I reiterated that I would be happy to continue working with Tony but would understand if he decided to find an alternative source of support.

We left the date for the third coaching session in the diary on the understanding that Tony would cancel if he decided not to proceed.

As Tony walked out of my room, I did not expect to see him again.

Supervision

I was quite shaken by this session and a little worried that I had overstepped the mark. I needed to see my supervisor again to talk things through. My supervisor asked me to talk through my approach and asked me whether I believed that I had been justified in taking the approach that I did. I did believe that it was a justifiable approach; however, Tony's reaction to my approach had surprised and worried me. I am not naturally very comfortable with confrontation and this session had felt very confrontational to me.

'How do you think Tony feels about confrontation?' my supervisor asked.

'He's probably more comfortable with it than me. It sounds like he has a lot more experience of confrontation than I do,' I replied.

'Was there any unconscious leakage in this confrontation? We may sometimes say things we regret when we get heated but we may also accidentally let out what we really feel.'

'Well, Tony didn't really answer my question. Instead he spent a lot of energy telling me what he **didn't** want.'

The ways in which individuals motivate themselves can be characterised as either *'towards'* motivation (towards what the individual wants) and *'away from'* motivation (away from what the individual does not want).

'It sounds as though Tony is very *'away from'* motivated,' my supervisor suggested.

I was beginning to suspect that Tony was perhaps too driven by what he was striving to get away from in his life and in business and was lacking a clear idea of what he was trying to move towards.

I thought that it might be helpful to Tony to highlight the concept of alternative motivational drivers in order to help Tony realise which motivational system he was primarily using, and to help him to evaluate whether this was helping him. If it wasn't, then I would try to help him to adopt an alternative motivational system. My supervisor reassured me that the confrontation that I had experienced with Tony in the previous session was something that could ultimately be helpful to my coaching work with Tony.

Session 3

Somewhat to my surprise Tony did attend the next session. He said he had decided to give coaching another go and would let me 'do it my way' this time. If he hadn't experienced any results after six sessions, he would give up on it, but he was here and willing to try something new.

Tony apologised for the abrupt end to the previous session, admitting that my 'blunt and forceful' questioning came as a shock to him because he had always been surrounded by 'yes men'. This was probably one of the reasons why the business had failed; Tony had not employed anyone to replace the energy which Tony provided when he was 'hands on'. I wondered why Tony felt so threatened by the idea of anyone disagreeing with him or challenging him or simply having a different opinion to Tony's.

We had obviously arrived at a turning point as now, instead of having to listen to Tony continuing to tell me about how great he was and how great his life was, I listened to Tony's self-recrimination, his regret, his guilt and his despair about the future. It was a dramatic turnaround of emotions.

'I should have just learned a trade or got a normal job in a bank when I left school like everyone told me to, but I wanted something better for my life. Looking back now I think it would have been a lot easier if I had done what was expected of me. I wish I could go back and start all over again. I have had enough of the stress that comes with owning and running businesses. As you know, this isn't the first time.'

'First time for what?' I asked.

'Liquidation.' Tony looked directly into my eyes for the first time, shrugged his shoulders and made an embarrassed face. 'Another business of mine failed about twenty years ago, you must have read about it in the press? I thought I had learned the lesson then. I certainly didn't expect to be making the same mistakes again, yet here I am twenty years older and supposedly wiser but in the same damn place, having to face everyone and start all over again. I just don't know if I have the energy for it.'

Tony went on to tell me that his marriage had ended when his first company failed and he hadn't had a regular relationship since then.

I asked Tony once again what he was here for. He said that identifying some next steps would be really helpful but he didn't know if he had the energy to do it all again. If he did do it all again, he wanted to learn the lessons from his past mistakes. He didn't want to find himself back here again in another few years. I asked Tony why he had started a business in the first place and what drove his ambition.

'I didn't want to be poor, like my parents were. I didn't want to do a boring dead-end 9-5 job. I can't bear routine or boredom. I didn't want to do what everyone expected me to do either. I wanted to break away from my background. I like nice things and I wanted fast cars, a big house and a good standard of living. That's what drove me.'

I noticed that Tony's first words were about what he didn't want and not what he did want. Only at the end had he talked about what he wanted. This supported the hypothesis that I had developed in my supervision session regarding Tony's typical motivation drivers, so I thought this might be worth exploring with Tony.

I asked Tony to tell me a bit more about the business and what he thought had brought about its demise. He talked for a long time about the pleasure he got from setting up the business, its early growth, the fondness he had for the staff he had recruited and how it had constantly surprised him that he had created such a great business. However, he had never had a business plan or any real growth strategy and he felt that this could have contributed to the business failing. He realised as he spoke to me that he had not planned ahead at all and he also realised that when the business was up and running he had 'taken his eye off the ball'. He had put in a General Manager and Tony had spent most of his time playing golf and organising charity fundraising events for the local Rotary Club.

'Once it was established, I thought it would just carry on like that and, to be honest, I got a bit bored with the business. I lost interest in it a bit and I thought it could survive without my input.'

I speculated that maybe he only feels motivated when he needs to get away from something. This resonated with Tony who acknowledged that he started to 'lose interest and energy when things are going smoothly'. We both recognised that Tony had been motivated to come for coaching because he had found himself in another 'back against the wall' situation. I mentioned that many business people engage coaches to work with them during the good times as well as the bad.

I suggested that we might need to do some work on goal-setting and *'towards'* motivation. I wasn't sure that this was by any means all that we needed to do, but it was a useful starting point for our coaching sessions. I asked Tony to do a piece of homework before our next session based on trying to get him to start with the end in mind. I asked him to write a 'nirvana letter' *(see Chapter Eleven: Searching For Fulfilment)* as if he were writing a letter towards the end of his life when he was living the life of his dreams and had achieved everything he wanted. I asked him to address his 'nirvana letter' to someone who mattered to him, whose opinion he valued, and to tell that person what he had done in the years between now and then to achieve this imagined state of fulfilment or nirvana. For more detail on how to use the nirvana letter idea see Tom Preston's book *'Coach Yourself To Success'. [Ref 22]*

Session Four

I was thrilled to find that Tony had done his homework. Although Tony told me that he had found the nirvana letter exercise difficult, he admitted that he had found it powerful and useful. Tony proudly produced his handwritten nirvana letter for me to read. He said that when he first sat down to write he didn't know what he was going to say, but soon he was writing about a successful Internet-based social media business which he had sold for a huge sum of money just five years after starting it.

My heart sank a bit when I had finished reading Tony's letter. I have seen many examples of nirvana letters and the most powerful letters all reference more 'meaningful' things, such as family, friendships, hobbies, travel, a feeling of appreciation, contentment or satisfaction, and sometimes even a zen-like feeling of making peace with oneself. However, there was no sign of any of this in Tony's letter - just more golf, more parties and more famous people.

I reminded myself that I should try to remain non-judgemental, should not impose my philosophical views upon Tony and should strive to maintain an attitude of unconditional positive regard for my client. My client seemed very pleased with himself.

'I know what I need to do now and, more to the point, I know who can help me with it. One of my business associates already owns a successful internet-based business and has agreed to invest in my new business venture. So I think you have solved my problem for me - I have a plan and someone to do it with and I am raring to go!'

I was torn. On the one hand I should be happy for Tony – he clearly had a great deal of enthusiasm regarding his new plans and appeared to have achieved what he wanted from coaching. On the other hand, I felt the coaching had been unsuccessful. I had a strong feeling that I was getting the brush-off from Tony.

'That's great, Tony,' I said. 'But we have still got a lot of work to do on keeping you motivated when things are going well, as opposed to in times of crisis. We have identified a pattern in your life that you only motivate yourself effectively when things are not working out well. I'm worried that you might once again lose motivation when things are going well for you. We have just started working on this and it might be helpful if we could dig a bit deeper to see if we can work out how this pattern arose. For example, I wonder if, deep down, you still see yourself as the 'little boy from the wrong side of the tracks' who grew up in poverty? If this is the case and you have not adjusted your self-image to embrace the successful man you are today, that could be contributing to your inability to maintain your success.'

'I hear what you are saying,' Tony said, becoming visibly irritated once again, 'but I'm really not interested in getting into therapy with you. No offence, but it's just somewhere I don't want to go and, to be frank, I don't think it's somewhere I need to go.'

'Fair enough, Tony,' I said, reluctantly, 'I want you to know that it doesn't become therapy just because we are talking about your childhood, but I hear you and if that is outside our remit then I'm OK with that.'

It may be possible for a coach to enable a client to achieve real transformation by exploring and identifying the root causes of unhelpful repeating patterns of behaviour.

Even though Tony was now aware of the concept of moving towards something rather than away from something, I still felt he had not really addressed any of his core values or beliefs about himself.

'I've got one more thing I'd like to try that I think might be helpful to you,' I said, 'and it doesn't involve anything to do with your childhood.'

Tony smiled, which I took as permission to continue.

'Do you think there is a risk that you might get bored with this new business venture also at some point? That you might perhaps take your eye off the ball once again?'

'Sure, there's always a chance. But I think this one will be different,' he said.

'Well one thing that might help is explicitly stating some of the beliefs you have about yourself. I want you to come up with some statements about yourself that will help you keep your eye on the ball. These statements should either already be true or you would like them to be true.'

These identity-based statements are a way of helping people tailor their behaviour patterns by changing or reinforcing what they explicitly believe about themselves. Tony was surprisingly happy to have a go at this and came up with the following:

- I am the kind of person who succeeds.

- I am the kind of person who is secure enough to avoid hiring 'yes men'.

- I am the kind of person who notices when he gets bored.

- I am the kind of person who looks for new challenges for his company as soon as things start to plateau.

- I am the kind of person who keeps his company ahead of the curve.

I said that this was a wonderful start and the challenge for Tony now would be to incorporate these beliefs into his daily routine so that they would stick. This can be difficult for people to do on their own and coaching can significantly increase the chances of these new beliefs taking root. I expressed my desire to continue coaching Tony.

'I hear you, I really do, but I think you've already done more than I expected. I'm really confident that I can take it from here.'

I was unconvinced but felt Tony wanted to go it alone from this point. So, I wished him luck and assured him I was there to help if needed.

That was the last I saw of Tony. I like to observe the careers of former clients when I can, and as a result of Tony's high profile he was easier to keep track of than most. Unfortunately, it turned out that Tony had not mastered this particular pattern of his. His new business went the same way as his previous businesses. I have spent a lot of time reflecting on whether I could have helped Tony more. I believe that there were signs of progress in just four coaching sessions and I continue to wonder whether, if Tony had been willing to work with a coach over a longer period of time, he might have had a chance of breaking the patterns of a lifetime.

TOOLS AND TECHNIQUES

Tony's reluctance to engage with coaching came from his *'away from'* motivational system, which was also limiting his success and creating a repeating negative life pattern. Sometimes having a compelling reason to flee from something undesirable is a powerful motivator. Sometimes we don't know what the right answer is but we do know that staying where we are isn't an option either. In those instances getting away from the current situation is good enough and acknowledging what is wrong with where we are right now is the right thing to do.

While *'away from'* motivational drivers can be very effective in the short-term, they have their limitations. If you only have an *'away from'* pattern, you are unlikely to be able to motivate yourself in the good times. Similarly, if you only have a *'towards'* motivation pattern, you tend to get stuck when the goal is unclear. We have found that being able to utilise both patterns in the appropriate circumstances is key to maintaining motivation over the long-term.

The techniques in this section may be helpful in raising awareness of your client's behaviours and help them to achieve realistic and healthy motivation, whether it be *'towards'* or *'away from'* or, ideally, a combination of both.

Know How

One way to help your client take action is to help them create and evaluate two alternative potential futures that they can visualise and choose between.

This exercise requires no props or equipment other than three chairs. Introduce the technique to the client by explaining that there are different ways to motivate ourselves and this technique will allow them to experience the power of both *'away from'* and *'towards'* motivational drivers. This technique can be used to help the client find their motivation in relation to any situation.

Invite the client to sit in one chair. Set up two additional chairs so that they are facing the client, ask the client to define their goal for the coaching session and ask them to describe their present situation.

1. Ask the client to look at the first chair and think about a time in the future where they haven't changed their behaviour, actions, beliefs or thought patterns. Be sure to ask the client what a reasonable timeframe feels like. Once they have this image in mind, give them the option to sit in that chair and act as if they were that future version of themselves. This can evoke a strong and emotional response in some clients and they may choose not to sit in that chair. The other option, therefore, is to simply look at that chair. In either case, ask them to describe in detail how they feel about their situation and themselves. As coach, your main job is to keep them associated and prompt them to visualise and experience the specific details, paying close attention to the feelings that are evoked.

2. Once they have finished in this chair, ask them to come back to their original chair. This is to dissociate them from that future state and bring them back to the here and now.

3. When they are ready, ask the client to look at the second empty chair and think about an alternative future where, instead of things staying exactly as they are, they have made some changes to their behaviours, actions, beliefs or thought patterns and achieved all that they want to. Ask them to sit in that chair and encourage them to build up as vivid a picture as possible, talk about what they will get, where they will be and how it will feel.

4. When they are ready, ask them to move back to their original chair again, bringing with them all the wisdom, advice and learning their future selves have just given them. Ask them which of those two experiences had the biggest impact on them to motivate them to change.

Work with the client to determine some initial steps towards that desired reality and remind them that every decision they make will take them closer towards one of those two chairs.

Powerful Coaching Question:
If you could reward yourself for completing an arduous task, and had no constraints, what would your reward be?

Push Me Pull You

One objective of coaching may be for the coach to 'hold the mirror up' to the client to enable the client to raise their awareness of their behaviours, thoughts and beliefs.

As both *'away from'* and *'towards'* motivational drivers may be useful in the appropriate context, it may be useful for a coach to help their client explore their current motivational patterns.

1. Ask your client to look back at anything they have attempted in their life which has involved significant challenge, effort or willpower, or which has taken a long time. For example, studying for qualifications, losing weight, learning a new skill like a musical instrument.

2. Place those attempts into two columns – one for things at which the client was successful and one for things at which they were unsuccessful.

3. Ask the client to think back to each of those challenges in turn and reflect on whether they were adopting a *'towards'* motivational strategy or an *'away from'* strategy at that time.

4. Invite the client to identify any patterns. Are there certain types of activity where an *'away from'* strategy works for them and others where a *'towards'* strategy works for them? Are there any examples where they have used both?

5. Now ask the client to think of something that they would like to change and to list any factors that are pushing them away from their current reality and any factors that are pulling them towards the desired change.

6. Ask the client to score each factor out of ten by reference to the extent to which that factor resonates with them. Does one set of factors score more highly than the other?

Powerful Coaching Question:
How much would you say that you enjoy the destination compared to the journey?

Creative Goal-Setting

Sometimes we need to break outside of the normal, linear patterns of thinking and get a little abstract.

Here are some techniques that may encourage clients to be more creative when setting goals.

Invite your client to:

- Make a drawing of how you want your life to be. Make it as bright, colourful and imaginative as you can. You can create drawings for each area of your life – work, home, relationships, money, etc. or create one big picture. Put lots of details into it and when it's finished, sign and date it, then pin it on your wall so you so that you can look at it every day. This can be a powerful method of making your goals come to life.

- Imagine that your life so far had been turned into a book or a movie and you were in charge of writing the sequel. Map out the storyboard of the rest of your life. Remember the key elements of a story:

    Characters – hero, allies, villains.

    Plot – with drama, a twist and a resolution.

    Themes – What values are evident?

    What is the moral of the story?

- Imagine you are at a party and people are talking about their work. What might you hear that would really excite you and make you want to join in the conversation?

- Create a treasure map that represents the journey of discovery upon which you intend to embark. Treasure maps might have not only an X that marks the spot but also a number of landmarks that you must navigate around or through and sights that are worth seeing on the way. Draw these and mark them out.

> **Powerful Coaching Question:**
> Think about times when you have been successful and have achieved what you wanted. In those situations, what was driving you?

THE INTERVIEW

Carl Llewellyn

It is important to remember that avoiding pain and disappointment is not, in itself a bad thing, but if this becomes our default driver for motivation then it can become destructive. We interviewed Carl Llewellyn – one of horse racing's most successful jockeys, and dubbed the King of Aintree for his Grand National successes – who told us how, throughout his career, he had used the positive aspects of this habit to his advantage and had attempted to mitigate the aspects that weren't helpful to him.

In addition to his successes at Aintree, Carl has won both the Scottish and Welsh Grand Nationals and he won the Whitbread Gold Cup in 2000 by the biggest winning margin in the race's history. After retiring from racing Carl was a trainer for three years, during which time he trained the winner of the Scottish Grand National and the Bet 365 Gold Cup. He is now assistant trainer to his long-time friend and boss, Nigel Twiston-Davies.

'I remember one day at the start of my career when I was schooling a horse, teaching him to jump. The horse was called Absolute Beginner and he was a clumsy, horrible horse; nobody liked riding him. At one jump, he fell and stepped on my stomach. I was in agony and scared because, for a while, I couldn't catch my breath and I could see my boss who, instead of coming to help me, just turned and walked away.

'I was 23 and had been riding for this trainer for about a year. Like all the jockeys who worked for him, I knew that if a horse fell he believed it was always the jockey's fault. So we all rode the horses in fear of what would happen if we made a mistake, rather than trying our best to win.'

I am speaking to a man who has won 995 horse races, including two English Grand Nationals, a Scottish Grand National and a Welsh Grand National. Surprisingly, he describes his overwhelming feeling when winning a race not as elation but as, 'Phew! Thank God I made it round and didn't mess that up!' Carl believes it all stems from the formative years he spent riding for this trainer, who he says bullied him.

'Before a race, everything would start with **don't**: *'Don't go too early'*, *'Don't hit the fence'*, *'Don't do this'*, *'Don't do that'*. That's no way to get someone into the right frame of mind to win a race is it? You ride better when you are having fun, but we weren't allowed to have fun.'

Carl tells me how he has always been driven by an overwhelming fear of failure; a pressing sense of responsibility to others – the owner who bought the horse, the trainer who spent years training the horse and had chosen him over other jockeys to ride it and even, to a degree, the punters who had bet their money on him.

'I don't mind the horse losing if it's not my fault. I can accept the horse not being fast enough or being unlucky, but if I've made a mistake I would hate myself for letting people down and would beat myself up horrendously about it. I would be shouting, screaming and swearing at myself after the finish line. It's the worst feeling.'

The calm person talking to me seems completely incapable of the bursts of raw emotion that he was describing, but Carl says that he thinks it is one of the main things that drove him to be successful.

'I was a percentages rider. I never took big risks, I would grind it out and people knew what they were getting from me, whether it was Monday at Plumpton or Saturday at Cheltenham, which is important I think. A dead hero is no good to anyone,' he says and then goes on to tell me how, over the course of 20 years, he kept his weight between 135 and 137 pounds whereas other jockeys would binge eat and then manically try to sweat it out to get back down to riding weight.

'I would always eat healthily, mainly chicken, pasta and fish. Occasionally I would treat myself to a bar of chocolate but I knew that it was really important to stay at my riding weight. Other jockeys were surprised at how I was able to eat just one biscuit and then stop, but I couldn't see why they would put themselves through all that pain of having to lose weight really quickly.'

He describes what he did as common sense, but it was all knowledge that he soaked up during an injury-hit start to his career when, at 22, he was told he should retire.

'I saw a lot of doctors and physios and I picked up information about how to avoid injuries and reduce the time it took to recover. I made sure I was always well hydrated and was one of very few people to wear a gumshield so I rarely got concussions like the other jockeys. It was just common sense really.'

It was this regime that allowed him to get back to riding only eleven days after breaking his collarbone, although he now admits that his attempt to ride in the Grand National a week after breaking his leg was 'a bit stupid'.

Carl says his fear of failure never left him, even when he moved to work for Nigel Twiston-Davies, an environment which he describes as being 'like heaven because he allowed me to ride how I thought I should'. Carl says that he also liked the fact that Twiston-Davies never praised him, possibly because he knew it was a trade-off for never having to worry about being shouted at as he had been by his previous trainer.

'I never allowed myself to get cocky and genuinely never believed I was good. The old adage of 'you're only as good as your next race' was one that I believe in firmly to this day and even after I had won the Scottish Grand National, the very next day was a blank slate. I had to prove myself all over again.'

I ask him whether he has any regrets and he admits, 'It would have been nice to go out there and think 'I can't fail' but I think it's a good thing that I was always trying to prove myself.' He also concedes that the fact that he viewed winning as more of a relief than a joy meant he had not enjoyed his career as much as he might have done.

A fear of failure can be a positive thing. Carl's career is proof of that. But how did Carl stop it becoming a paralysing fear? How did he mitigate this self-limiting belief that he might screw up?

'I trained myself to become great at blocking things out by focussing on the present. I would give myself small windows of time in which I would allow myself to worry about the race, maybe ten minutes on the morning drive to the racecourse, but then that would be it. After that I would read the paper, talk to a stranger or someone in the yard, anything to bring me back to the present and away from the impending race. I knew jockeys who would spend all week worrying about a big race coming up but I didn't see the point in that.'

'Likewise after that bout of swearing when I'd lost the race because of a mistake, as soon as I was back with the press, the trainers and the owners, that would be it. I would be back in the present, talking calmly and normally, which became one of my key skills.'

This compartmentalisation is a theme in other areas of his life too. He tells me that 90% of his house is 'immaculate, like a show home' but that he has two rooms where he can be as messy as he likes.

'If I got really worried or down on myself, I would stick on a video of a race where I did really well – I've got everything on tape – and that would be enough to remind me of my capability. I know some jockeys who would watch mistakes they made over and over again, winding themselves up more and more. I don't see the point in that. I don't need to be reminded of what I did wrong and I don't think that helps.'

He also talks about how he has made sure that, since moving to work with Twiston-Davies, he has become friends with the trainers, the owners and their families.

'I think it makes a difference if I'm riding for a friend rather than a boss,' he says. 'I suppose, thinking about it, it was another way of me reducing the pressure on myself. If the trainers and owners liked me then they would go easier on me if I didn't do well.'

Finally, I ask him what he tells the young jockeys that he coaches when they are nervous.

'I tell them that they *should* be nervous. Everyone is. And the cocky ones with their bravado are the most nervous; they are just putting on a front. The point is to make sure that you give yourself time to get that anxiety out of your system and then focus on the technical side of your job. So I tell them all of the things that they are good at, remind them what they can do rather than fill their heads with what *not* to do. At the end of the day, the best way to overcome a fear of failure is to succeed. So I tell them they can't let their fear of failure stop them, they need to just shut it out and let their talent talk.'

CHAPTER SEVEN

Ostrich Syndrome

'We don't see things as they are, we see them as we are.'

ANAIS NIN

THE CASE STUDY

'Richard's self-assurance was quite something. I've coached many people who are at either end of the self-confidence spectrum but I was beginning to sense that Richard was something else.'

While working on a corporate engagement, I came across a team leader, Richard, who had recently been removed from his position and 'moved sideways' to a new, smaller team in a different department. Management officially explained this move as 'the team requiring some fresh ideas', coupled with a drop in morale and some high-profile people leaving.

Richard was aware of my presence as I had been coaching some of his colleagues. Although I was not officially available to his new department, Richard asked for some internal budget for coaching to help him settle in to his new role. After many discussions with his previous manager, his current manager, the HR department and others, eventually it was agreed that his previous department would fund his coaching for six sessions.

In his first session Richard couldn't wait to tell me that he felt extremely hard done by and how certain people had 'manipulated the situation' in order to 'get rid of him'. He was very clear that he wanted to use coaching in order to work out why people had treated him badly and how he could restore his reputation.

'I've been a successful team leader for nearly ten years – a really popular one as well – and, all of a sudden, out of nowhere and with no warning, it all gets taken away from me.' Richard said, angrily. 'I'm seriously thinking about taking up a grievance with Human Resources about it.'

'I can tell you are very upset about this,' I replied. 'It must be a huge blow for you. Although, as I understand it, you are still a team leader, right?'

'Well yes,' he reluctantly agreed, 'but it's definitely a demotion.'

Richard told me how another member of his team had twisted the output of meetings in order to make him look bad and had gone behind his back to undermine him and impress management so that he could get Richard's job. Richard was so angry at the 'sneaky politics' of the company that for twenty minutes I barely had the opportunity to speak.

There is very little chance of any progress being made in coaching while the client is highly stressed because, during periods of high stress, clients are in 'survival mode'.

When someone is in 'survival mode', their 'fight or flight' response is fired *[Ref 23]*, leading to a number of changes within that person. Firstly, because their focus is very much on themselves and their immediate needs, there is a significant loss of empathy and conscience: they are forced into black and white thinking, assuming that one party must win and one must lose.

As you can probably imagine, this is unhelpful for a coaching relationship. A coach's first priority in such circumstances is to reduce the client's stress levels and help the client to reach 'competency mode'. This begins with letting the client 'vent' and get things off their chest.

There was so much passion in Richard's complaint though that it was hard not to get drawn into his story. I had only met his old manager during the negotiations to set up the coaching and he seemed like a decent person, not someone who would be hoodwinked by a tell-tale or deviously manipulate Richard out of his position and into another department. However, listening to Richard, I was becoming less certain.

Having the opportunity simply to talk this through in an uninterrupted way seemed to have a calming effect on Richard and we could then start to explore what was really going on. I reminded Richard that our sessions would remain confidential and asked him if what had happened was actually as surprising as he had first thought. Confidentiality is an important part of the coaching contract to ensure trust and partnership, and exceptions should only be made in extreme circumstances or if otherwise agreed.

I attempted to engage Richard's rational side and asked him to evaluate his boss as objectively as he could: was Richard's boss truly a manipulative person who had it in for Richard, or was it possible, for example, that he might simply have acted with incomplete information? As regards Richard's colleagues: were they definitely ganging up on Richard unnecessarily or might they, in some small way, have reason to feel aggrieved with him?

'Looking back, Richard, with the benefit of hindsight,' I tentatively began, 'and if you were being perhaps overgenerous to your previous manager in your interpretation of events, was there any way that you could have seen this coming do you think?'

'So you believe all this crap too do you?' he replied, then added, sarcastically, 'Great!'

'Not at all. I really don't know what has happened. So far, I only have your version of events and I'm wondering what the other side of the story might be, that's all.'

This was a tricky balancing act for me. On the one hand, I aim to act as a partner for my clients so that they know they always have someone alongside them. This is a key component in people being able to change – knowing that they are not doing it alone and that they have an ally. On the other hand, it is useful to be aware that you may be only getting one, often extremely polarised, view of any situation. I believed that, at some point, Richard was going to have to face up to how others had viewed the incidents in order for him to reconcile things for himself.

'Have you had any similar feedback in the past that has questioned your leadership style?' I asked.

'Sure. No leader worth his salt pleases everyone all of the time,' he replied, still full of confidence. 'But it's always been from people I have had to let go or people who were lashing out because they hadn't got their way.'

'What kind of things did people say when they were lashing out?' I asked.

'Oh you know, the usual. Alleging that I was power-hungry and controlling. Someone even called me devious once.'

'Interesting,' I said. 'And how would you say the majority of your team would describe you? The ones who don't have a reason to lash out?'

'Visionary, nurturing, inclusive,' he reeled off.

Richard's self-assurance was quite something. I've coached many people who are at either end of the self-confidence spectrum but I was beginning to sense that Richard was something else. In fact, the person who was coming to mind more and more was the lead character from the television series The Office.

I hadn't made any progress in my attempts to get Richard to consider anyone's perspective other than his own, but I decided that I had pushed enough for one session. If I pushed any more then I risked losing any rapport that we had and, without rapport, there would be no chance of my being able to help him.

I asked Richard how he would like to proceed and he came up with an interesting suggestion.

'Why don't you come along to one of my team meetings? You could see for yourself whether you think I deserve the treatment I've had.'

This was certainly something different and the type of opportunity which only really tends to present itself when the coach is working directly within an organisation. I was a little unsure how to respond. My first thought was that this would be a great opportunity to see Richard in action, but on the other hand while I was observing Richard he would be on his best behaviour so I wouldn't get a true picture. Nevertheless, my curiosity won out and I took him up on his offer.

Session Two – The Team Meeting

The meeting was something to behold. I was introduced as an observer and sat behind Richard at the front of the room, making myself as inconspicuous as possible. I was conscious that just the presence of an observer will inevitably have an influence on what is being observed; I thought, however, that if I could stay out of Richard's line of sight and 'melt into the background' then everyone, particularly Richard, would eventually act as if I were not there.

Richard regularly talked over people, tried to outdo his own team-members with shows of one-upmanship and even took credit for a suggestion that someone else put forward in the meeting. He did a lot of good things as well, but I was amazed that he couldn't see how his behaviour was undermining and demotivating those in the meeting.

Session Three

We had scheduled our next session immediately after the team meeting. This was so that anything which came up in the meeting would be fresh in our minds. Two of the keys to effective feedback are to be specific and to be timely. Leaving too long between action and feedback will dilute the impact and increase the chances that one or both of you will forget some of the specifics.

'So what did you think?' Richard asked, getting straight to the point.

'Well, before I reply, this is the only time I have seen one of your meetings so I don't have anything to compare it to. How would you say it went? Would you say it was typical?'

Richard said that, while there was no such thing as a 'typical' meeting, nothing out of the ordinary had happened in the meeting and, on the whole, he was pleased with it.

'What does 'on the whole' mean?' I asked.

'Well I would rather it hadn't dragged on quite so long and I would have preferred it if a few more people had got involved, but it was probably because I'm relatively new to the team,' he rationalised.

'Is that the only reason they didn't get involved?' I asked.

'From that leading question, I guess not!' he replied, immediately on the defensive.

'I'm getting the sense that you feel I am out to get you, but I want you to know that this is not the case,' I said. 'I want to be very clear that my only desire here is to help you with the goal you stated when we first met, namely to use coaching to work out why people had treated you badly and how you can restore your reputation.' I paused briefly. 'Is that still what you want?'

It is important to use the client's own words as accurately as possible.

Restating the client's declared objectives in their own words can be particularly helpful. This not only builds rapport, it also avoids the coach putting their own 'spin' on the coaching objectives.

'Yes. I guess I'm just feeling a little victimised at the moment,' he explained.

I could certainly understand why Richard might be feeling victimised, even if I didn't agree that he was being victimised. At this moment, Richard's perception was the key. I needed to get across to Richard that I understood where he was coming from while simultaneously opening his eyes to other interpretations.

'You mentioned that you would have preferred it if the meeting hadn't dragged on quite so long. You seem like somebody who likes it when people get to the point. Would I be right?' I asked.

'Absolutely. I can't stand it when people fuss around and use a hundred words when ten would have done.'

'My observation arising from that meeting was that you displayed some behaviours which were not consistent with how you describe yourself as a leader,' I began, wondering how well Richard would take my feedback. Some clients who put on a strong front may be insecure and fragile underneath. My aim here was to provide direct feedback to Richard on his leadership style based on what I had observed.

'Such as what?' he asked.

I decided that I wasn't going to sugar-coat my feedback because clear, direct and well-intentioned feedback has integrity and can have the most impact.

'There are three things that I would like to play back to you. Firstly you talked over people on a number of occasions, for example when Stefan was talking about the project dashboard they used to use. I got the sense that Stefan had more to say but gave up when you started talking. This became something of a pattern during the meeting.'

I paused and then decided to list the other two pieces of feedback now rather than let Richard keep wondering what else I was going to say later on.

'There were also a couple of occasions when you seemed to want to out-do your team members. When Ian told you how many stakeholders he had to deal with, you told him you had managed a project with even more stakeholders.'

I could see that Richard's demeanour wasn't changing, although I did feel as though he couldn't wait to rebut my feedback with explanations or excuses.

'And the third thing I observed which did not seem consistent with your definition of you as a leader was when, at the end of the meeting, you seemed to attribute the credit for the week's successes to your having joined the team as leader rather than congratulating the team itself.'

I waited for Richard's reply, and I wasn't too surprised when he gave explanations for each of the examples I had given him.

'Oh me taking the credit was just a joke,' he said. 'And I was reassuring Ian that, while managing a team with many stakeholders may seem difficult, it is possible. Plus, there was no point in Stefan talking about the previous system which they had had in place because I was bringing in a new system. It would only have wasted time. To me, these are examples of a strong leader with practical experience and a sense of humour.'

Feedback can be hard to internalise immediately and clients often go through four stages when receiving feedback.

These stages of response to feedback can be illustrated in the 'SARA' model below:

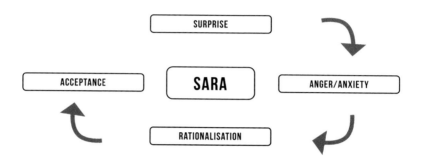

First of all, people are generally surprised by feedback because they don't expect anyone to find anything wrong with what they are doing. A common response here is, 'Really? You think I did that?'

It's important that the person being coached can trust the coach's feedback. One way I increased this trust was by accurately recalling specific examples from the meeting. However, it can still lead to anger: either with the person giving feedback ('How dare you!'), or internalised anger ('How could I be so stupid!'). Both of these reactions can lead to anxiety, causing worry about the consequences, as well as over-dramatising and catastrophising.

Depending on how experienced the person is with receiving feedback and how comfortable they are with themselves will determine how long they take to move on to the rationalisation stage. Here they will attempt to explain why things happened the way they did; to find a way of interpreting their actions that paints them in a positive light and aligns with their self-perceptions.

The third stage is also sometimes labelled 'rejection'. This is where our rationalisation can be so powerful that we choose to ignore the feedback as irrelevant or, even worse, we twist it to match our world-view.

The final stage is where some or all of the feedback eventually hits home and we come to accept that there may be some truth in it after all.

Richard seemed to be very good at rationalising the feedback I had given him. He had gone through the emotions of surprise and anger in our first session and was now very firmly in the rationalisation stage. Unfortunately, though, there was little sign that he was going to do anything other than just dismiss every observation I had made.

There are two main reasons someone will reject feedback. The first is that they don't have sufficient respect for the person giving the feedback. The second is that they have such a strong internal reference system. This impenetrable sense of self-belief prevents the assimilation of a contrary message into their worldview. Many people also have the view that they have been successful so far and so what need is there to change?

I was hoping that there may be a little crack in Richard's resistance due to recent events, but I was still of the opinion that both of the first two factors were in play here. Richard had a strong internal reference system, such that he judged the quality of his work and made decisions about himself and his behaviour based on his own internal standards. Someone with a strong external reference system would judge the quality of their work based on outside feedback. Most of us use a healthy combination of external and internal referencing to make judgements about our own behaviours. I also knew that Richard didn't yet have enough respect for me to take my feedback on board.

I switched tack and decided to introduce the Johari Window *[Ref 24]* - a technique designed to help people develop a better understanding of their relationships and to highlight blind spots in how others perceive them. I briefly introduced the technique to Richard:

'I will give you a list of adjectives that could be used to describe you and you must decide which six of these you think describe you best,' I explained. 'Then, with your permission, I would like to ask some members of your team to select the six adjectives that THEY believe best describe you and we will see what patterns, if any, come up. How does that sound?'

Richard agreed and set about the activity with enthusiasm. Within just a few minutes he had picked the following adjectives: able, confident, helpful, knowledgeable, trustworthy and wise.

We then agreed that I would ask a selected few people from both his previous team and his current team to participate in the exercise before discussing the results in our next session.

Before our next session, however, I bumped into Richard's boss who asked me to his office for a chat later that day. Our meeting was positioned as a general catch up, but it was clear he was very interested in how things were going with Richard in particular. I explained that I don't disclose anything about my clients unless it was agreed in advance or the client has given their express permission for me to do so and Gerry understood this. However, he couldn't help himself dropping into the conversation something that put me in a very difficult position; namely that unless he saw any change in Richard soon then he would be sacked. He stressed that there was no pressure or expectation on me to do anything, as the company would be able to justify the decision having given him every opportunity to improve – including coaching.

This wasn't the first time that I had seen an organisation use coaching for ulterior motives but I still felt manipulated and used. In fact, because of the disingenuous nature of the coaching arrangement, I felt more determined than normal that the coaching would produce a positive result for Richard. My only problem was that time was against me. I refused to believe that Richard was incapable of becoming a great leader, but I was also convinced that it would take time for him to get his head out of the sand and come to terms with his destructive behavioural blind spot.

I told Gerry that I thought he was being too hasty and that I believed, with time, Richard could still be a great asset to his organisation. I pointed out some of the past successes Richard had mentioned and some of the positive and encouraging signs I noticed in his team meeting. Gerry seemed to soften a little but I was not convinced that he was prepared to give him a chance.

Supervision

Until meeting with Richard's boss, I had not felt much anxiety about this engagement. Richard's extreme self-confidence was interesting, but there was nothing out of the ordinary or anything to make me doubt that the coaching would be successful.

'I'm worried because the clock is ticking now.' I told my supervisor. 'I don't think Richard is making progress quickly enough.'

My supervisor challenged me about how much responsibility I was taking for the outcome of the coaching; for getting Richard to uncover his blind spots and for trying to convince Richard's manager that Richard could change.

'Do you think Richard is coachable?' my supervisor asked me.

My supervisor suggested that the behaviours which I was describing might be termed 'Ostrich Syndrome', a useful and easily understood term for people whose behaviours are characterised by denying, ignoring or refusing to acknowledge awkward facts. A client with Ostrich Syndrome will habitually react to challenging situations by 'sticking their head in the sand', like an ostrich is often claimed to do, and hoping the problem or issue will go away

My supervisor went on to to ask, 'Do you think the Dunning-Kruger effect may be relevant in Richard's case?

The Dunning-Kruger effect *[Ref 25]* might be seen as an extreme form of Ostrich Syndrome. It can also be useful to think of it as the opposite of Impostor Syndrome [see Chapter One]. People suffering from Impostor Syndrome tend to be talented individuals who underestimate their own ability and also tend to assume that other people are as able as – or more able than – they are themselves. People who suffer from the Dunning-Kruger effect are individuals who overestimate their own ability and tend to assume that others are less able than they are themselves. Clients who suffer from the Dunning-Kruger effect may not be capable of acknowledging their own poor performance or incompetence and are likely to discount or disregard negative feedback.

'I don't think that Richard is incompetent and the fact that he is engaging with the Johari Window technique is encouraging evidence that he can be reflective. I do think that Richard's behaviours are a bit 'head in the sand' and ostrich-like. I have coached one or two clients who I did think suffered from the Dunning-Kruger effect but I do not think Richard's behaviours are quite like that.'

We then discussed other potential strategies, one of which was provocative therapy. This is an approach, developed by Frank Farrelly *[Ref 26]*, which uses humour, teasing, mimicry and reverse psychology to bring about positive change in the client. I was trained in provocative approaches to coaching so was confident to go down this route.

It is vital to create a 'safe container' for the coaching relationship, and this is even more the case when the coach is using techniques such as provocative therapy which might appear shocking and a significant departure from what might be regarded as usual coaching behaviours.

The work should be undertaken with an overriding positive intention and regard for the client and their interests, and a belief in their resilience and capacity for change. Frank Farrelly described the approach as 'working from the heart'. He compared this way of working to 'the affectionate teasing banter between close friends' and stressed the importance of proceeding 'with a twinkle in the eye and affection in the heart'.

The word 'provocative' derives from the Latin word 'provocare' - to elicit or call forth - and the positive intention of a provocative approach is to call forth resources in the client. By gently teasing or challenging the client, the coach is aiming to call forth the client's own ability to assert themselves, to defend themselves, to demonstrate a sense of their own self-worth, to engage with their vulnerability for a positive purpose, and to take responsibility for their own change.

I was torn as to whether I should share what Gerry had said with Richard. It seemed only fair that Richard should know the situation he was in, but I decided that it wasn't my place to tell Richard and I did not believe that telling him would help the coaching process. My main concern was whether the contractual agreement had changed and, technically, it hadn't. All that had changed was that I was now more aware of the mindset and perception of one of the parties involved – Gerry – and had a little less time than I had thought.

I had made my point to Gerry and my supervisor agreed that it was acceptable for me to carry on my coaching with Richard without increasing his anxiety any further by telling him what Gerry had said about his job being at risk.

Session Four

In our next session, Richard and I were able to go through the results of the Johari Window exercise together. The colleagues Richard had selected to complete the exercise had all returned their results directly to me. The differences between how Richard saw himself and how others saw him was quite stark - at least from my perspective.

	KNOWN TO SELF	NOT KNOWN TO SELF
KNOWN TO OTHERS	OPEN	BLIND SPOT
NOT KNOWN TO OTHERS	HIDDEN	UNKNOWN

A JOHARI WINDOW TEMPLATE

Of all the adjectives that were available to describe Richard, there was only one which both Richard and his colleagues had selected – 'confident'. There were a number of other characteristics which others had seen in Richard, in particular 'independence' and 'pride'), while Richard saw some characteristics in himself such as 'wisdom' and 'helpfulness' which none of his colleagues had observed .

I put Richard's results into the Johari Window and asked Richard what he thought when he saw them.

	KNOWN TO SELF	NOT KNOWN TO SELF
KNOWN TO OTHERS	CONFIDENT	INDEPENDENT PROUD LOGICAL SELF-ASSERTIVE COMPLEX INTELLIGENT
NOT KNOWN TO OTHERS	ABLE HELPFUL KNOWLEDGEABLE TRUSTWORTHY WISE	This box is for the words that nobody selected and represents 'future potential' that nobody has noticed yet. We weren't going to focus much on this box.
	RICHARD'S JOHARI WINDOW RESULTS	

'That's pretty good,' he said. 'I do take pride in my work, I am very logical and it's good that they notice my intelligence.'

'And what about the fact that they didn't pick out most of the characteristics which you used to describe yourself, such as helpful, knowledgeable, trustworthy and wise?' I asked.

'Well they were only allowed to pick six, right?' he half-joked.

It is true, of course, that just because someone doesn't pick the characteristic 'trustworthy' in their six it doesn't mean that they don't trust you. However, Richard had picked it as one of his 'big six' and the fact that *nobody* else had done so could suggest a mismatch in perception.

I sensed this was my moment to experiment with provocative therapy. I knew that ideally there should be good rapport between coach and coachee to ensure a safe environment. I wasn't sure if Richard and I were at that point yet but we didn't have a lot of time. It was a huge risk but, given how I had assessed Richard and how I had seen him operate in his team meeting, I thought there was a chance it could work anyway.

'Yeah, you're right,' I began, remembering that one of the underlying ideas behind provocative therapy is for the coach to say what the client is thinking deep down within himself, to bring into the open the client's irrational fears and beliefs. 'You've got all of these skills and they know that. They probably just picked these things at random so the exercise is really meaningless.'

'Well, I didn't say that. I'm not superman!' he said.

'No I don't believe even kryptonite would have an effect on you. You are definitely the most complete leader that any of your colleagues have been lucky enough to work for. If they aren't able to notice how trustworthy, helpful and wise you are then it just goes to show why you are a team leader and they aren't.' It takes a lot of courage to use a provocative approach but I trusted my experience and reminded myself that I had a positive intention so I continued. 'And as for the people who demoted you, they are plainly lunatics who don't know a good thing when they see it.'

Richard looked a little confused by my complete change of approach. For once he seemed almost lost for words.

'Are you having me on?' he asked.

'Why would you say that? It's true isn't it?' I responded, still in character.

'Well I have to admit to thinking that at times but, no, it's clearly not completely true.'

This was the first time that Richard had given any ground and was the first sign of reflection on his part. I asked him to tell me more about this and, to my surprise, he did. It seemed that by arguing against my exaggerated comments Richard became more reflective and more self-aware.

Richard acknowledged that the traits which he had immediately seen as positive could also be viewed as negative. When others had described him as proud, self-assertive and complex, he wondered whether this was their way of saying he was actually headstrong and hard to read.

The provocative therapy approach seemed to have flicked a switch in Richard. He had taken off his self-confident armour and was now looking for the injuries he might have underneath. Reflection and self-awareness are essential for people to develop emotional intelligence, but there is also a danger of becoming self-aware to such an extent that we start finding faults with ourselves that aren't really there. Initially my job had been to help Richard acknowledge certain blind spots which he had about himself, but now it seemed to be to keep Richard from going too far the other way.

I explained my provocative therapy stance to Richard and how it was aimed at shifting his thought process in a playful way, hopefully bringing to the surface some of his more irrational thoughts and beliefs. Once Richard understood the process he had experienced, he was able to look at his situation from a more balanced perspective. We then looked at how Richard could begin to help others see parts of his character of which they were currently unaware, as well as bringing into Richard's consciousness some of the characteristics that others saw in him.

Final Sessions

This was a breakthrough for Richard and it took a lot of courage for him to accept this new perception of himself. He worked hard at changing some of his behaviours and I believe made a lot of progress. Unfortunately, Gerry and others at the company didn't see enough of a change and Richard left the organisation.

I believe, in retrospect, that this decision had already been made before the coaching agreement was put into place. I was really pleased that, after this employment had ended, Richard decided to fund further coaching out of his own pocket. Within weeks Richard had found a new job where he could start with a completely clean slate and in which he was both successful and happy. We ran the Johari Window exercise within six months of Richard starting at the new company and the results this time around showed a much greater overlap in perceptions, indicating that Richard was being more successful in showing his true self to his team and that this was being noticed and well received.

TOOLS AND TECHNIQUES

There is certainly something to be said for dogged self-confidence. It is impossible to please everyone and if we spend too much time trying to adjust our behaviours to accommodate others' opinions, then we risk becoming chronic people-pleasers or bouncing from one critic to another.

Having enough confidence in yourself to withstand criticism can be a valuable and useful trait.

Coaches, of course, do not want to undermine the self-confidence of their clients. However, if clients consistently ignore feedback regarding their behaviours or performance this can significantly affect their progress and how they are perceived.

As coaches we seek to 'raise the mirror' to our clients so that they can become aware of any self-limiting blind spots. This can be done tactfully or provocatively, directly or indirectly, depending on the client and the levels of safety and trust which have been created within the coaching relationship.

Traditional psychometric tests can be a good place to start. Some of the following techniques may also be used to help your clients develop greater self-awareness.

Try Something New

If, as with Richard, a client's lack of self-awareness is manifesting as over-confidence or a blind spot, then a coach may choose to focus on helping the client to develop their humility.

Extreme lack of self-awareness is often termed the Dunning-Kruger effect after studies run by David Dunning & Justin Kruger from Cornell University.

Dunning and Kruger concluded:

'Ignorance more frequently begets confidence than does knowledge.'

They also found that incompetent individuals:

- Tend to overestimate their own level of skill.

- Fail to recognise genuine skill in others.

- Fail to recognise the extremity of their inadequacy.

- If trained to improve their own skill level substantially, they can then recognise and acknowledge their own previous lack of skill.

This is, in effect, the opposite of Impostor Syndrome (See Chapter One). It might also be termed Ostrich Syndrome.

One of the most effective ways to help raise awareness within a client who is over-confident is to encourage them to try something completely new. This will allow them to experience the feeling of learning as they navigate through the 'conscious competence' learning model *[Ref 27]*.

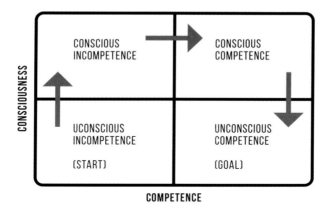

When a client begins the process of learning a new skill they quickly become conscious of their incompetence.

Through teaching, coaching and practice, they will develop skills which they can apply, when they think about it. This is the zone of conscious competence. With enough practice these skills can be internalised to such an extent that they become competent without conscious application.

If they can persevere sufficiently to improve substantially in this newly acquired skill, they may be enabled to recognise and acknowledge their own previous lack of skill. The self-awareness developed in this learning process is often transferable to other areas where there are currently blind spots.

Powerful Coaching Question:
What would be the worst possible piece of feedback that anyone could give you? Why would that be so bad?

Dream Journaling

If we avoid or repress something in our conscious mind then there is a good chance that it will surface in our unconscious mind, sometimes in our sleep.

Keeping a dream journal can be a useful technique to use with a client if you suspect they they are ignoring an aspect of their behaviour.

Ask your client to keep a notepad and pen beside the bed for two weeks and, when they wake up, to note down as much as they can about any dreams which they have had.

Ask your client to focus not just on the location, people and objects present in the dream but also how the client was feeling during the dream.

While we are not suggesting this is an exact science or that you should be looking for literal interpretations of dreams, this can provide another perspective or metaphor through which the client can view their situation or themselves.

It is not your role as coach to interpret the dream but rather to ask your client how they interpret the dream and how it might relate to the reasons that they have come to you for coaching.

Below are some tips which your client might find helpful to enable them to recall dreams:

- Write dreams down as soon as you wake up, even before visiting the bathroom or getting out of bed.

- Consider keeping a voice recorder by the side of the bed instead of a pen and paper.

- If you are someone who talks in their sleep there are smartphone apps that you can set to record while you are asleep.

- Avoid setting an alarm that involves speech, for example the radio, TV or music as this can interfere with your recollection of the dream.

- Don't expect to remember your dream as if it were the storyboard to a Hollywood movie. Sometimes you can just remember snippets – this is fine.

- Don't expect it to make sense – just capture what you can. You can interpret it later.

- Try giving each dream a title as a way of summarising and then later referring to the dream.

- It becomes easier with practice. You may find that when trying to recall dreams has become a habit you remember more of your dreams and remember them in more detail

Powerful Coaching Question:
Who do you want to be? How close are you to who you want to be? How can you find out more about yourself?

360° Feedback

Asking your client to obtain feedback from a wide range of people can help to bring blind spots and patterns to the conscious awareness of our client.

Organisations often have a 360° feedback tool of preference and, if this is the case, this can be a good place to start. You might also wish to investigate becoming trained and licensed to use a particular tool. Our preference, however, is to create a bespoke questionnaire that is relevant to the situation at hand. You can use your experience and intuition to develop your own questionnaire or you could use something like the model below:

1. Identify a selection of people from whom you will invite feedback regarding your client. Work with your client to find approximately 5-10 people who they have various relationships with, for example:

   - People to whom they are subordinate in the organisation.

   - People over whom they have positional power or authority.

   - Colleagues and peers.

   - People with whom they have less deep relationships (perhaps customers to whom they only speak infrequently).

   - Also include people outside work for a more rounded view of the client.

2. Once you have selected the people from whom you will be seeking feedback on your client, inform them of what you are doing, ensuring that they know this is being done for the benefit of your client, with the client's full knowledge, and that responses will be anonymous.

3. Ask each person (including your client) what he or she thinks the feedback survey should be trying to find out about the client and use their answers to craft some questions.

4. Ensure, wherever possible, that each question has a range of possible answers (for example Strongly Agree, Agree, Neutral, Disagree, Strongly Disagree) and an opportunity for the respondent to add comments to give some context to their answer.

5. Issue the questionnaire to each of the respondents and collect the responses. Also ask your client to complete the questionnaire themselves.

6. Compile the answers to show the range of responses and the average response. Compare these to how the client scored themselves.

7. Work with the client to explore the results and pay particular attention to the questions where the client scored themselves significantly differently to how the others scored them.

8. An optional variation is to ask your client what they think each person said about them. This is often enlightening enough in itself.

Powerful Coaching Question:
If you could be another person for a week, who would you be?

THE INTERVIEW

Lewis Moody

Ostrich Syndrome may involve burying your head in the sand and ignoring something that somebody else is telling you, as was the case with Richard in Part One. It can also involve acknowledging something that you are fully aware of but have failed to deal with.

Alternatively, as you will see in the following interview with Lewis Moody, former captain of the England Rugby Union team and World Cup winner, it may involve bringing to the surface something that we know on a subconscious level but haven't quite rationalised yet.

In all, Lewis played 71 times for his country, played in two World Cup finals and also represented the British and Irish Lions. At a domestic level he also won seven Premiership titles and a Heineken Cup with Leicester Tigers. In 2004 he was awarded the MBE in the Queen's New Years Honours List.

'I love Lewis. He's great. But I never know what he's going to do on the pitch.'

This was what England coach Andy Robinson said to Lewis Moody's wife Annie shortly after her husband became the first England player to be sent off at Twickenham.

'I was just back from being banned after punching someone in a reserves match that I was only playing in to prove my fitness. It was completely out of character for me - I had been aggressive on the pitch but never violent before,' Lewis says in his defence.

Lewis, who was given the nickname 'Mad Dog' for his all-action, physical style of play, then tells me of the moment when he 'lost it'. After seeing his England teammate Mark Cueto fouled and then punched, he retaliated.

'The red mist descended, my emotions took over and I was raging,' he says as he describes the moment that he hit his Leicester teammate, Samoan Alesana Tuilagi.

'I got a lot of stick from the media after that - quite rightly - but I also got a lot of offers of help, from my agent and from my club. But my reaction was that I didn't need help. Rugby is a physical, combative game and I was defending my team-mate. I don't have anger management issues.'

Eventually one of his sponsors recommended talking to a sports psychologist and, although Lewis admits to being highly sceptical about it all, he gave it a go.

'It got to a point where so many people were saying I should do something that I was pretty much doing it to shut them up, just to say that I'd done it. We looked at why I had these moments and what else was going on in my life that might be contributing to it.'

As well as being given the nickname 'Mad Dog', Lewis also picked up a label of being 'injury prone' - a label he hated although he admits that he can see why. With 14 major operations in 16 seasons, it is reasonable to say that he spent more than his fair share of time on the sidelines.

'Being injured is the worst thing for an athlete because you can't do the one thing that you really love doing and are good at doing. You have to do more training than if you were fit yet you don't get the release of actually playing.'

Lewis says that by working with a sports psychologist he eventually realised that the frustration of the injuries, regaining fitness and proving himself time after time was taking a huge toll on him. For a long time Lewis had failed to acknowledge this.

'There was a eureka moment for me when I realised that I had subconsciously been putting the frustration on the back burner so that I could focus on getting fit. Rugby had taught me that if you can't deal with your own mental issues then that's a sign of weakness, so I repressed it. You had to be tough.'

Lewis acknowledged that, in many ways, this requirement to be tough worked for him as it pushed him on but, every now and again, it would leak out and he would be unable to control his emotional and ultimately physical outbursts on the pitch.

This tough-guy culture in rugby, coupled with Lewis' catalogue of injuries, meant that for years Lewis hid a severe bowel condition from his teammates, club officials and even doctors. Even after he was diagnosed with ulcerative colitis - a condition that led to him losing 10Kg in weight through lost blood - Lewis continued to hide his condition from the rugby world in case it increased the impression that he was physically unreliable.

'It took my being sent off twice and the subsequent work with the sports psychologist to realise that actually wanting to deal with my psychological and behavioural issues wasn't a sign of weakness but was actually a way of improving myself - just like going to the gym.'

So what did the trick? How did a sports psychologist help Lewis Moody to tame this aspect of his psyche?

'It's really simple and you'll think it's silly. All he got me to do was realise when I was starting to bubble over and then to look at the referee. It was simply a direction to distract myself and re-focus my attention. I've always been good at taking direction and focusing.'

And did it work?

'Absolutely. I never got even a yellow card after that and this was despite the fact that teams were now targeting me as they thought they could play on my temper.'

He tells me of a game against the New Zealand All Blacks in 2008 when he remembers using this technique.

'We were in a ruck and Ma'a Nonu knee-dropped me and tried to pin me down. I reacted and got on top of him thinking to myself, 'He's going to get it', when I realised and looked straight for the referee. The referee told us to stop acting like children and get on with the game.'

Lewis believes that acknowledging his emotions and getting them under control was key to him being named England captain because Robinson then had faith in what Lewis would do on the pitch.

'I always tried to go through my career as if retirement was just around the corner. I didn't want to have any regrets or think 'I wish I had tried a bit harder'. In every training session I had the attitude of proving myself.'

When you look at Lewis Moody's record I think it is safe to say that he can be more than satisfied with his achievements. Especially because, if what Lewis tells me is true, he wasn't the most talented player in his position.

'People would often come and say to me that they were more talented than me at school and so they should be where I am. And they probably were but they don't realise what it takes. It's not just about talent. I prided myself on being one of the hardest workers.'

He does have one regret though and that was not dealing with his frustration and subsequent anger earlier.

'I could have been ready for the England captaincy much earlier in my career if I had,' he says with a wistful look in his eye.

Lewis is now passing on his wisdom in his role as Director of Rugby at Bradford-on-Avon Rugby Club and by coaching youngsters through his Mad Dog Sport programme. Helping players cope with injury is also high on his list of passions.

'There was only one time when I thought of quitting. I actually called my wife in tears from a Wagamama and said 'I've had enough'. I'd just been told that I had snapped my ankle in two places and needed a metal plate inserted. This wouldn't normally have been so bad but I had just come back from six months out of the game after a hip injury that had itself followed a ruptured achilles injury. This would be my third operation in 18 months and I didn't think I could do it any more. I was only 29 but I was so close to just quitting.'

'Just like it was for me at that moment, people often can't see past their current injury and sometimes they just need someone - like I had with my wife - to say 'Don't be silly. You'll get over this and come back stronger'. I like to tell my kids that no matter how hard it gets, if you want it enough, you can come back.'

CHAPTER EIGHT

Perfectionism

'*Striving for excellence motivates you; striving for perfection is demoralising.*'

HARRIET BRAIKER

THE CASE STUDY

'I have high standards and I like to push myself and do everything to the best of my ability.'

Sally worked for a large multi-national telecommunications company that provided one-to-one executive coaching for all its Director-level employees. Each Director had three sessions with a coach to use as they saw fit and in a way that would be most beneficial to them. I had a brief 'chemistry' session with Sally to establish whether we felt we would work well together and to consider a focus for the coaching sessions.

Sally looked like a model, immaculately groomed and classically dressed. I watched her making detailed notes throughout our meeting in perfectly neat, small handwriting and I marvelled at the quality of her accessories including a leather-bound notebook and Mont Blanc fountain pen. I looked with a degree of embarrassment at my ballpoint pen (one of many acquired from regular hotel stays) and scruffy old notepad, covered in my big scrawling writing. I actually wondered whether she would choose to work with me because I didn't match her level of neatness. I know that generally people like people who are like themselves and I didn't think we were at all alike. I had made a couple of feeble attempts at humour and Sally had not responded to them. I realised that she was a very serious person.

Sally was very business-like in her manner as she asked me, 'In order to understand whether we can work together, I would like you to tell me more about yourself and your background, please.'

Later I learned from Sally that it was my response to this question that confirmed her decision to select me as her coach. She told me that she was impressed with my academic qualifications, the breadth of experience I had and the seniority of the people I had coached.

Sally wanted to be coached on how to be a better leader. 'I am relatively new to this level of leadership and I want to be a real role-model within the organisation. I am also keen to explore my career progression. I am very ambitious and would like to map out where I go from here.'

We arranged the dates for all three sessions in advance and I left the building feeling as though I had passed a tough test. I also felt determined to do my best to live up to Sally's high standards.

Coaches should always notice their own responses to their clients because these could be clues as to how other people tend to feel in the presence of the client.

Of course, there are two people in a coaching relationship and so my response could have been more about me than about Sally. I didn't yet know much about Sally but I made a mental note to be aware of my responses to her in our first coaching session.

Session One

As I waited for Sally to arrive for our first session, I was aware that I was feeling a bit of 'performance anxiety'. I wanted to make sure that this was a really good session.

When she arrived, Sally told me that she had taken the initiative of doing some preparatory work for the session. She produced a leather binder in which she had her CV, her academic and professional certificates and some recent 360-degree feedback she had received in her current role. She wanted me to have some background knowledge about her in her professional capacity. I thanked Sally and congratulated her on having acquired three

Masters degrees while pursuing her demanding career. I then asked her, 'How did you manage to achieve all this with such a busy schedule?'

She immediately replied, 'I have high standards and I like to push myself and do everything to the best of my ability. One of the things I want to get out of the coaching is to learn how to motivate others to be as conscientious as I am. I find it really frustrating that people are so sloppy about their attitude to work. I can't believe how people make mistakes and shrug their shoulders, even when I give them strong feedback about it. I hate making mistakes and, if I ever do, I beat myself up about it really badly and work even harder to ensure that it doesn't happen again. I would really like to know how to coach others to get the best out of them too.'

I assured Sally that we would certainly be able to look at ways in which she could coach and motivate her staff. Before moving on too quickly, however, I suggested to Sally that, although the coaching was being sponsored by her organisation and the focus of the coaching was her leadership style, it was often useful in the first session to take a look at a client's whole life, as all the elements of our lives are inextricably linked. This could also highlight any other areas for coaching work over the next few sessions. I was careful to seek Sally's permission to move into more personal coaching territory and she agreed to complete an exercise called 'The Wheel of Life' as background to and exploration of her working life.

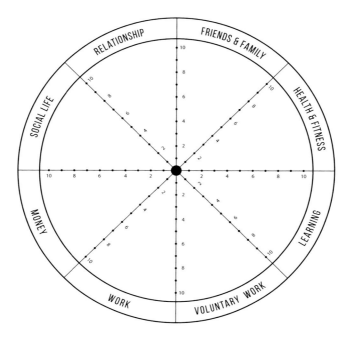

We often use this exercise in a first session so that the client can see a visual 'snapshot' of their life. The exercise is very effective in allowing the client to see what is working well in their lives and what isn't going so well. It also highlights how each area of their life has an impact on the whole, and how changing one aspect may affect others – for better or for worse. Goals can be set for each area of the client's life and doing this exercise in a first session means that the client can use it as a reference point throughout the coaching sessions, enabling the client to see 'at a glance' what has changed and what progress they are making. Like most of the best ideas, it is simple and effective.

Sally dutifully completed this exercise and I learned that, in addition to holding a senior leadership role, she was married and had a young child, was the Chair of the Governors at a local school, taught a fitness class at the local leisure centre one evening a week, was currently attending an evening class to learn how to bake and was a regular competitor in triathlons. Sally gave a high score to all areas of her life and, although pleased to see her achievements on paper, seemed to be going through the motions with this particular exercise.

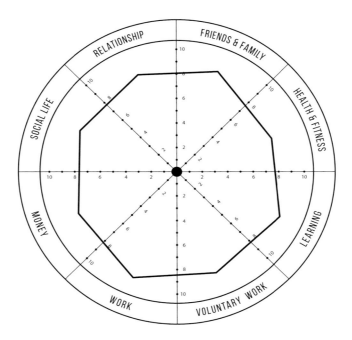

I couldn't help remarking that I had rarely seen anyone achieve so much and said that I wondered whether Sally was putting a lot of pressure on herself to manage all this? As soon as I had said it, I could tell that this comment had ruffled Sally's feathers.

'I thought you would know, better than others, how anything is possible if you set your mind to it,' she said, somewhat indignantly. 'I think people want an easy life these days. They expect things to be given to them on a plate, but success means hard work, discipline, focus and blood, sweat and tears. Think about top athletes and how hard they work to get to the top of their game. Well, I aim for the best in the same way in all that I do. Is there anything wrong with that?'

I replied that there was absolutely nothing wrong with that and that I admired her for what she had achieved to date.

At that stage I decided to abandon the other questions for Sally that had been in my mind. These had included asking Sally what she did to relax and what it cost her to have such high expectations. Instead I replied to Sally that I was really impressed with her achievements and self-discipline. I had registered that Sally was uncomfortable with any implied criticism of her lifestyle. I suggested that in the second half of this session we should return to her objective for the coaching programme and start to have a look at leadership styles so that she could consider what type of leader she was and what type of leader she wants to be. We would also be able to see how different leadership styles could be used to motivate others. Sally seemed keen to explore this and I introduced her to a leadership model we often use, developed by Daniel Goleman in his book *Primal Leadership: Unleashing The Power Of Emotional Intelligence [Ref 28]*.

Leadership Styles

Goleman identified six leadership styles, all of which are appropriate in certain situations and, while everyone will naturally have a preferred style, effective leaders will adopt the style that is most suitable to the situation at hand.

COERCIVE	This style is mostly about command and control. It is appropriate in an emergency or turnaround situation or in order to deal with poor performance.
VISIONARY	In contrast to the coercive style, the visionary leader attempts to engage their followers with a picture of a compelling future. The leader inspires the team and invites the team to join them on a journey.
AFFILIATIVE	This style focuses on building great morale and a team spirit. Affiliative leaders focus more on the wellbeing of the team than the task. This is an appropriate leadership style for bringing groups together in the early stages or relieving stress within a team.
DEMOCRATIC	A democratic leadership style is participative and facilitative, involving all members of the team in planning and decision-making. Using a democratic style of leadership means learning to listen well and facilitate team thinking.
PACE-SETTING	The pace-setting style relies on setting high standards and modelling them. It is effective for improving technical performance and showing poor performers how things should be done.
COACHING	A coaching leadership style involves leaders developing their employees through questioning, listening, challenge and support. A coaching style of leadership encourages self-responsibility and independent thinking.

Sally was excited by this model and I realised that she was very comfortable with structured coaching work and did not respond well to conversational coaching with no apparent process.

She was quick to identify that her preferred leadership style was pace-setting and we discussed the benefits of such a style, both for her and for her team. A pace-setting style can be particularly motivating for highly-skilled teams who need little direction and who are focused on growth or achieving clear targets. In the right conditions, this style will help teams to meet or exceed expectations.

The leader will step in if necessary to address poor performance or to show the team what to do.

It was clear to me from the look on Sally's face that she liked the sound of this but that look disappeared when I asked her why this might not always be an effective strategy. To her credit, though, she was surprisingly reflective about it.

'Well I suppose if the team doesn't have the necessary skills then they could become anxious and if they don't know exactly what to do then the lack of direction could be dangerous,' she suggested.

'Yes,' I agreed. 'And there is often a risk with this style that the team feel that they are being driven too hard and that the leader only cares about results rather than the people in the team.'

I wasn't sure how Sally was going to take this last comment. I was a little worried that she would take it too personally but, again, she surprised me with her reflective capacities.

'I think I may have become carried away as a result of my own track record - which they all respect - and the fact that I am the most experienced and knowledgeable person in the team. I can see, though, that I don't give people a chance to think for themselves, or do things their way. In the end I guess that can be demoralising for them and they can't develop if they simply have to copy me. '

'What would you say it means to be a leader?'

Sally was stumped for a minute or two. 'Do you know, I had always assumed that I had to know more than my team and be better at doing what we do than anyone else so that I could show them the way. Now I can see that being a leader means that sometimes you don't know as much as your team members about the day to day work, but you are an expert in managing people and motivating them.'

It is not unusual for people appointed to a leadership role to respond in this way, particularly if what got them promoted was their technical expertise. My concern now was how Sally would react. I could already see some typical behaviours of a perfectionist emerging as Sally started to berate herself for not having realised all this before. She knew that she hadn't made a great impact on her team and she was keen to learn as much as she could about how to be a great leader and how to coach her team to success. She asked me to recommend some reading, which I did, and I also suggested that she reflect on the Goleman leadership styles and gather some feedback from her team.

Sally agreed to take on the following pieces of homework:

• Share the Goleman leadership styles with her team members and peers and ask them to identify what they thought was her preferred leadership style.

• Ask team members what they needed more of from her and what they needed less of.

• Reflect on what she thought was the right style at that moment for her team.

• Consider what she needed to do to build flexibility to adopt other styles.

• Consider in which contexts other styles might be appropriate.

• Consider what early warning signs she could look for that would tell her she had adopted an inappropriate leadership style?

As I was seeing Sally to the door she said, 'I don't think I could ever do the touchy-feely affiliative style though!'

We encourage coaches to look out for the 'door handle moment' - the apparently throw-away comments clients often make when they think the session is over and are leaving the room.

In these last thirty seconds clients will often be less guarded and may reveal deep-seated thoughts or anxieties, often with their hand literally on the door handle. In Sally's case I remained curious about her comment and made a note to hold it in my mind when we next met. I thought it was probably an unconscious message for me from Sally that she wanted me to keep the coaching focused on professional matters, and not to stray into emotional territory.

Supervision

The first point that my supervisor brought to my attention was that I had virtually forced a technique on Sally when she had clearly identified a goal for our coaching. She had categorically stated that she wanted to understand more about the sloppy attitudes of some of her team and how she could coach them to be more conscientious and get the best out of them. Yet I had pushed that to one side, assuring her we could come back to that, and had insisted that she complete the Wheel of Life exercise.

My immediate response was to explain that often clients will want to focus on something superficial and distract attention from the real underlying reason and also that the Wheel of Life gives a good overview to the client and provides a good opportunity to spot patterns.

'Or spot something that interests you as the coach?' my supervisor suggested.

Was he right? I would have liked to think not but there was something about this particular client that was different for me and I was struggling to put my finger on it. Perhaps it was because I was worried about the standards to which Sally would hold me up as her coach. Perhaps it was because I had never really 'gelled' with other perfectionists, since it was not one of my traits. Perhaps I would have felt more comfortable looking at another aspect of her character or perhaps I was even jealous of her success.

I genuinely didn't know what was driving this feeling but it was interesting to explore it a little, even if we didn't come to a resolution.

Most habits that we develop through our lives can have a positive impact and Sally's perfectionist streak was certainly working for her in many ways, there was no denying that. One factor in the degree to which people can make perfectionism work for them is where they sit on the adaptive/maladaptive perfectionist scale *[Ref 29]*. Perfectionism in itself is not a bad thing. Almost all great works of art, important discoveries and scientific developments have resulted from people striving for excellence. The key, however, seems to be how people who are striving for perfection react to situations where they don't quite meet their own goals or standards.

Adaptive perfectionists manage to maintain a healthy self-esteem, do not berate themselves excessively, regroup and try again. Maladaptive perfectionists often react badly and 'lash out' at themselves and others.

My supervisor asked me where I thought Sally sat on that scale and also where I thought I sat on that scale. The fact that I saw Sally as being much further towards the adaptive end of the scale than I perceived myself gave me another indication that perhaps I was jealous of her greater ability to handle this trait. Although Sally had a tendency to beat herself up over mistakes she made, she was able to limit the amount of time she spent doing this.

It is always important as a coach to recognise your own feelings towards your clients and their traits as this can have an impact on your ability to coach them effectively.

I still believed that, although perfectionism was a largely effective strategy for Sally, the fact that she was so strongly associated with a pace-setting leadership style was a sign that she might not be as adaptive as she had the potential to be.

Session Two

Sally was keen to tell me about her progress since the last session. She had gathered feedback from her team and this had reinforced her sense that she had a pace-setting leadership style. She had learned that her team respected her but felt that whatever they did was never good enough for her.

Since then she had read a number of coaching books and was already beginning to see the benefits of changing her leadership style; relationships with her team members were better and, now that she was listening to her team, she was discovering that they had some great ideas. In short, Sally was a total convert to a coaching style of leadership and in a matter of weeks she had successfully learned and adopted a coaching approach. This may seem too good to be true but one of the potential benefits of coaching a perfectionist is that they can try very hard to be perfect coaching clients too.

Sally wanted to spend the rest of the session learning more about coaching from me. She particularly wanted to learn some more techniques for giving feedback and having difficult conversations in a coaching style.

Sally made copious notes and seemed very pleased with the session. She went away with lots of information and more homework. However, I felt manoeuvred into having delivered a training session rather than actually coaching Sally herself. I was definitely experiencing her strong need to be in control and I was confused about what my response to this should be. One of the fundamental principles of coaching is that the client should set the agenda for the session but usually this means that the client determines the focus of the session rather than how the session should run. I decided to take this dilemma to my supervisor.

Supervision

I was becoming a little concerned about this particular coaching relationship. In theory I agreed with the principle that the client should be in charge of where they want coaching to take them, but for some reason I was resisting this with Sally. My supervisor's response was not comfortable for me to hear.

My supervisor suggested that I might be looking for something from Sally that she was unlikely to provide in coaching and that we were both destined to be frustrated by our relationship. He reminded me that Sally, as a perfectionist, was unlikely to ask for help or readily show vulnerability or 'imperfection'. In her 'door handle moment' she had reinforced that I should not expect any deep, 'touchy-feely' – or transformational – coaching. As a result, I should not expect anything more than transactional coaching with this client.

If I wanted transformational coaching while Sally wanted transactional coaching then we were destined to disappoint one another.

Transactional coaching brings about change purely at a behavioural level and its effects may therefore be short-lived whereas transformational coaching brings about change at the deeper level of beliefs and is usually more enduring.

'What scares you about giving Sally what she wants from coaching? What is conflicting about improving her use of a range of leadership styles and, in particular, her coaching ability?' he asked me.

The accusation that I was scared seemed extreme to me, but I knew from experience that my supervisor chose his words very carefully so I searched myself for feelings of being scared or frightened.

The first thing that came to mind was that I was feeling insecure and threatened by Sally's interest in coaching. Could I be worried that she was after my job? Was I even worried that she might be better at it than me?

It is not uncommon for clients to want to imitate the coach; certainly if the client has respect for the coach or sees the coach as holding a position of authority. It wouldn't be a surprise if Sally were to aspire to this. In fact, in many ways, this is what I hoped for when working within an organisation because it can be the quickest way to establish a sustainable coaching culture with the company. So why was I scared?

I reflected that perhaps I was anxious that, given Sally's track record and her ability to handle her perfectionist tendencies in a more adaptive manner than I could, Sally might become a more effective coach than me. This could be making me feel insecure.

My supervisor suggested that I continue letting Sally set the agenda and pay attention to my own feelings about this. After all, Sally was satisfied with her progress and change was happening. The question my supervisor posed for me at the end of our session was: 'What more did I need and why?'

Session Three

When Sally arrived for the final session she updated me on her progress and reported that she was enjoying practising her new-found coaching skills with her team. She had received more positive feedback from colleagues and her fellow board members had noticed the change in her. She had even organised a cake baking team-building event, which had been a great success. She told me that she was finding that she did not have to micro-manage her team any more and this was leaving her more time in which to focus on the strategic aspects of her role. She had decided to enrol on a postgraduate coaching programme in her spare time and she had convinced the organisation to sponsor her training. She intended to establish a coaching culture within the company and, once again, wanted to pick my brains on how she should go about this.

With my supervisor's words ringing in my ears, I decided to accept the fact that I should follow Sally's agenda and stop looking for dysfunction or pain in Sally's life. She seemed to be a highly adaptive perfectionist. However, I could help her in a true coaching style to think about how to establish a coaching culture and this meant asking Sally some coaching questions.

'Sally, instead of me telling you how I would do it, which would be a pace-setting way of proceeding,' I said, 'I could use a coaching style and ask you some questions. Are you happy to give that a go and that way you will be able to experience a coaching style of leadership in action?'

Sally was happy to work in this way but requested that, if she could not come up with any ideas, I should tell her my thoughts.

I asked Sally to imagine that she had succeeded in establishing coaching within her organisation and to picture the organisation in two years' time and describe what was happening there. She didn't have to think long before she replied:

'I have completed my academic qualifications in coaching and I am heading up the coaching team at work. We have drawn up selection criteria for external coaches and we have a preferred supplier list of coaching companies. Directors have regular access to external coaches and less senior people can request coaching for specific issues. There is a specialist team of internal coaches, all of whom have completed an internal coach-training programme and who meet six times a year as a team for supervision and Continuing Professional Development (CPD). The internal coaches provide coaching for delegates on our talent programmes and they also provide regular one day coaching workshops for line managers.'

'That sounds great, Sally. Tell me more about how coaching has been embedded within the organisation,' I prompted.

'We have coaching resources on our intranet and all line managers attend a coaching workshop and are expected to use a coaching approach where possible in one-to-one meetings, team meetings and appraisals. Every employee is familiar with the leadership styles as they are introduced in our induction programmes and we base some of our employee engagement measures around this model. I am speaking at conferences telling other organisations how we have successfully used coaching within our company. We have also developed our own way of measuring the return on investment for coaching, which is creating a lot of interest in the industry at large.'

Sally stopped speaking and looked at me in astonishment. 'Where did all that come from?' She asked.

I smiled. I responded:

'Coaching can provide the right conditions and the right questions to help people generate their own answers. After all, how could I possibly have come up with all those ideas that are specific to your organisation? You are the expert on your situation.'

We moved on to think about how Sally was going to turn these good intentions into actions and, in doing so, considered questions such as:

- What could get in your way? How would you overcome these obstacles?

- What support will you need?

- Who will be the best sponsor or advocate of this project?

- What will be the costs of doing this – financial or otherwise?

- What resources – financial or otherwise – will you need?

- What haven't you thought of?

- What other options do you have?

- What will be the benefits of doing this – financial or otherwise?

- How will you measure success?

- What will be your first steps and when will you take them?

Sally was delighted that she had the beginnings of a plan and also that she had benefited from understanding how coaching can help people to generate their own solutions. She felt that she had enough ideas to put together a proposal for her board. She said that she was happy to leave the discussion there.

'We have some time left in this session. How would you like to use the rest of the time? We could use some of it to review the session, if that would work for you?'

Sally was happy to have the opportunity to review the session and give me some feedback. As I suspected, she liked a structured coaching approach and admitted to feeling like she had embarked on a therapy session when I had used the Wheel of Life in our first session. She had learned that her preferred style of coaching was goal-oriented and outcome-focused. She had felt uncomfortable discussing non-work aspects of her life with me. Sally hesitated for a moment and then said:

'Now I feel a little more at ease with you, I am going to tell you something. I cheated when I did the Wheel of Life. I didn't want to discuss my personal life with you because I didn't see the relevance and therefore the exercise was meaningless to me at the time. I gave a high score for my relationship and for my social life and neither of those were true at the time.'

'My relationship with my husband was very strained when I came to see you and we were not socialising as a couple as a result of the difficulties we were facing. Whilst I didn't feel it was appropriate to address this with you, especially as my company is paying for the coaching, I did go home and ask my husband to complete his

Wheel of Life, which gave us the opportunity to have an important conversation about our relationship.'

'In addition to this, in the next session I had a big realisation about my pace-setting style at work but what I didn't tell you was that I also realised in that session that I was using a pace-setting style at home. I am a quick learner and I like to do things properly so I have been reading lots of coaching books and have also been adopting a coaching style at home. It is making a big difference so far - we are not 'there' yet but things are a lot better. I wanted to let you know that the coaching has had a wider impact than you could have known. If you had pushed me on the personal stuff I wouldn't have continued with the coaching but, because you didn't, I was able to take the techniques for myself and apply them at home.'

With some clients as much change happens outside the coaching sessions as within them and Sally's experience was a clear example of that. Sally took the tools and techniques that I had offered her at an organisational level and applied them to her own personal situation. Sally didn't feel the need to share this in the coaching sessions. A coach will never be wholly aware of what is going on for their client in their sessions and will never know the full scale of change that occurs.

As coaches, we are looking to create independence within our clients, not dependence or even co-dependence, and we should celebrate any evidence that our clients are demonstrating the ability to self-coach.

TOOLS AND TECHNIQUES

As the saying goes, *'Shoot for the moon, because even if you miss, you'll land in the stars'*. Setting high standards can drive us to achieve things we never thought possible. The key to the degree of effectiveness is how we react to 'landing in the stars'. Do we see this as a great result? A stepping stone to something greater? Or do we view it as failure?

People whose perfectionism trait has become a trap often focus exclusively on end results, are unable to enjoy the journey and, as a result, lose joy in their work. Setting high standards will often lead to great achievements, but if those standards become unrealistic then dissatisfaction is the likely result.

In the case study, Sally was an 'adaptive' perfectionist; she largely reacted well to her own efforts and used them to drive herself further forward. If she hadn't been able to do that, the most common results are either procrastination (in order to avoid failure) or defeatism (which may lead to depression if left unchecked).

The techniques here are aimed at helping clients to explore their definition of perfection, and include alternative perspectives to help redefine it.

Define Perfection

A great place to start with a client who may be struggling with their perfectionist tendencies is to ask them what 'perfect' means to them.

We would recommend asking this question both at a general level and also at the level of a specific task or challenge that the client is facing. It is also helpful to ask the client to define 'imperfect' from their point of view.

By looking at these definitions objectively, we can start analysing them with a view to making them a little more realistic. For example, a perfectionist might expect their presentation to be flawless, with no pauses, running perfectly to time with no stumbling over pronunciation and incorporating a perfect answer to every conceivable question. However, a more realistic expectation would be that they might pause where necessary and mispronounce the odd difficult word because everyone does. The presenter might run two minutes over time and this, again, will be acceptable. Even if the presenter does not have the perfect answer, they might still be able to talk knowledgably about their topic.

A major issue for people who let their drive for perfection get out of control is the difficulty of living up to what the perfectionist believes is expected of them by others. Often this is based on a number of false assumptions and a coach can help draw attention to, and analyse, these assumptions. For example, in the context of giving a presentation, these assumptions may be along the lines of:

- I am assuming that if I give a bad presentation then people will think I am an idiot.

- I am assuming that if I stumble, forget what I am supposed to say or mispronounce something people will laugh at me.

- I am assuming that everyone knows more than me about the topic of the presentation.

- I am assuming that people will want to ask me questions to 'catch me out'.

- I am assuming that if I give a bad presentation my chance of a promotion will be missed and I may even lose my job.

It can be surprising how many things we subconsciously assume about a situation. It can often be helpful to list all of the assumptions we have about a scenario and to analyse ruthlessly which assumptions might be false or unhelpful. Once we have identified false or unhelpful assumptions we can consciously adopt a new assumption that is more true and/or more helpful.

A coach may seek to enable their client to replace an unhelpful assumption with another, more helpful, assumption. In our example, the client might form the more helpful assumption, 'When I am relaxed, and not worrying about what people think, I give my best performances and that is the best strategy for success'.

Powerful Coaching Question:
What would be the impact of reducing by 10% the standards you set for yourself?

Inner Boardroom

**One approach to tempering a client's excessive perfectionism
is to enhance the client's ability to take into account different
perspectives.**

The 'Inner Boardroom' exercise is a technique that can be useful
in many different situations. Invite your client to imagine that they
have a board of directors governing their lives. On this board are a
number of people – real or imaginary – who influence your client's
life.

Encourage your client to notice who appears in their boardroom, to
be open-minded and not to exercise any editorial control over who
is there. Your client may wish to describe who they see on their
board and/or may like to do a sketch. This technique is not about
who they would like to be in their boardroom – although that is
a good direction for this exercise to move – it is about who they
currently have in their boardroom, whether they like it or not.

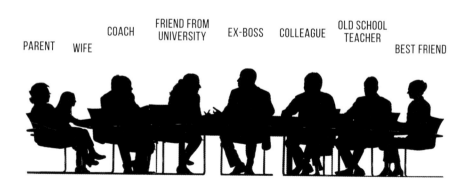

Once they have their boardroom set up, some questions that might be useful are:

- Who is in charge?

- Who else is there?

- Who is holding back your progress?

- Who is being listened to most?

- Who is not being heard?

- If you could have anyone in the world on your board of directors, whom would you invite?

- Is there anyone who you would like to remove?

- Would changing their positions around the table affect things?

- Do you have too many (or too few) people on the board?

- Do you have the right balance of positive and negative (or optimistic and cautious) voices?

Powerful Coaching Question:
How could making mistakes become less painful for you?

The Wheel Of Life

The Wheel of Life is a tool designed to enable the client to determine how satisfied they are with various aspects of their life.

Ask your client to label each segment of the wheel with an area of their life or their personality. Then ask them to rate how satisfied they are with each of these areas. Some people might want to give a score out of ten for each area.

Once they have assessed all eight areas, consider asking your client:

• Does anything stand out for you?

• What is your overall feeling, looking at your wheel?

• What would you like to talk about, or look at, first?

It can also be used as an ongoing resource throughout the coaching sessions. The initial creation gives both coach and client a visual record of their present state, or baseline. It can then be used as an ongoing metric of progress throughout the coaching relationship. As with Sally, the client may not be completely truthful until they feel safe, so it may be worth revisiting it at a later date, and being prepared for lower scores even though they are in a better place.

It is useful to bear in mind that your client may prefer to discuss areas of higher satisfaction in the first instance and may seek to avoid more sensitive areas until more trust and rapport has been developed between coach and client.

One final thing to bear in mind is the client's state of mind at the time of completing the wheel. If they are generally quite 'low' then expect low scores. It they are feeling fairly positive then scores can be unnaturally inflated. The most important thing for a coach to focus on is not the absolute scores but more the relative scores across themes and over time.

Powerful Coaching Question:
Imagine you are at the end of your life looking back on what you have achieved. What did you learn from the things that you did not do perfectly?

THE INTERVIEW

Alec Stewart

Redefining perfection is a key technique to help people make the most of their perfectionism trait. As you will see with our interviewee Alec Stewart, England's most capped Test cricketer and a former captain of both the Test and One-Day International sides, perfectionism as a driver is great but perfectionism as a permanent state of being is not. Altering your focus and reducing the pressure is a great way to make the most of the positive aspects of this trait and avoid it becoming a trap.

Alec, who was named Wisden Cricketer of the Year in 1993 and awarded the MBE in 1998 and the OBE in 2003, shows that being able to celebrate your achievements along the way is essential and reminds us that, in reality, 'perfect' doesn't exist.

'I was brought up to believe in myself but you never know if you are actually good enough until you produce a match winning contribution, or at least make a major contribution and then back it up quickly with another one.'

Alec Stewart is very grateful for his upbringing and believes that a lot of the mental strength that serves him so well came from his family. He tells me how his father always told him to 'Be the Guv'nor', not in an arrogant way but to give the impression that he belonged.

'I was five foot ten but I always tried to give the impression that I was six foot five.' He admits that, at times, it was a bit of a bluff but he says belief is important in sport.

'You always have to believe that you *can* win. If you don't think you can then you've already lost, but if you think that you *will* win then you run the risk of being turned over.'

His Dad instilled a couple of other important aspects of his psyche as well, namely to be able to partition things off and to give his all.

'My motto was *'Leave nothing to chance'* and I ensured that I had done everything I possibly could so that I could do my best. I hated losing and still do, so I trained my hardest so that I knew I couldn't have personally done any more.'

So was he one of those sportsmen who obsessed to the point of perfectionism? He says he wasn't.

'I don't believe perfect exists. There's a saying in cricket that 'you've never got enough'. You may have scored 130 but you could have got 230.'

We discuss the difference between aiming for perfection and aiming for excellence and this resonates with him. For all of his achievements, accolades and self-belief he comes across as a humble man.

'Really I should have scored 30% more hundreds than I did. I got out too often between 50 and 99. I still don't know why that was but 80% of a batsman's dismissals are self-inflicted.'

We talk about his early days back in the late 1980s when an England call-up was for the first time within the realms of possibility:

'It was well-known that the selectors paid attention to hundreds. 99s didn't get noticed.'

I suggest that maybe Alec put so much pressure on himself to get those targets that he forgot his own goal of 'do the best you can'. Perhaps he was focusing too much on the perfection of the 100?

'Maybe' he says, looking out of the window.

I ask him if he did anything differently to get over that hump and he tells me about the routines that he developed.

'These probably sound like superstitions but I started twiddling my bat and then taking a walk in-between balls. It was like a reset.'

Perhaps he was using his strength of always striving to do his best and applying it at the micro level to every delivery the bowler sent down at him?

'Yes I suppose so,' he agrees, thoughtfully. 'I have always been a big creature of habit. For example, and you will probably think this is a silly superstition, I always put my left foot on the pitch first. That was my way of saying to myself 'I'm at work now' and I'm switched on.'

We talk about the difference between doing something because you think that you will be lucky (which we would say is superstition) and doing something to get yourself into a particular state of mind.

He admits to a couple of things that fall into the category of superstition. 'If I scored a hundred in a particular shirt, I would wash it but I would make sure that I wore it next time as well!'

How else did he tame this potentially unhelpful striving for the externally-defined 'perfection' of scoring 100?

'I broke it down so that I wasn't going out to score 100. I started building my innings in tens. Get to 10, then 20, then 30.'

He also seemed to have redefined success in his own terms, which was really important.

'Sometimes a draw can feel like a win,' he says and then puts forward a hypothetical race between myself and Usain Bolt. In this race Bolt obviously wins but, in defeat, I beat my personal best while Bolt doesn't run his fastest.

'You have to ask yourself 'who is the winner?' because, to me, you both are,' Alec says.

He believes that it is a real challenge for people to change the way they think but also that he judges people (and himself) by how they react to adversity.

'That is when you get a true reflection of someone's character. And character is so important in a sport like cricket.'

And how did he respond to adversity? If he was out to a bad decision or a bad shot, did he smash up the dressing room?

'No. I never threw a bat. In fact I get angry with the youngsters who do. I think it's for show. I got all of that out of my system on the walk back from the middle to the dressing room. I called myself all the names under the sun but by the time I was back in the dressing room I was calm.'

I asked Alec whether he ever sulked.

His response seemed to me to suggest that Alec had achieved a balanced view of perfectionism: 'Yes I sulked but not for long because you can only control the controllables. As a cricketer you always have to be looking at two things. On the one hand, you have to give yourself a pat on the back for doing the best you could while, on the other hand, you have to give yourself a kick because you've never got enough.'

CHAPTER NINE

Procrastination

'Procrastination is one of the most common and deadliest of diseases and its toll on success and happiness is heavy'

WAYNE GRETZKY

THE CASE STUDY

'Help - I leave everything to the eleventh hour!'

Tom came to me because he was running out of time to complete his professional qualification as a surveyor. 'My boss is on my back to get this done,' he said. 'He suggested I get a coach to give me the kick in the pants I need to get started.'

Tom had registered for the qualification some years ago, with every intention of completing it. However, by the time he came to my office he had just three months to submit his dissertation and he hadn't even started it. 'All of my peers have finished this already, which really bothers me. I do this to myself all the time and I'm sick of it. I need to learn to stop procrastinating, once and for all,' he told me.

As Tom continued to talk about all the times he had procrastinated, I began to feel I was getting mixed messages. On the one hand, he appeared excited and optimistic about his ability to work under pressure. On the other hand, he was angry with himself for leaving things so long and wasting years doing less important things. He explained that this had been his pattern all his life and he wasn't really sure whether he should try to change it or embrace it. 'After all,' he said. 'Eventually, I manage to finish everything - although usually by the skin of my teeth. I do like the rush of the impending deadline. It seems so boring to plan everything and plod along day after day. People that do that make me crazy—I don't want to be like that.'

Procrastination is the delaying or postponing of an action so that there is a significant time lapse between when someone intends to do something and when they actually do it.

People with a tendency to procrastinate employ various conscious and unconscious tactics to avoid doing something, including:

- Filling their time with unimportant jobs, rather than getting on with more important and pressing tasks.

- Finding 'displacement behaviours' which prevent them from doing the work which they need to do almost immediately after sitting down to tackle the work. For example, making a cup of coffee, checking social media, reading emails, listening to music, watching television, or going for a walk to help 'clear their mind'. Sometimes even domestic chores can be an attractive proposition when faced with the task they have been putting off!

- Waiting for the moment to be 'right' before they tackle the task.

On our university-accredited postgraduate coach training programmes, we have observed many of our students procrastinate over writing their essays. What we find perhaps most interesting is that many students who put off writing the essays predict that they will procrastinate from the outset. If students are aware of this behavioural tendency, why can't they overcome it? This question came to mind as Tom described his casual disregard for his career-limiting habit. I began to consider the many reasons for procrastination, which range from simple to complex.

Simple causes of procrastination can include:

- The task appearing overwhelming.

- Not possessing the knowledge or skills to complete the task.

- Lack of time-management skills.

- Inability to prioritise.

While these relatively simple causes of procrastination can often be addressed simply through skills training and acquisition, the more complex reasons for procrastination are worth looking at in more depth and are likely to require a coaching approach. They include:

- Fear of failure.

- Perfectionism.

- Lack of assertiveness.

- Lack of autonomy.

Fear of Failure

We instinctively seek to protect ourselves from failure, often without realising we are doing so or acknowledging the consequences.

By delaying things, people who procrastinate due to a fear of failure may be unconsciously changing the question 'Am I able to do this?' to a different question, 'Am I able to do this with very little time?' After all, if we fail because of time pressure, we aren't failing due to our own shortcomings. The message that such procrastinators are telling themselves, and others, is:

'It's not that I failed, it's that I didn't have enough time to succeed.'

It may be obvious to the objective observer that procrastinating due to fear of failure is self-defeating. To clients experiencing fear of failure, however, failing because they run out of time is much more palatable than failing because they weren't good enough. Surely it is better to be judged as being under too much external work pressure or even as being disorganised than being judged as fundamentally incapable?

Perfectionism

Those who exhibit perfectionism often have unrealistically high standards and expectations of themselves.

Perfectionist procrastinators will often delay doing something because they don't believe they will be able to do it to their own exacting standards. They often struggle to make decisions because they are always looking for the perfect outcome. Alternatively, they may want to delay their actions until the external conditions are perfect for optimal performance, for example waiting until they have a block of time when they have no distractions. Many students do not submit draft essays for review by our tutors because they want even the draft essays to be 'perfect', so they are unable to understand or take advantage of the benefits of early feedback and constructive criticism.

A key coaching approach for people who procrastinate is to help them break down unrealistic expectations into small, achievable steps. *[For more on perfectionism, see Chapter 8.]*

Lack of Assertiveness

Procrastination can also be linked to a lack of assertiveness, which can lead clients to say 'yes' to too many things and too many people.

Those who suffer from lack of assertiveness find it difficult to say 'no' without feeling guilty, and struggle to express their own opinions and feelings or ask for what they want. This type of procrastinator will tend to put other peoples' needs before their own and will often just be too overcommitted to be able to complete the task. Some may argue that this is more to do with poor planning than procrastination, but taking on too much can certainly compound the issue of procrastinating behaviours. *[For more on lack of assertiveness, see Chapter 2 on People Pleasing.]*

Lack of Autonomy

Procrastination can also stem from the client feeling a lack of control. The client may be delaying a task as a means of seeking to exert some autonomy over a situation.

If a task is considered onerous or is imposed upon us then we may rebel against it and one form of rebellion is to delay undertaking the task as long as possible. It is a feature of human motivation to want to try to take control of our own destiny. *[For more on this topic, see Chapter 4 on Fierce Independence].*

Tom, however, didn't seem to fit any of these typical profiles of the procrastinator. He didn't lack assertiveness or self-esteem. He exhibited no signs of fear of failure or of being overwhelmed. On the contrary, his whole attitude seemed cavalier, as if achieving the qualification didn't matter to him at all. I asked him about his ability to manage his time and to say 'No' to unimportant things. He expressed no difficulty with either and, although his boss was 'on his back' to get the qualification completed, it was clear that working towards this professional qualification was something which Tom had taken on voluntarily for his own benefit.

Tom said that he believed he always gets things done in the end and that he often worked at his best when he was up against the pressure of an impending deadline. This type of belief has the potential to be self-limiting and to be an obstacle to a client breaking their repeating patterns of procrastination.

Coping strategies which clients have evolved to counter limiting habits or behaviours can be an obstacle to tackling those behaviours.

As I could not yet see where the roots of Tom's procrastination might lie, I was not immediately able to help Tom to understand and address his procrastinating behaviours.

I did observe that Tom changed topics a lot, fidgeted, avoided answering some of my questions, and made light of his situation. He seemed bored with the coaching process and more interested in his surroundings than his situation. He got up frequently to wander around the room and examine the fixtures and fittings. About halfway through the session, Tom told me that if his boss had not insisted, Tom would never have called me because he considered coaching a waste of time. Tom's whole attitude was off-putting, making it difficult to warm to him.

Towards the end of the first session, Tom abandoned his initially-stated desire to overcome his lifelong habit of procrastination. Tom said, 'I appreciate you meeting with me and listening to me vent. I just panicked with the deadline getting close. I can get this done at the last minute, just like I always get everything done,' he explained, shrugging off the problem. 'And even if I don't, so what? I can succeed in the world without the qualification.'

I acknowledged this as a possibility, but reminded Tom that he had come to me for help with what he had said was a lifelong habit not just a particular issue, in which case conquering it might be more difficult than he was suggesting. I proposed that we meet again in two weeks, just to make sure that Tom was on track and making progress. I also proposed that before our next session Tom try a few strategies and exercises that I often offer as first steps for clients struggling with procrastination.

Activities to combat procrastination

- Write down all the reasons for delaying the task. Then create a convincing argument against each one.

- Break the task into small, manageable 'chunks.'

- Tell other people what they are going to be doing in order to introduce an element of accountability and peer pressure.

- Schedule a realistic time slot each day to get a little bit done. Plan a small reward after completing each time slot.

- If the task seems overwhelming, remind themselves of all their past achievements so that they know that they are also capable of succeeding in this task.

Tom said that these would be useful and that he would implement them, but I was not sure that he would. I was also sceptical that Tom would start his essay or submit for his final assessment. All in all, I was disappointed about the session and my own reaction to Tom's attitude.

Following the session, I couldn't stop thinking about how bored Tom had seemed to be, which was a new experience for me. I was also struggling because I had not managed to maintain an unconditional positive regard – my belief in the intention and potential of my client. In fact, I didn't like Tom very much. I found him fickle, arrogant, and dismissive. His little-picture thinking and short attention span had irritated me. I needed a session with my coaching supervisor to help me understand what was going on and how I could be of service to Tom – always assuming that Tom kept his appointment to come back to see me!

Supervision

In my supervision session, I explained that I didn't think that Tom fitted any of the classic explanations for procrastination. My supervisor's initial response was to ask me what I thought about this quote from Carl Jung *[Ref 30]*:

'Everything that irritates us about others can lead to an understanding of ourselves.'

Immediately, I had a 'wow' moment. As I reflected on my strong negative reaction to Tom, I recognised that some of Tom's patterns of behaviour were patterns of behaviour which I shared. I too can be over-confident. I too have a short attention span and crave constant new challenges and stimuli. Like Tom, I get bored all too easily. I realised suddenly that, when I was looking at Tom, part of what I was seeing—and judging—was myself.

As I explained my eye-opening realisation, my supervisor reminded me of how Jung used the term *shadows* to refer to the parts in each of ourselves that we judge to be undesirable and which we try to conceal.

One of the underlying objectives of coaching, therapy, or change work is to enable the client to bring their 'shadows' into their conscious awareness so that they can come to terms with themselves through greater self-awareness and self-acceptance.

I was reminded once again of the continuing need for coaches to be coached themselves and have the benefit of regular supervision. During my supervision session, I was enabled to critique and analyse my shadow aspect in order to generate greater insight into Tom and, more importantly, into how I could help him.

As a result of the insights which I had gained at supervision, I wondered whether Tom's procrastination was, like mine, the result of a low tolerance of frustration. Low Frustration Tolerance, a term coined by Albert Ellis *[Ref 31]*, who developed the concept of *Rational Emotive Behaviour Therapy*, is our inability to tolerate difficulties, discomfort, or anything that appears painful or unbearable to us. Those who suffer from Low Frustration Tolerance exhibit agitation and poor attention span, and often resolve their discomfort by walking away from situations. Low Frustration Tolerance is characterised by seeking immediate pleasure or avoiding immediate pain, notwithstanding the longer-term consequences and is sometimes referred to as 'short-term hedonism'.

The following questions may be useful to enable a coach to identify whether they, or their client, may have 'Low Frustration Tolerance'.

DO YOU HAVE LOW FRUSTRATION TOLERANCE?	
Do you believe that life should be easy and comfortable?	Y/N
Do you find being bored intolerable?	Y/N
Do you find yourself saying 'I can't live without that' or 'I just can't bear this'?	Y/N
Are you bored easily?	Y/N
Do you choose short-term pleasure over important duties?	Y/N
Do you often feel lethargic?	Y/N
Do you have episodes of feeling 'hard done by'?	Y/N
Do you have a history of starting lots of things but not finishing them?	Y/N

A technique which my supervisor now used with me to help me to address my own Low Frustration Tolerance was to help me to develop some identity-based goals – or, more accurately, to redefine some of the identity-based goals which I had already subconsciously developed. Over time, I had come to believe the following about myself:

- I am over-confident.

- I have a short attention span.

- I crave constant new challenges and stimuli.

- I get bored too easily.

Having enabled me to become consciously aware of this 'self-talk', my supervisor then helped me to re-write my definitions of myself. I came up with the following:

- I am confident and know when this will affect people positively.

- I have bursts of passionate concentration.

- I can find ways to make monotonous things interesting and challenging.

- I love new things and ideas.

These beliefs, no less true but more helpful than the previous beliefs, have become a real source of energy and motivation for me. I decided that I would try to adopt a similar approach with Tom in our next coaching session. I remained wary, though, that I might have made a premature 'diagnosis', so I made a conscious effort to hold this idea as a hypothesis rather than as a solution.

Session Two

When we met again, Tom reported that he hadn't had time to do any of the exercises. He also admitted that he still hadn't started his dissertation, although he had been thinking more about it. He was still confident, however, that when he was right up against the wire he would do it.

I asked Tom to tell me about his life in terms of things which he had completed and things he had given up on. Because Tom liked to be up and about and active, I asked him to do this by standing up and using a flipchart to draw a timeline of his life. I explained that he should populate it above the timeline with things which he had completed and below the line with incidences of his having walked away from things.

When Tom had finished, he stood back, shook his head and swore. 'I've walked away from so many things!' he exclaimed. He had left University before completing his degree; started several businesses and closed them; entered into commercial partnerships with friends and quit; been close to getting married but, as he put it, 'cried off at the last minute'; embarked on lots of professional and recreational courses but never finished them; had opened several savings accounts, all of which were empty; and had spent a fortune on golf clubs, tennis racquets, scuba diving kit, and gym equipment, all of which were sitting at home and never used.

Above the line there was a drawing of a house, signifying a completed house purchase; some good long-term friendships; and three years working in his current role as a property surveyor.

Walking away from things may not necessarily be a bad thing— it may be evidence of ability to exercise discernment and to make decisions.

I suggested this to Tom and then asked him how he felt when he saw a visual representation of his life.

'It is powerful and eye-opening. I have made some good decisions, particularly with regard to calling off the wedding, but I have just realised that I have trouble making the right decisions in the first place.' Tom went on to explain that he loved the excitement of starting new things so much that he was often drawn into projects without really thinking them through. He identified for himself that he needed to stop and consider what a new hobby or idea would give him before charging headlong into it, investing money and time only to discover it wasn't what he wanted after all. He also admitted that there were times when he didn't complete certain tasks, like his degree, when they became difficult or too painful.

I took that as an opening to discuss Low Frustration Tolerance and my notion that it might be the root cause of Tom's habitual procrastination. Tom nodded. 'I think you might be on to something. I need to make better decisions, not only about which activities to start, but also about which ones it is important for me to finish!'

I then asked Tom if there was a theme in the items above the timeline. He looked at the flipchart again and it jumped out at him – property. He loved the property market and he loved his job in property surveying. In fact, his dream was to have a property portfolio of his own. He also recognised that he had worked hard to maintain some good long-term friendships.

I asked Tom to think about how he had made the decision to complete these things. How had his thinking and behaviour differed from when he had walked away from things? We all have internal strategies, which are often unconscious, and bringing them into conscious awareness can enable us to utilise them more readily. I asked Tom to consider his behaviours when he had decided to complete something, what he had said to himself, what mental images he had made, who else he had involved and how he had felt. I then asked him to do the same for times when he had walked away from something. He saw that his two sets of internal strategies were very different.

Much of coaching is about helping our clients draw on resources which they already have. Coaches can often do this by helping clients look at past successes.

By identifying what they did to achieve success, clients can begin to replicate the same behaviour patterns in the present and the future.

'Do you see that when you love something, when there is a compelling reason to finish it, you have demonstrated that you are willing to put up with a little pain in order to achieve a goal?' I said.

Tom nodded. He paused for a moment and then said, 'I really want this qualification—and I'm willing to go through the pain of studying to get it.'

I thanked Tom for his hard work and honesty. We agreed that, as a first step towards tackling the qualification, he would look again at the strategies which we had discussed during our previous session and actually implement them before we met again.

Session Three

In our third session Tom reported that he had kept almost all of his two-hour writing appointments over the past two weeks. I applauded his progress and told him that I wanted to walk him through a technique called 'Know How' to build on the great work which he had already done and to reinforce his commitment to action.

I asked Tom to sit in one chair and imagine how his life would be in three years if he kept his procrastinating behaviours. He entered into this exercise readily and his descriptions were vivid. He imagined himself feeling even more frustrated with himself, feeling as though he was being passed by, feeling a failure, not being able to progress in his career without a qualification, spending money and having no savings, and potentially slipping into destructively hedonistic behaviour or addictions. These images visibly upset Tom.

I then asked Tom to get up, to physically 'shake off' those feelings and to sit in a different chair to imagine how his life would be in three years if he had succeeded in making the changes he wanted to make. I reminded him that these were quite small changes — ones that involved Tom considering whether to embark on a course of action and then sticking with it through any possible discomfort. It was noticeable that Tom was vividly imagining a future self in this second chair. Tom vividly described himself progressing in his career, having enough savings to buy his first buy-to-let property, having increased self-esteem because he was proud of his achievements, and managing his life better. These images really encouraged Tom because he saw and felt that it was possible for him to achieve these things.

I asked Tom to hold these two sets of images in his mind, in particular the image of him buying his first buy-to-let property, and to ask himself *each day* as he went about his business,

'Is my behaviour today taking me closer to my desired outcome or further away from it?'

Having completed this exercise, Tom came up with a number of strategies for himself. When faced with doing something, he would ask himself the following questions:

- Does this get me closer to my goal?

- What would be the cost of doing this, or not doing this?

- Does this require any planning or support or can I do it right away?

- What worthwhile benefits would come about from my doing this?

- How quickly would I do this if my life and my future depended on it?

Further Sessions

Tom and I met for four more sessions to ensure that Tom completed his dissertation and, perhaps more importantly, that he changed his thinking patterns about putting things off because they felt too painful or boring for him. It was clear to me by session five that Tom had made huge progress. The turning point for Tom had been recognising a repeating behavioural pattern and seeing the long-term costs of those behaviours and the long-term benefits of his new ones.

I noticed a real change in Tom. He was calmer, more patient, and he listened more. His self-confidence was quieter and more authentic than before. He completed his dissertation in good time and achieved a respectable mark. He also didn't slip back into old habits but went from strength to strength and seemed to grow in confidence and maturity because he had finally learned to tolerate discomfort in order to achieve the rewards he deserved.

Tom had discovered that, if he could work out whether his choices were getting him closer to his goal, then there was no difficulty in making a decision - therefore procrastination or 'not finishing' was no longer an issue for him. Through taking action, Tom had discovered that he had the ability to stick with something after all and he no longer needed to bail out at the first signs of discomfort.

TOOLS AND TECHNIQUES

We all procrastinate at some points in our lives and, although procrastination has a bad name, there can be some positive aspects to it. If we never procrastinated then we might make many rash and potentially bad decisions. As we saw in Chapter 2, individuals with a strong people-pleasing tendency often just say 'yes' without thinking through the ramifications of their decision.

However, taken to excess, procrastination can lead to missed opportunities, missed deadlines, an appearance of weakness and extreme frustration and dissatisfaction for both the procrastinator and those who have to deal with them.

The following techniques may be used help clients who have a habit of procrastination. Techniques set out in related chapters may also be useful, particularly techniques set out in the chapters on People Pleasing, Perfectionism and Fierce Independence.

Step Up & Speak Up

Through enabling the client to identify clear goals and to focus on the wider benefits of achieving the goal, coaches can enable clients to greater commitment to the goal and reduced procrastination.

One reason we succumb to procrastination is because we haven't clarified the true benefit which we might get from doing what we have been putting off. 'Stepping up' can be a big help here by helping us to think about something bigger than the immediate outcome.

In a *New York Times* article Joseph Epstein *[Ref 32]* refers to a study that claims 81% of Americans say they want to write a book while less than 1% of them actually do so. This looks like procrastination on a mass scale.

Rather than simply stating 'I want to write a book', one technique might be to help the aspiring writer to 'step up' and identify the reason why achieving this goal would be valuable to that individual. If the coach enquires with genuine and gentle curiosity, the client will feel able to offer a genuine response, which might be 'I want to write a book because I want to be famous'. The coach could then ask the client what benefit they would get from being famous. The client's answer might be, 'So that I can leave a legacy and be remembered' and perhaps they might go on to say, 'I would feel as though my life had had meaning'.

Making explicit commitments is a key part of getting things done. This does not necessarily need to involve anyone else, simply verbalising commitments can increase their power. Often just saying something out loud, to yourself, 'I am going to call James today, tell him my thoughts, and ask him for some feedback', can be enough to set that wheel in motion.

The power of setting down objectives in visual form should not be underestimated. Many people make a to-do list and some clients might like to go one step further and create a progress chart or a progress wall with sticky notes, big green ticks or smiley faces to encourage progress.

Powerful Coaching Question:
What could you do to increase a sense of responsibility and accountability?

Identity-Based Goals

Procrastination is not just about the task we are putting off, but also about our relationship to that task and how the task relates to our personal drivers.

One technique to help your client to 'dig down' and access the identity-based drivers which could help them to get past a habit of procrastination is to ask your client to finish the sentence:

'I am the kind of person who...'

Encourage the client to do this a number of times. Ask the client to include both their current perceptions of themselves and one or two aspirational ones, things they would like to be able to believe and say about themselves, making sure that the client talks positively about what they do rather than about what they don't do.

As an example, our procrastinating author might come up with:

- 'I am the kind of person who *has a lot of valuable experience to share.*'

- 'I am the kind of person who *likes to share their experiences with others.*'

- 'I am the kind of person who *believes in the educational value of books.*'

- 'I am the kind of person who *likes the idea of being a published author.*'

- 'I am the kind of person who *does what they say they will.*'

- 'I am the kind of person who *always finishes what they start.*'

These types of identity-based goals tie into our personal drivers, affirming much about ourselves and what we want. Because people with a tendency to procrastinate often have a level of insecurity about their identity, they also tend to over-personalise and catastrophise the consequences of their actions or non-actions. A student writing an essay, for example, may take constructive feedback of their draft essays, intended purely to support them in a specific learning task, as critical and negative personal evaluations of their worth as a human being. The student may think, 'If I write an essay and they don't like it, then I am a bad person and they don't like me.'

To an observer, such a reaction might seem overly dramatic and out of proportion. However, self-limiting beliefs can take quite extreme forms while they remain unconscious: it is only when such beliefs are verbalised, particularly in the presence of a listener such as a coach, that we see them to be unrealistic. Coaches can help their clients to work out realistic definitions of success and failure through bringing unhelpful assumptions and myths to the surface.

Powerful Coaching Question:
How does it feel when you have completed something from your 'to do' list?

Shrink It Down

Making things smaller can enable quicker progress.

Having a large task ahead of us can feel overwhelming and can make us not want to tackle the task at all. A daunting task can produce an adrenaline-induced 'freeze' response which can physically stop us from pursuing the task. By breaking the task into smaller, more accessible parts, we can limit that feeling of being overwhelmed by the size of the task, and can make progress both more easily and more quickly.

You can help your client to work out all the steps involved in getting something done and breaking a large task into a series of smaller steps which the client feels that they can take. Battling procrastination is largely about maintaining some momentum so ensure that the client is able to initiate and to maintain some forward movement, however small. What is the smallest step the client can take?

When writing this book, for example, we took it one chapter at a time, deliberately starting with the procrastination chapter — we love irony! For the book as a whole we knew we wanted to include a number of elements: case studies, analysis, tools and techniques and a number of interviews with successful people.

For each of the chapters, we knew we would want a little bit of each of those elements; so the daunting prospect of 'writing a book' was broken down into a more manageable prospect of writing one chapter, and the task of writing one chapter was broken down into a series of yet smaller parts. Completing just one of the elements required, such as a case study, enabled us to maintain forward progress - and what a feeling of achievement it gave us when we finished a complete chapter!

Another useful concept to bear in mind when considering procrastination is that of 'decision fatigue': a phenomenon which may occur where people who have a large number of options to choose from become overwhelmed and make bad decisions or avoid making decisions altogether. Since people who procrastinate often have particular difficulty finding the confidence to make choices, your client may be experiencing decision fatigue.

We have found that constraining options can significantly help clients to make forward progress. You might encourage your client to try introducing some constraints on their decision-making processes. For example your client might try following the following 'rules' for a period:

- I will not spend more than 20 minutes analysing any decision.

- I will not exercise for more than 10 minutes a day.

- I will not write more than 500 words each day.

Another consequence of decision fatigue is that it becomes harder to make tough calls later in the day or when we are tired. For example, a study by Danziger, Levav and Avnaim-Pesso [Ref 33] reported that there was a 67% chance of judges approving parole applications at the start of a decision-making session, but that this steadily decreased to ZERO by the end of the session. After a break, however, the proportion of applications for parole which were accepted went right back up again. This type of study suggests just how helpful it might be to help your client to think not just about limiting and constraining their options, but also to consider the timing of their decision-making.

Powerful Coaching Question:
What is the smallest step you could take to make some progress on this issue?

THE INTERVIEW

Roger Burden

In all of our interviews of successful people we noticed something: not one of these successful people was aware of suffering from procrastination. We found this very interesting. One could infer from this that if you procrastinate then you won't become successful! Of course, this may not be true, but it does seem likely that excessive procrastination can inhibit achievement.

One of the challenges which procrastinators face is acquiring the confidence to make decisions. Roger Burden is Vice Chairman and Vice President of The Football Association and former Chief Executive and Chairman of Cheltenham & Gloucester Plc. Our interview with Roger provides some great insight into the strategies of successful decision-makers, which keep procrastination at bay.

Roger Burden believes that making sound decisions requires self-confidence that has been acquired through research and reflection. 'Confidence is built on data,' he says. He explains that this data is collected, consciously or unconsciously, throughout your life.

Roger gives the example of attending a lecture. 'If you pay attention in class and take dutiful notes,' he says, 'you can feel confident that any questions you ask will be good ones. You don't have to hesitate. Because you were diligent during the lecture, you already know whether the material was covered or not. The decision about whether to raise your hand and ask is an easy one because you have the data to make it.'

A common reason for procrastinating over an impending decision is lacking the confidence of our convictions and this, coupled with the fear of our decision being thought of as 'silly' can be enough to force people to put things off. What we learn from Roger is that being thorough in your research and then trusting yourself is key.

Another factor which Roger has learned to integrate with his habit of thorough research is reflection. 'I reflect upon every decision I make, more than once,' he says. 'One question that I will always ask myself is 'What more could I have done?" Roger acknowledges that it is impossible to get it right all the time and, once he had accepted that fact himself, it became easier to learn how to make better decisions. Learning from his mistakes, and those of others, gives Roger even more data to use for future decisions. 'And,' he quips, 'I much prefer to learn from others' mistakes than my own!'

Roger's view is that the more information you have the easier it becomes to make the right call. 'It's incredibly valuable to be sure that, even if other people don't agree with my decision, it is indeed the right decision.'

Over the years, Roger has developed a strategy for battling procrastination over decision-making which involves a few key steps:

- Categorise the decision.

- Define (or re-define) 'successful' outcomes.

- Solicit opinions from people you respect.

- Make the decision, reflect, and store the data.

Every decision, Roger says, can be categorised as either easy or hard. 'There's no point losing any sleep worrying about the easy decisions, just make them and move on,' he explains. 'But there's also no need to worry about the hard decisions. They are hard for a reason — you can make a strong case for and against. So again, just make the best decision you can based on your research and move on.'

Roger then considers the positive outcomes of each decision. He finds that when he is hesitant to take action, it is often because the outcomes need to be reframed. As an example he describes how, in his first managerial job, there was a team member who was not being very constructive and was undermining another member of the team.

'It was very subtle, but it was clear to me that something had to be done. I had to confront him about it. A big part of me didn't want to because I could see a number of outcomes: maybe he would agree with me, accept he had been wrong, and agree to change his ways. But he might also disagree with me, tell me how he was the victim, and start a confrontation. There was also a chance he would go to my boss and complain about me. And it was just as likely he might throw his toys out of the pram and quit. I didn't want to lose him, or lose face with my boss, or have a confrontation so, on the face of it, I had identified three unwanted outcomes compared to only one favourable outcome.'

To move out of this mindset, Roger re-framed the potential outcomes.

'If he argues with me, then I will have more information and will learn something. If he goes to my boss, then I will get an insight into how my boss thinks and how he would handle it. And if he quits, then perhaps he's not the kind of person I want in the team.'

By reframing it in this way, Roger explains, all of the potential outcomes became positive, so it became much easier to move forward with confidence.

Another strategy Roger finds helpful when making decisions is to surround himself with people whose opinions he respects. 'Soliciting the opinions of others gives me as much information as possible with which to make my decision. But be careful not to delegate the decision-making power to these advisors. The final decision must still be one you support and can defend. Even if everyone suggested one route and I alone thought another, I would back my judgement and take responsibility for the decision,' he explains.

The last part of the decision-making process, as Roger sees it, is to store every good decision as further data to help him to make tough decisions in the future.

'I keep a mental database of things that I have done and decisions that I have made,' Roger explains. Then, when a similar situation arises, he can pull up a relevant experience and use that to help him make the best decision in the present. 'It's very easy to remember the ones that went wrong, but that's often not very helpful. When I'm struggling, I consciously look back at my track record of decision-making and pull up all the examples of good decisions.'

Working hard, paying attention, and continuously learning are the building blocks which Roger has used to arrive at quick, confident decisions, and to escape the paralysis of procrastination.

'I might lose some sleep before I make the decision because I am ruthlessly thorough in researching the decision that needs to be made. But I don't lose sleep after I have made the decision worrying if I have made the right one, because I know that I have done.'

CHAPTER TEN

Performance Anxiety

'There are always three speeches for every one you actually gave. The one you practiced, the one you gave, and the one you wish you gave.'

DALE CARNEGIE

THE CASE STUDY

'I just froze – it was horrible.'

It often happens that previous clients contact us some time in the future looking for coaching on a new topic. This is usually a positive experience for us as coaches as we can pick up our previous relationship and need not spend as long developing rapport and trust. One such client was Kelly. I had previously coached Kelly when she had been promoted into a new, senior position at work, helping her with the challenges of establishing herself in the new role. About two years after we had finished our coaching, Kelly contacted me to ask if I would coach her on something completely different.

Session One

Outside work, Kelly had always enjoyed her hobby of singing in a band with some friends. They had a regular routine playing a few local pubs and clubs. It was always a great source of release for her and, from what I could gather, the band was very good too - so much so that they had occasionally toyed with the idea of quitting their jobs and going professional. She told me that the band had been given a huge break recently when they had been asked to replace a support act for a big performance in London. However, for some reason, Kelly had got stage fright.

'I just froze; it was horrible,' she said. 'I didn't feel right before we went on. My heart was going, I was sweating and I was really nervous. About half way through the first song, I completely forgot the words; my mind went blank. Luckily Jamie covered for me and eventually I caught up and we finished the song. But the next song was even worse. I missed a couple of notes and my voice was wobbly. I never miss a note. After that I said to Jamie that I wasn't feeling well and they carried on without me.'

'That certainly sounds out of character,' I said. 'Were you ill, do you think?'

'No. I don't know why it happened. I went backstage and I felt as though I was having a panic attack. I was almost hyper-ventilating.'

The first thing I wanted to do was to help Kelly to realise that what happened to her was probably nothing to worry about but rather a simple case of nerves.

Many performers are likely to be affected by a form of stage fright at some point.

I told Kelly that I thought it would be more unusual if she *didn't* get nervous when performing. Even some of the most famous and successful performers experience stage fright – John Lennon reportedly used to vomit before every live performance and Barbra Streisand struggled with performance anxiety for years.

Perhaps the most common form of performance anxiety – or stage fright – is associated with giving a presentation or a speech in public, but other situations where this is common include job interviews, exams, customer meetings or even football's dreaded penalty shootouts. Common symptoms include:

- Shallow and uncontrollable breathing.

- Unclear thinking.

- Dry mouth.

- Nausea.

- Moist hands.

- Impaired sense of time.

- Trembling.

- Muscle tension.

- Loss of balance.

It is estimated that 75% of people have a fear of 'performing' in public. Some neuroscientists have suggested that we are hard-wired to seek to avoid such situations in order to preserve our reputations as social animals.

When faced with the prospect of a public performance and a perceived threat to our reputation and social status, our most primitive response may be triggered – commonly labelled the 'fight or flight' response, a term coined by Harvard University physiologist Walter Canon in 1915 *[Ref 34]*.

When faced with danger, our instinctive reactions are triggered to prepare us either to fight off the danger or to run away as fast as possible. Powerful chemical and physical changes in our body occur in association with these primitive responses. Our heart rate intensifies, adrenalin is produced, our digestive system shuts down and our muscles tighten in order to prepare us for either defence or retreat.

However, 'Fight or flight' is probably more accurately described as the 'fight, flight or freeze' response because if neither fight nor flight are possible responses, we are left with a third possible response – to freeze, and hope the danger passes us by. When we see ourselves as under threat, the survival-focused area of our brain called the amygdala takes over from our frontal cortex where, among other things, speech is activated. This might explain why it would have been difficult for Kelly to sing or to recall her words.

I asked Kelly whether there was any reason she had felt that this particular audience were more threatening to her than her usual pub crowd.

'Apart from the sheer difference in numbers, no. Obviously I didn't get to speak to them, and they weren't actually there to see us, but I certainly didn't feel threatened by them. I did feel under more pressure than normal because it was a proper performance rather than just one of our regular gigs, but we had been practicing more and everything was fine in rehearsals.'

'How have you been since the performance?' I asked, curious as to how she responded.

'I've been haunted by it. I keep playing it over and over again in my head. I haven't sung since. We've cancelled a few of our normal gigs. I really don't think I can put myself through that again.'

'That sounds tough,' I sympathised. 'Do you miss singing?'

'Sure, and I feel really bad for the rest of the band,' she said. 'I need to sort this out because they really want to get back to playing this weekend.'

I wanted to make sure that she wasn't doing this solely for the band but that she actually wanted to get back to singing as well. She was adamant that she wanted to keep singing but needed her confidence back.

I asked Kelly to close her eyes and think about the end of her nose.

She looked at me very strangely but we knew each other well so she went along with me and did as I asked.

'Have you got a mental picture of the end of your nose?' I asked.

'Yes' she replied.

'Good. Now you must not imagine the end of your nose. Stop thinking about the end of your nose. You must not let the image of the end of your nose back into your head,' I said.

'Well if you keep saying those words, that's all I will be able to think about,' she said, opening her eyes.

'Exactly. Deliberately trying not to think about a particular thing generally just doesn't work – instead that thing will be all you will be able to think about. At the moment you are filling your head with an image, or a belief, which you are not allowing yourself to get rid of. What is that image or belief?' I asked.

'That I forgot the words, that I panicked and got stage fright.'

'Right. And you keep re-living that story, re-telling yourself those things. You need to change the message that you are giving yourself to be a more positive one. So what else do you know about yourself as a singer?'

'That I have sung hundreds of times; that I know how to breathe from my diaphragm, which I have to do to be able to sing well; that I know the lyrics to over a hundred songs; that I enjoy singing and people think I'm good,' she began.

'Excellent. You can use this aspect of your mind to your advantage. What you tell yourself will be in your head and it can become difficult to shift it. So being very careful about what you are putting into your head is useful.'

'There is one more aspect to this technique. When you're performing and your mind wanders – because this may well happen, and you may start thinking those negative thoughts again – you can train yourself to force those thoughts out of your head by focusing on something else, maybe even the end of your nose.'

With that in mind, we explored the differences between the one-off gig where Kelly had experienced stage fright and the usual gigs which she had been playing successfully for years.

'You said that you felt under more pressure than normal with this performance. Why was that? Were you singing new or different songs?'

'No, nothing like that. We even had slightly fewer songs to sing than normal as we were just the support act, but these people didn't know our material so we sang a few different songs that we thought that particular audience would like. Like I said though, they didn't pay to see us.'

'And what about the customers at the pubs where you play; have they specifically asked you to play there?' I asked, slightly provocatively.

'Well, no, not all of them anyway. Most of them just turn up for a drink and expect some live music, but we have some regulars who know we play on certain dates and come specifically to watch us.'

We talked about the similarities and differences between the regular gigs and this one-off performance. They were similar in that the mechanics were largely the same – the same instruments, the same people in the band, the same songs and roughly the same performance time - and while there were some differences in the venue and the people who were listening, the main difference seemed to be that this was a one-off performance.

'What was your definition of success for this particular event?' I asked.

Kelly thought about this before answering. 'Well obviously I wanted us to perform well and wanted people to have a good time, dancing and singing along. I also hoped that this would be the start of something bigger, that we would get more of these types of request and we wouldn't just be playing in the same pubs with the same routine.'

One of the key reasons performers struggle to replicate their practice performances on stage is because they focus too much on the future. By looking at this as 'the start of something bigger' Kelly was making this performance far too much about what would happen next rather than what was happening at the time. I asked Kelly to describe her routine gigs and it was clear why she felt very little anxiety about them when she said, 'Those gigs are just singing some songs with the guys in a pub.'

Athletes who struggle to repeat their practice performances when it really matters often cite the main difference as being that in a match, race or event they only have one chance, whereas in practice they can do it again if something goes wrong. By focussing on the future too much, they forget the purpose of all the hours of practice which they have undertaken in preparation for the event – to automate the actions which they need to replicate in the match or race. Successful athletes speak of just trusting their muscle memory and 'being totally in the moment'.

A secondary factor with Kelly was that because of this 'event' she had now introduced herself to the second most common reason people get performance anxiety – living in the past. It would be very tempting for her to revisit her past 'failure' and become anxious about the possibility of this repeating itself.

We spent the rest of the session developing Kelly's 'present moment focus' – noticing when she found herself projecting either forward or backward in time and consciously bringing her attention back to 'the end of her nose', to the present moment.

This is an easy technique to practice but can be a difficult technique to master. Kelly would berate herself for losing her focus but this only made it more likely that she would lose her focus once again. To become skilled at this technique, it is important to acknowledge that it is inevitable that your mind will wander from time to time so there is nothing to be gained by metaphorically 'kicking yourself' when you notice it happening; just accept it, and bring your attention back. We developed a signal to help Kelly to practice this refocusing, to help her to build a mental 'muscle memory' which would help her deal with performances.

I remained silent while Kelly attempted to maintain her focus on the end of her nose. Every time Kelly's mind wandered to the future or the past, she would slightly raise her hand and then bring her attention back to the present. I would keep track of these hand movements and tell Kelly how long she had been able to maintain her present moment focus. During the course of the session Kelly went from one second to 28 seconds, which was excellent progress. By the end of the session Kelly felt confident enough to play another of her 'routine' gigs and her homework was to practice staying 'in the moment' as much as possible during the gig.

Session Two

In our next session, Kelly told me she had performed at the gig but was disappointed that it 'wasn't like it used to be'. She had made use of the 'present moment awareness' technique, which had helped a little, but she had not enjoyed the performance as much as usual and had felt more anxious than she ever had for a pub gig.

'I was really stressed,' she told me, 'and I didn't sing well, which made me even more stressed. In the end I couldn't wait for it to finish.'

When we are tense and anxious, we are not in our optimum physical state to perform well; our muscles, blood flow and heart rate are all working against us. In our coaching session Kelly and I focused on developing a pre-performance routine which Kelly could follow to get her into the best possible state to perform.

I wanted to see Kelly's current pre-performance routine, so I asked Kelly to try to re-create it in the coaching room. Kelly felt comfortable enough with me to do this and we created an imaginary stage area.

'Imagine that you are backstage and will be going on in about ten minutes,' I said. 'What are you doing?'

'Well I would probably be pacing around like this, going over the lyrics of the songs, having a drink of water, having a pee, having another drink…'

'Stop!' I said, quite loudly. 'Stay exactly as you are, as if you were playing musical statues.'

I took a quick photograph of Kelly with my phone and showed it to her.

'How would you describe your posture?' I asked.

Kelly was hunched over, looking down at her feet; her shoulders were high and her hands were clasped together in front of her chest.

'Wow,' she said. 'I look like an old lady!'

We sat down and I started a conversation with Kelly about the 'Three Ps of Performing' - posture, pace and preparation.

I explained that her body language was sending messages not only to those around her; it was also sending messages to Kelly herself.

'What messages do you think this body posture is saying to you, yourself?' I asked.

'That I'm scared, small, insignificant…', Kelly said.

'How would a confident person stand? Imagine someone who is destined to go out and give a great performance - how would that person stand?'

Kelly made some adjustments to her posture, standing straighter, holding her head higher, and smiled.

'Good. Now take it one step further. I want you to stretch your arms up and out and look up and tell me what you feel as you do that.'

Kelly stretched and commented that she felt good.

Successful performers are sometimes said to have a 'stage presence' – they look and act as if they belong on the stage, almost as if they 'own' it. I asked Kelly to act out what she would look like if she owned the stage and belonged there. This included Kelly finding a comfortable pace for her movements which would enable her to breathe fully. When we are stressed, we often rush and don't pace ourselves properly. The third 'P' referred to preparation, not just preparing for the performance in a general sense, but also identifying a few things which might go wrong, and then preparing how she might cope with any such difficulties if they arose.

Kelly's homework this time was not only to practice the songs, as she always had done, but also to practice the Three Ps.

Session Three

Kelly told me that the next gig had been more comfortable for her. Kelly said that she had felt much more confident, even though she said her confidence was 'partly an act'. Kelly had noticed that she spent longer 'in the moment', had engaged with the audience and had enjoyed it again.

'But we've been asked to do a corporate party. I'm glad that I've got my confidence back for the regular gigs but I don't want to freeze again when I do something a bit different.'

There seemed to be a number of things going on with Kelly here and we spent some time 'unpacking' them together.

Firstly, Kelly had been back in her comfort zone. This was a good thing in many ways as it had allowed her to do what she did well and with confidence. However, she was now faced with the prospect of stepping outside of that comfort zone to play a corporate event. We might refer to this type of situation as the 'stretch zone'. The stretch zone is an area in which we experience some degree of discomfort but is the area where learning and growth is most likely to occur and where confidence may grow.

If we 'stretch' too much or too soon, however, then we can end up in the 'panic' zone where we are unlikely to be capable of learning or growth.

I explained this model to Kelly and suggested that perhaps the support act gig had been a little bit of an over-stretch for her at that particular time. However, by consciously putting herself into a stretch zone now, she could gradually expand her comfort zone and get to the point where an event like the support act gig would not induce panic.

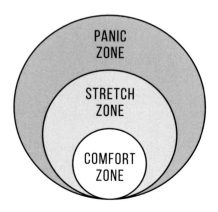

Kelly liked the idea of this and we agreed to pursue a strategy of gradual exposure to stretching situations.

We also agreed to work on augmenting Kelly's strategies for managing her anxiety.

One part of this strategy was to address the fact that Kelly was unconsciously using an 'away from' motivational approach. She was looking at how things might go wrong and was focusing her attention on trying to avoid the negative result which she feared.

Our first step here was to 'normalise' the situation. Kelly admitted that it was highly unlikely that anyone attending the corporate party would actually want to see her fail let alone make her fail. The audience effectively would all be 'on her side' - if Kelly did well then they would have a good time.

Kelly agreed that having a 'towards' strategy would be more beneficial to her than her current 'away from' approach. I therefore asked Kelly to describe and visualise what a great outcome might look like, particularly in relation to the audience.

'When I'm on top form, the audience join in, singing and dancing. Then I tend to feed off this and perform even better. It's a virtuous circle,' she reflected.

Many performers attempt to ignore or marginalise their audience in the hope that this will reduce the pressure they are feeling. They will avoid eye contact and 'get through it' as quickly as possible. However, many successful performers we know, whether in the boardroom or on a stage, find that doing the opposite works better for them. They deliberately attempt to connect with their audience rather than ignoring them.

Some performers say that connecting with an audience helps them to avoid feeling isolated and exposed on the stage so Kelly and I worked on strategies which she could use to engage the audience more and earlier, such as talking to the audience directly.

Many performers crank the pressure up on themselves by demanding unrealistic perfection from their performance. It is rare for anybody to deliver a presentation or complete a gig without missing a beat, tripping over a word or some kind of technical glitch. The irony is that worrying excessively about the prospect of this happening only increases the chances of mistakes as the levels of performance anxiety increase.

When talking about this, Kelly remembered how powerful it had been for her to see Beyonce, who was a heroine of hers, admit to forgetting her lyrics and offering the microphone to the crowd, then laughing about it afterwards.

By the end of the session Kelly was happy with the approach of stretching herself and she had the beginning of a strategy to manage her anxiety. The memory of her stage fright was still fresh, however, and she asked if our next coaching session could be at the gig. Kelly explained she would feel much more comfortable if I was present for the performance.

I thought about it. I couldn't immediately see any reason why this would be a problem, so I agreed.

Session Five

The gig was a success and Kelly was happy that she had stretched herself. She had engaged with the audience and not only had she performed well, she had enjoyed it too. At the 'afterparty', the band was talking about trying to get a spot at one of the big festivals, which Kelly was really excited about.

The only problem was that Kelly had attributed a lot of her success to the fact that I had been present at the gig. Kelly asked me to come along to the next one as well. I could see why she wanted me there. Many athletes, performers and other people will develop attachments to routines that have been successful. Sportsmen such as Alec Stewart in Chapter Eight will often follow routines and rituals such as wearing the same items of clothing after a great performance. Kelly was trying to recreate the exact conditions of her successful performance at the corporate function.

'It's flattering that you think my presence there was part of the reason that you were successful, and I certainly enjoyed the show. However, logically you know that I had nothing to do with it. It would be a bad idea – not to mention unethical – for me to encourage you to have any kind of dependency on me,' I explained.

Our job now was to recreate whatever benefit I was giving Kelly without my presence being necessary. We achieved this through the process of anchoring. I asked Kelly to recall as vividly as she could and in as much detail as possible the feelings which she had experienced at her last performance and to create an 'anchor' so that she could recall those positive feelings at will. *[For more on anchoring, see the Tools and Techniques section that follows at the end of this chapter].*

Supervision

While I did not have any direct supervision with this coaching assignment there certainly would have been plenty of potential for useful supervision with this client. In particular, Kelly asking me to attend her gig raised questions as to professional boundaries. Not all coaching interaction needs to happen in a formal one to one office setting. We like to be open to new and different ways of working with our clients if that is appropriate and in this situation it seemed to me that it was appropriate.

When judging whether something like this is appropriate or not, there are no hard and fast rules. However, we tend to find that there are a number of questions which it is helpful to consider:

Firstly, is following the particular course of action likely to be more helpful to the client than the alternative? If it isn't, then the consideration stops there.

Secondly, are you confident that you will be able to maintain your professional capacity and appropriate standards of conduct in this situation? For example, we wouldn't recommend getting drunk and crowd-surfing at Kelly's gig! On this point, a coach should always treat this type of session as they would any other chargeable session.

Thirdly, is there a risk of the course of action creating undue dependency for the client? There was clearly some risk of Kelly developing a dependency upon the coach in this situation and coaches should always be alert to and manage such risks.

Supervision can be particularly helpful to the coach in considering and thinking through ethical issues of this kind.

TOOLS AND TECHNIQUES

There are a number of theories about how to deal with performance anxiety – from the old 'imagine the audience in their underwear' idea, to trying to ignore the audience or even scanning the room for a friendly looking face and focusing on them. We don't believe there is one right technique but we have noted some common patterns.

Seasoned performers learn to expect and work with their anxiety. They don't try to fight it off entirely or expect to get through the performance without feeling nervous. Even people who love public speaking (and they do exist!) may experience some degree of anxiety when they present. It is perhaps impossible for most of us to remove performance anxiety completely.

Many performers suggest that they need a certain degree of nervous tension to push them to prepare effectively and to generate the levels of adrenaline and excitement which they need to perform at their best. So a coach's job may not be to eliminate the anxiety associated with a performance entirely, but rather to bring it down to a level which is manageable for their client.

Power Pose

Adopting the body posture of someone who is confident and powerful can generate feelings of confidence and power.

Jessica Tracy observed that congenitally blind athletes have the same physical responses to winning and losing races that sighted athletes do, suggesting that displays of pride and shame are likely to be universal and instinctive *[Ref 35]*. Thus, by adopting the physical postures which we unconsciously associate with pride, we can take a 'short cut' to the positive emotions and mindset which are unconsciously associated with those physical postures *[Ref 36]*. Even simply gripping a pen between your teeth will force you to smile thus making you feel happier. Try it!

Amy Cuddy's TED.com talk (with over 20 million views), shows how adopting a 'Power Pose' for just two minutes positively alters the hormones produced by your body, giving you a more positive and powerful presence with reduced levels of anxiety *[Ref 37]*. Of course coaches may worry that this exercise might seem to be inducing clients to 'pretend' to feel something which they do not authentically feel.

Cuddy herself was very aware of the risks of a 'fake it till you make it' approach. However, the technique has an entirely positive purpose and can have positive effects. With this technique we are tapping into the psychological benefits of a particular state of mind in order to make it easier for your client to adopt this behaviour as a reality. This is what Cuddy describes as 'Fake it till you *become* it'

Powerful Coaching Question:
"How will this moment seem to you when you look back at it in 10 years' time?"

Prepare and Practice

Help your client to leave as little to chance as possible and to think through some contingency plans.

The first step for your client to being confident about their performance is for them to be confident that they know their material or their skills inside and out. Help your client to automate the recall process as much as possible both by practicing and by trying to recreate in practice the atmosphere of the real performance so far as is practicable.

As well as practicing the speech, the lyrics or the dance moves, great performers also prepare and plan for the unexpected. The singer who forgets the words gets the crowd to join in; the presenter who trips over his words says, 'That's easy for you to say, let's try that again'.

The chances are that your client may not need these plans, but the confidence gained from knowing that they have considered some contingencies and that they were able to come up with solutions may prove invaluable.

Encourage your client to get additional support from nutritionists or dieticians. Preparation for a performance could also include looking at dietary factors. Nutritionists suggest that caffeine and sugar intake on the day of the performance, while very tempting, is usually a bad idea as this can increase your nervous energy at the outset and leave you with an energy drop in the middle of your performance. Even worse is the myth of *'Dutch courage'* so it is prudent to avoid alcohol as well! Other advice from dietary experts includes eating a low fat meal with complex carbohydrates, such as a pasta or rice dish, a few hours prior to the performance to ensure you have the energy you need to perform, whilst also handling the energy-sapping consequences of stress and anxiety.

During our interviews for this book, we came across one strategy that many people employed as part of their preparation – compartmentalisation. Carl Llewellyn and Alec Stewart, among others, both gave themselves a fixed amount of time in which they permitted themselves to worry about their next race or match. Once that time had elapsed, that was it. They would also give themselves a fixed amount of time after the performance in which to critique the performance, before moving on.

Worrying about a performance can be helpful as we have said, but setting a time limit constraint upon that worrying can be a very effective strategy for achieving a healthy balance for this trait.

Powerful Coaching Question:
If your stress level was marked as ten out of ten, what would it take for you to lower it to a nine?

Anchoring

Coaches can help their clients to develop strategies to manage the inevitable tendency for focus to drift off into the future or back into the past.

Coaches can help their clients to practice consciously bringing their focus back to something in the present moment. Coaches can also help their clients to achieve present focus with a Neuro Linguistic Programming technique known as 'anchoring' *[Ref 38]*.

An 'anchor' is a small movement or action – for example squeezing your left earlobe or tapping your foot – that is deliberately associated with a particular feeling or state of mind so that, after enough practice, simply repeating the action can bring about the desired feeling or state of mind.

This is a process that happens automatically and unconsciously. Some of the most powerful anchors are associated with the sense of smell. Have you ever caught the smell of freshly baked bread or freshly cut grass and been 'taken back' to a time in your life years ago? This is the anchor of the smell evoking a memory, a feeling or a state of mind. By working with our clients to enable them to create an anchor for themselves, we can help our clients develop an internal resource which can be helpful in managing their performance anxiety.

Guide your client into a deeply relaxed state and then ask them to:

1. Recall, in as much detail as possible, an experience from the past when your confidence and self-esteem was really high or when you felt really calm.

2. Re-live the experience, slowly and fully, physically and emotionally.

3. Recapture all of the sensations which you experienced at that time. Spend some time enjoying these feelings while at the same time making a small movement (pressing your hands together,

squeezing your earlobe or just pressing your index finger and thumb together.)

4. The trigger movement you choose should be one which feels comfortable to you and which is discreet so that nobody would notice you doing it in public.

5. Repeat on several occasions until you find that when you use your physical anchor this generates an automatic response of a feeling of calm, confidence, self-esteem or whatever emotional state you have chosen to anchor.

6. Repeat this a lot – keep at it! Eventually you will be able to use this small trigger to anchor yourself to feelings of calm or high self-esteem whenever you need to.

Powerful Coaching Question:
In what situations are you very calm when that situation would cause other people anxiety? What is your strategy in those situations?

THE INTERVIEW

Craig Campbell

There are many situations where people may face performance anxiety: presenting a report at a team meeting, making a speech at a wedding, or performing a standup comedy routine on stage in front of thousands of people. Fear of public speaking – or glossophobia – is so common that it is believed to be the most common of all fears or 'phobia'.

We interviewed Craig Campbell, a standup comedian who is a regular at the Edinburgh Comedy Festival. Craig has appeared on many primetime comedy TV shows and comedy festivals in the UK, North America and Australasia and has had the experience of playing to an audience of over 300,000 while touring in 2010. Craig has also written and performed his own one-man play.

Craig told us how he has consciously built up a strategy over many years to enable him to be confident enough to put himself 'out there' on the stage every night.

'They don't know your show' – these are the words that stand up comedian Craig Campbell holds dear to him and he remembers vividly when Rich Elwood gave him that advice back in 1991. A joke might have died but so long as you don't acknowledge it, the audience won't know it.

Craig admits to always having been unusually philosophical for his age but to being at the same time very naïve.

'I can remember the first time I ever saw a comedian tell the same joke twice.' (He actually does remember because he tells me the name of the comedian). 'And I thought, 'Woah, it's really true! What looks like pure improvisation can actually be practiced.' It was a massive 'naïve' moment for me and my career has been full of them.'

Craig has a wonderfully human, almost child-like enthusiasm for life that comes through in his story-telling both on stage and off. His glass half-full perspective shines through in the tales of his adventures, which are his comedy trademark.

'I didn't want to be the Canadian who just knew about Canada. I wanted to learn about cultures that the audience knew and cared about. I needed adventures – that's my material.'

So he tells me about his time hunting reindeer in Norway and his desperate taxi ride across a river delta in rural China. He not only saw the exciting and positive side of these experiences at the time, but also managed to turn them into material for his performances.

This has always been Craig's style of comedy, telling stories that people can relate to and find funny, rather than 'telling jokes'. Craig's first performance was in a local comedy competition in his native Canada, when he was aged just 18. He came second.

'I was absolutely terrified but I was also amazed that people could do this, and that I could do this,' he says.

So how did Craig cope with the nerves? It seems as though he has accumulated a number of techniques over the years.

'First of all, you need to prepare for different circumstances,' he explains. 'You need to be able to tell a joke in many different contexts so you ask yourself, 'How do you tell it if…' - like, 'How do you tell it if half the audience hear it but the other half don't?' - because you can't just repeat it each time verbatim.'

'I always practice just by talking to people. I'll talk to the bus driver, the waiter…' And he strikes up a conversation with our waiter about Kathmandu in Nepal where he's about to do a charity gig at Everest base camp.

'He doesn't know it's a punch line,' he says to me, 'so if you can make him laugh then of course an audience will like it. And you've worked it through so you are prepared.'

It sounds to me as though Craig might be a perfectionist but, having just seen his show, I wouldn't be surprised if it was all spontaneous. He tells me this is another of his techniques to avoid performance anxiety.

'If you come out with an ice-breaker joke and it dies then you're in trouble. But if you come out and just talk to someone… well if it's funny then it was a joke, but if it's not funny then you were just talking.'

Another strategy that he has employed to reduce the pressure on himself is that he introduces himself onstage rather than having a compère do it.

'By bringing myself on, I'm in control and I will always be ready. I've known some compères who deliberately try to trip you up.'

But of course it doesn't always go perfectly. Craig tells me of gigs where the crowd have physically threatened him, people have walked out of the exits right at the front of the room and also occasions when he has been heavily criticised by the media for 'political jokes above his station'. How do these things affect him?

'Well they certainly made me think more about my delivery and the reactions to what I do, which made it harder,' he says. We discuss the importance of staying in the moment and being able to leave the past behind and not worry about the future.

'I only worry about controlling the controllables now. I used to really stress if I was stuck in traffic but now I'll say to my support act, 'They're not going to start without us!"

I ask Craig what had been his biggest challenge as a comedian and he says it was his second tour.

'I felt that I had 22 years' worth of material to pull from for my first tour but within 12 months I was back on the same stages playing to the same crowds and I had significantly less to pull from. I didn't want to say the same things but I didn't know what I told them last time.'

He describes this as being more terrifying that being an 18-year-old on stage for the first time.

'I always set my target at pleasing the hardest punter, not the easiest. I wanted to win over the curmudgeon. And it took me a while, but eventually I realised that audiences don't remember what I said last time. Sure a few do – some of them even take notes – but generally they don't.

'I also learned to look at it as wonderfully emancipating to have to come up with new stuff and that means having new adventures!'

Craig's final piece of advice is sage-like as he explains that he deliberately leaves gaps in his knowledge and will happily admit when he doesn't know what the audience is talking about.

'It's almost as essential to have ignorance of the frivolous as to have knowledge of the important.'

CHAPTER ELEVEN

Searching For Fulfilment

'You will never be happy if you continue to search for what happiness consists of. You will never live if you are looking for the meaning of life.'

ALBERT CAMUS

THE CASE STUDY

'I want to look forward to work; I want to enjoy what I do.'

'I'm just bored and I've got this feeling that there's something more out there that I should be doing,' said Julian. 'I'm doing fine in my job, in fact I'm doing more than fine. I'm well paid and I'm good at what I do,' he continued, 'but it doesn't really do anything for me any more, you know? I want to look forward to going to work; I want to enjoy what I do and do something that interests me. I mean who can get really get passionate about running a software department in a bank!'

Julian is one of many clients who present with this issue, an issue which arises repeatedly irrespective of the client's role, level or sector. We have had experience of senior managers and middle managers, technicians and developers, architects, lawyers and traders who all say pretty much the same thing: 'I need a purpose'.

One question which I often ask people in these situations is:

> **'If money were of no consideration to you, and you had no current ties, what work would you choose to do?'**

It's a simple question. There is nothing clever about it, and the fact that people struggle to answer it is telling. In fact, Julian's answer was fairly typical:

'I don't know really. I just know that this isn't it'

'So then how do you know that there is something more out there for you?'

'Because I know people who have quit their jobs and followed their dreams, and they're happy.'

There appear now to be a significant number of people who are sufficiently financially comfortable to contemplate 'chucking it all in' and 'following their dream'. I asked Julian to tell me about the people he was referring to and while it appeared to be true that some of them had written a book or developed an app that had been successful, it appeared that most of these people were financially reliant on savings or on a partner while they attempted to follow their passion. Julian told me about a friend of his who had quit his job and set up a new online retail company selling hiking gear and how it had grown into a community.

'Not only has he made a load of money out of it but he's working in the hiking world, something that he adores,' Julian said with a sigh.

'You sound envious Julian and, when you paint that picture, I can see why,' I said. 'So what's your equivalent to 'hiking'?'

'I'm not sure. I've never really given myself time to think about it,' Julian replied.

Some companies are hesitant to provide coaches for their employees in case they realise that they want to leave and set up a business of their own. Of course, if businesses are providing something which is aimed at developing employees' self-awareness then there is a risk that those employees will start to feel that they should really be working elsewhere. However, the benefits which businesses can gain from a self-aware workforce may well outweigh the downsides of losing one or two employees. As the old management joke goes:

'What if we spend all this money developing our people and they leave?' which prompts the reply, 'What if we don't develop them and they stay?'

People who have a slow-burning passion may reach a tipping point or notice a sudden opportunity in the marketplace that makes it 'now or never' and, because they have years of bottled up energy and drive behind them, they may do well when they make the decision to follow a new path.

My intuition told me that Julian was not one of these people but was a case of an employee with a general feeling of 'itchy feet' or needing to address something incongruent at work. I remembered some of the words which he had used in our sessions to date, including his initial explanation of why he was coming to me for coaching. He used words which implied an obligation rather than a passion – that he 'wanted' to make a change or that he 'should' make a change.

'I'd like to give you an exercise to do which might tell us both a bit about you and about your values. This might help you to work out what your passion is.'

Julian agreed and I explained that I was going to give him 50 cards each bearing a value which might be important to him. I stressed that there were no right or wrong answers and that it was important that he did not worry about what he thought he should or shouldn't do but rather it was essential that he be as honest as he could be.

The first step was for Julian to go through the cards one at a time, and to put all the cards containing values which were important to him into one pile and to discard the rest.

I told Julian not to think too hard or take too long, but to try and go with his gut instinct. Once he had finished and was left with a smaller set of cards, I then asked him to do the exercise again using only the cards which he had kept, but this time to be even more ruthless.

Once again, Julian discarded some cards and kept others. I asked him to keep repeating the process until he was left with just five cards. He found this difficult but eventually ended up with only the following cards:

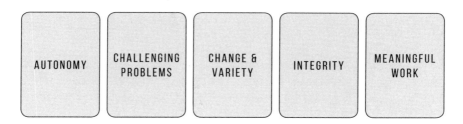

I congratulated Julian on having succeeded in narrowing things down to just five values – it is a lot harder than it might first appear – and then challenged him to put those five values into a sentence or two that described his ideal work. He came up with:

'I like my work to be meaningful and varied. I like solving challenging problems with autonomy and integrity.'

Julian said he was happy with this as a summary, so I followed up by asking him whether there was anything that surprised him about this.

'I wouldn't say anything surprised me as such but putting the words 'autonomy' and 'integrity' together in a single sentence sheds a whole new light on those words.'

'What do you mean?' I asked.

'Well, obviously I chose the word autonomy from the pile four or five times so it was definitely a conscious decision. But, when I say that I like solving challenging problems with autonomy and integrity, it makes me realise how much I value my independence. I think that's why the logical next step is to set up a business of my own.'

I stopped to consider what might be the best approach to take with Julian. There is, of course, a wide spectrum of coaching approaches, from the directive to the non-directive. Many coaches sit on the non-directive end of the spectrum, which means that they primarily ask questions to enable the client to make their own decisions and will seek to avoid providing solutions or determining the outcome of the coaching.

Coaches who adopt a more directive approach may seek to find ways of pointing out to a client if the client's goals appear to be unrealistic. This might be considered to be closer to a mentoring or consultancy approach.

Initially I took an indirect approach with Julian but, before I had even finished speaking, I realised it would have no effect on him. Julian was warming to his theme and warning lights were beginning to flash for me now. With everything Julian said, he seemed to be convincing himself more and more that setting up a new business was the answer to his situation. I was far from convinced.

'What else could it mean, apart from indicating that you should set up a business?'

Of course, Julian was so focused on this new world of possibility that there was no room for alternatives in his mind. In fact, he took what I had said as confirmation of his assessment, which was the opposite of what I had intended.

'You're right,' said Julian, 'there isn't any other interpretation. I now know what the aim of this coaching should be – for you to help me to set up a new business.'

I explained that I had not quite got my question across as I had intended but Julian wasn't interested in what I had to say. He seemed very excited and, despite not feeling as enthusiastic about this coaching engagement as Julian clearly was, I expressed agreement.

'Fair enough,' I said. 'I think it would be valuable for you to think about what you would like this business venture to be before we meet next time.'

Julian almost bounded out of the room while I felt quite deflated by the whole session – a surprising reaction for me and one that I decided to discuss in supervision.

Supervision

My 'flat' mood had continued all week and I felt that it had to have something to do with my coaching session with Julian. When I met with my supervisor I told him about this session. The first thing that my supervisor picked up was the mismatch between Julian's levels of enthusiasm and mine. I explained that I had seen this before and also my feeling that, although Julian was bouncing up and down like a puppy at the moment, the chances of his business being a success were minimal.

'What makes you say that?' he asked.

I reeled off some statistics about how many start-ups fail and I suggested that the fact that Julian didn't even have an idea for a new business yet meant that his chances of success were even lower.

I didn't need an invitation to continue as I went on to explain that I had coached many people who see setting up a business doing what they enjoy doing as being the ultimate form of career.

I remember being told once that if you choose a job you love then you will never have to work a day in your life. More and more people tout this as the dream but is it true? Once something becomes a job, it often ceases to become enjoyable. Our hobbies are enjoyable because they *aren't* a job. It's like that quote by Mark Twain: 'Work is what we are obliged to do. Play is what we are not obliged to do.'

'For some people, attempting to turn their passion into their career is a fast track to depression. They strip out the fun from their lives and potentially risk associating the thing they used to enjoy so much with a failed business.'

I then went on to tell him that this idea of nirvana isn't just restricted to those with big bank balances who can afford to write off a couple of years as a sabbatical should it all go wrong. I told him that I knew people who had taken out bank loans, double mortgages and put everything they have and more on the line in order to chase their dream.

'Wow. You've got some strong feelings there! Have you always felt that way about the self-employed?' my supervisor asked, half-jokingly.

'Of course not,' I said, a little bashfully. 'As you know I've coached many people who are setting up their own businesses but, the truth is, a lot of them recently have seen setting up a business as something they think they **should** do rather than what they want to do. And I've just seen too many people go into a new business without a really good idea or any real intrinsic passion and, in my view, you need both of those.'

'And you see Julian as another of those doomed to failure?' he asked.

'I'm not saying that he couldn't be a successful entrepreneur but I am saying that he has not got the ingredients for that particular recipe right now.'

'How quickly would you say you worked that out?' he asked me.

'Quite early on. To be honest, perhaps too early,' I reflected.

'Maybe even earlier than that,' my supervisor suggested. 'It sounds as though even Richard Branson might have had a hard time getting any support for a new business idea from you on that day.'

'Ouch,' I said as my professional pride took a hit. Thinking about it, I realised that I had become a little cynical recently and that possibly this had affected my neutrality with Julian. I had recently helped one of my clients to set up a new business that had failed and I reflected that this might be prejudicing my view of Julian's situation.

I resolved to make more of a conscious effort to treat each client as a unique case to be judged on its own merits.

Session Two

When Julian returned he was nowhere near as excited as he had been when he left the previous session. It emerged that this was because he had not decided what his business should be and this had left him deflated.

'I came up with a few ideas but nothing really clicked,' he said. 'Either there were already existing well-established businesses out there in that field or I didn't think there would be a big enough market for it.'

I had a choice to make as a coach and, given how biased I had been in our first session, I decided to put the options on the table and ask Julian how he would like to proceed.

'I can understand how that would feel frustrating but it's quite a normal reaction. It seems to me as though we have a choice as to how to proceed. We could use our coaching sessions to explore some of those options more fully, for example by exploring a niche for your business which might set you apart from the existing competition or by investigating market demand and developing a market proposition. You might find that by working these things through you begin to feel a bit more positive about your options,' I suggested. 'Alternatively, we could look at how else you might be able to live out your values and achieve greater fulfilment without setting up a business.'

'Such as what?' he asked.

'Well many people manage to create an environment at work that gives them many of the aspects of running a business without a lot of the risks - a sort of intrapraneurship if you like. Or we could look at other areas of your life to see if you could get some of the things which your job doesn't give you from elsewhere.'

'What do you think?' Julian asked me.

'I don't know you that well yet,' I explained, 'and this really is something that you should decide, not me. So let's see if we can work out what you think. The first question I would ask you is, when you think about setting up a business, do you think of this as something you would like to do, something you would love to do or something you think you should do?'

This was apparently a more powerful question than I thought it would be as Julian silently pondered this for what seemed a lengthy 20-30 seconds.

It's often tempting to fill the silence that follows a powerful question with another question but, more often than not, that interruption destroys the client's thought process.

In this instance, I was right to remain silent.

'I hate to admit it but I'm not one of those people who has always had a desire to own their own business. I don't think it would be something that I regretted not having done if I looked back on my life when I'm old,' he said eventually.

There was another pause and, once again, I fought the urge to speak and said nothing.

'I think I have looked at others who have gone down that route and made an assumption that it's the logical next step without really thinking whether it's something I want.'

Julian still hadn't answered my question directly, but he wasn't avoiding it and the reflection which had emerged was the important thing. I said to Julian, 'There was a psychologist called Albert Ellis who, among other things, coined the phrase *must*erbation *[Ref 39]* to explain the destructive thought pattern that we sometimes have whereby we say to ourselves that we *must* do something when actually that isn't strictly true. He was typically referring to things like feeling you *must* get revenge on a driver who cuts you up on the motorway, but I think the term could potentially be applied here.'

'Ellis felt that applying language like *must* is not helpful because you are effectively handing over control of your emotions to someone or something else rather than making a conscious choice about what to do and handle things in a more rational and helpful way.'

I could tell from Julian's face that he really liked this term and he also seemed to relate to the ideas behind it. I also reminded Julian that one of the very first things he had said to me in our first meeting included the word *'should'*, which might be another indicator of this type of unhelpful thinking.

Julian told me that he wondered what other options might be open to him in looking for a greater sense of fulfilment in his life. We agreed to start our exploration of this with a 'value alignment audit'.

We spent the rest of the session creating the tools for the audit – a simple sheet, based on the five values cards which Julian had previously selected. The sheet looked as follows:

	AUTONOMY	CHALLENGING PROBLEMS	CHANGE & VARIETY	INTEGRITY	MEANING-FUL WORK
MONDAY					
TUESDAY					
WEDNESDAY					
THURSDAY					
FRIDAY					

Julian's task over the next two weeks was to assess how much he found himself acting in alignment with his values at work. We talked through some options for Julian as to how he might like to complete the sheet including:

• A tally chart with a mark for each example.

• A smiley face, neutral face or sad face.

• Green, yellow, or red shading.

• A score out of 10 with 10 being perfect alignment and 0 being complete absence of alignment.

Julian decided that he would make an assessment once a day just before he left the office and use the smiley, neutral & sad face system. He seemed keen to do this audit and I was happy that the session appeared to have given him a little more insight and direction.

Session Three

This session was spent looking at and reflecting on the results of Julian's value-alignment audit of the last week. There was one clear pattern that jumped out at me when I looked at the sheet that Julian put in front of me.

'Wow. Thursday was a good day for you!' I said. 'Do you want to tell me about that?'

	AUTONOMY	CHALLENGING PROBLEMS	CHANGE & VARIETY	INTEGRITY	MEANING-FUL WORK
MONDAY	☹	☺	☹	😐	☹
TUESDAY	😐	☺	😐	☺	😐
WEDNESDAY	☹	😐	☹	😐	☹
THURSDAY	☺	☺	☺	☺	☺
FRIDAY	☹	😐	☹	😐	☹

'Well, Thursday was a complete break from the norm. We had a bit of a meltdown in production that caused a huge number of defects, unhappy customers and frustrated engineers. Nobody could work out why, but I thought it must be a process issue so I grabbed a couple of key engineers, commandeered a meeting room and we worked it out. It was brilliant.'

'What exactly was brilliant about it?' I asked.

'Well it wasn't the same old stuff that I get every day: it was mentally stimulating, I was in complete control of solving the problem and it was really important that we solved it.'

I could tell from both his general demeanour and what he was saying that he was completely energised. Just remembering the event seemed to be giving him a buzz.

'This is great,' I said. 'How would you feel about your job if you had more days like that?'

'I'd love it. I could happily stay working here forever if every day was like that,' he said. 'But it's not and it won't be,' he added.

'But if it were, then do you think you would feel fulfilled?' I asked.

'Yes.'

I wanted Julian to harness this vision of a desired future state for his job but needed to help him create a desired state that he believed was attainable. 'Would every day have to be like Thursday or would, say, one day a week be enough?' I asked.

Julian agreed that his initial statement was unrealistic and that actually a toned-down version would still be a fulfilling and exciting prospect for him. More importantly, it was a more realistic proposition. To me, this looked like a case of workplace redesign. We quite often work with managers who are looking for help in increasing the levels of engagement of a disgruntled or demotivated employee. An effective approach in such circumstances can be to coach the manager to experiment with the work environment to encourage greater intrinsic motivation.

A good place to start is Dan Pink's work on *Motivation 3.0 [Ref 40]*. Pink suggests that there are three elements necessary to create and sustain motivation – autonomy, mastery and purpose. It appeared to me that these were evident in Julian's decription of Thursday's events. I felt that if Julian could replicate and amplify these in his day-to-day working life then he would feel more fulfilled. However, as Julian was paying for this coaching himself, I did not automatically have access to Julian's manager. Instead, my strategy would be to coach Julian so that he felt able to approach his manager himself. First of all, I wanted to do a quick test to establish Julian's locus of control *[Ref 41]*.

I asked Julian to rate the degree to which he agreed or disagreed with a number of statements:

STATEMENT	SA	A	D	SD
Our society is run by a few people with a lot of power and there is not much the ordinary person can do about it.	1	2	3	4
Success hinges on being in the right place at the right time.	1	2	3	4
There will always be conflict in the world, however hard people work to stop it.	1	2	3	4
There is no point in voting, it won't change anything.	1	2	3	4
Everything which happens in life is predestined.	1	2	3	4
It's a waste of time trying to change people, they will always stay the same.	1	2	3	4
Whether I work hard or not it won't make any difference to how others assess my performance.	1	2	3	4
Leaders are born and not made.	1	2	3	4
Luck and chance play a key role in life.	1	2	3	4
Most of what happens in life is controlled by forces that we do not understand and can't control.	1	2	3	4

People who score mostly 1 and 2 are said to have a high external locus of control, believing that what happens to them is largely outside their control and is largely directed by outside agents, luck or fate. People who score mostly 3 or 4 are said to have a high internal locus of control, believing they have control over what happens to them through their own decisions and actions.

In order for any form of significant change to happen, clients need to have an appropriate level of belief that they have an internal locus of control.

Julian's scores indicated a moderate internal locus of control, which was a good sign. We spent the next few sessions working on developing his internal locus of control and developing a strategy for approaching, and ultimately influencing, his manager about changing Jeremy's working environment.

The main approach to developing a greater internal locus of control is to realise that you always have a choice – even if you choose to do nothing or don't like the choices in front of you, and even if that choice is limited to how you interpret an event. It is then useful to delay making a decision until you have developed a wider range of options as to how you might proceed.

The main focus in Julian's case was the language which Julian habitually used. Julian was accustomed to using absolutes such as *'always'*, *'completely'* and *'never'*. He also regularly found himself using phrases like *'I can't'*, *'it's impossible'* and *'I have no option'*. We worked on identifying these phrases and consciously changing them to phrases that emphasised his degree of control. So, for example, he would replace *'I can't'* with *'I choose not to'* and *'impossible'* with *'difficult'*.

This seemed strange and somewhat forced to Julian to begin with but soon became natural and had a huge impact on how he saw things. As one outcome of the coaching, Julian developed a sound, logical strategy to take to his manager. Julian was able to explain to his manager that he knew what motivated him and that he could add greater value to the organisation by becoming more involved with challenging and meaningful problems where he had autonomy. Julian's manager was very receptive, as people often are when employees proactively suggest ways in which the employee can add more value to their organisation. Julian's manager put him forward for a part-time role on the new cross-departmental, trouble-shooting team.

In our final coaching session, I reminded Julian of the reasons why he had initially said he had come to coaching and asked him whether he still felt he needed to set up his own business. His response was:

'I've realised that all I needed in order to feel fulfilled was to feel that I was adding value and being more myself at work. I also realised that this was as much my responsibility as my manager's and it was more in my control than I previously thought.'

Whenever we are doing something that does not meet our values and needs, we are likely to feel unfulfilled.

I congratulated Julian on having had the courage to confront the big question of fulfilment in his work and reminded him that he might well find himself searching for fulfilment at other times in his life. I said to Julian that my hope and anticipation was that, when this happened, Julian would have a greater understanding of his needs and values upon which to base his decisions. I also encouraged him to continue to take time out periodically to check whether his life was working for him and how far it was meeting his values and needs.

TOOLS AND TECHNIQUES

Our ability to question the meaning of things is perhaps one of the key characteristics which sets us apart from other animals. Our tendency to ponder, to philosophise and to look for a purpose and meaning in life has been instrumental in human evolution.

A desire to be part of a greater good and know that our efforts have a point is immensely valuable to people and society in general. It has led to great comfort, relief and peace for some, but can lead to endless frustration and dissatisfaction for others.

All of the greatest philanthropic acts in human history have arguably come from people looking to focus on something greater than their own individual journey in life. As we have developed more freedom in our material lives, the opportunity to look for a fulfilling career - rather than one simply to pay the bills - has increased.

This is perhaps the greatest example of personal reflection, which in itself is arguably our ultimate aim as coach. Therefore this certainly shouldn't be ignored or belittled. However, as we saw with Julian in the case study, there is a risk that clients have a sense that they *should* be doing something more worthwhile and fulfilling with their life without any clear sense of what that might be. Clients who appear to be leading materially comfortable lives but who feel that they should have a greater purpose in their lives and are unable to find such purpose or meaning can experience high levels of frustration and dissatisfaction.

In this section we share some techniques that we have used to help coach people whose trait of searching for fulfilment has become a trap.

Nirvana Letter

The best way to predict the future is to create it. The best way to create the future is to visualise it.

In his book *Coach Yourself To Success [Ref 42]*, Tom Preston describes a technique that his coach used with him many years ago and which he – and we – have been using very successfully with our clients ever since: The Nirvana Letter. In this technique the coach asks the client to imagine themselves 10 to 30 years from now, in their twilight years, when all their dreams for life have come true. Then the coach asks the client to write a letter to their best friend explaining in great detail what they have done in the time between now and then.

As with all of the visualisation techniques we have included in this book, the job of the coach is to keep the client associated and to encourage them to be as vivid, specific and reflective as possible. We also recommend that you emphasise to the client that, while they should keep within the bounds of relative reasonableness, the purpose of this exercise is for the client to act as if everything they have ever hoped for has already happened and to imagine that they are looking back on the most successful and fulfilling life they could have wished for.

The kinds of things that we encourage our clients to explore are:

- What kind of life have they led?

- What have they achieved in their career?

- What steps did they take to accomplish these achievements?

- What is the state of their family life?

- How have their hobbies or interests developed?

Tom Preston recommends starting the letter by describing the place where you are while writing the letter and specifying the date upon which you are writing it. Then work your way back from that moment to the present, outlining the major milestones along the way.

Powerful Coaching Question:
If you knew for a fact that you would be happy and content in twenty years time no matter what you did now, how would that change things for you?

---

50 Values

Helping your client to establish clarity regarding their values and to act more in alignment with those values can create an increased sense of fulfilment.

Ask your client to create their own personal list of values, perhaps using the following as a starting point. Write each value on a separate index card or print them out:

ACHIEVEMENT	HELPING OTHERS	QUALITY
ADVANCEMENT	HONESTY	RECOGNITION
CHALLENGE	INDEPENDENCE	RELIGION
CHANGE	INFLUENCING OTHERS	REPUTATION
COMMUNITY	INNER HARMONY	RESPONSIBILITY
COMPETENCE	INTEGRITY	SECURITY
COMPETITION	INVOLVEMENT	SELF-RESPECT
COOPERATION	JOB TRANQUILLITY	SOPHISTICATION
CREATIVITY	KNOWLEDGE	STABILITY
DECISIVENESS	LEADERSHIP	STATUS
DEMOCRACY	LOYALTY	SUPERVISING OTHERS
EFFECTIVENESS	MEANINGFUL WORK	WEALTH
EFFICIENCY	NATURE	WISDOM
EXCELLENCE	PERSONAL DEVELOPMENT	WORK UNDER PRESSURE
EXCITEMENT	FREEDOM	WORK WITH OTHERS
FRIENDSHIPS	POWER AND AUTHORITY	WORKING ALONE
TIMELINESS	PRIVACY	

Then ask the client to select the ones that they most associate themselves with and to discard the rest. Ask the client to repeat this process until they have narrowed it down to six values.

Looking at the six selected values ask your client to state how much, on a scale of 1-10, they believe they act in alignment with each of them.

Finally, ask the client to state what specifically they can and will do to increase their alignment scores.

Powerful Coaching Question:
How much do you believe in the statement 'We all have the potential to be whatever we want to be'?

The Caterpillar Question

'Who are you?'

In Alice in Wonderland, the caterpillar asks Alice this fundamental question and, just as Alice struggled to answer this question, so do many people who are searching for fulfilment.

Jung claimed that *'We are what we do, not what we say we'll do'* and therefore our actions and behaviours, not our intentions, are the best definition of who we are.

This technique requires a certain amount of trust and safety within the coaching relationship but can be very powerful. Introduce the client to the premise above and then ask them the following question:

'Based on all the actions and behaviours of your life so far, how would you objectively define yourself?'

Most clients will answer a slightly different question to the one you have just asked and will tend to over-inflate or undervalue their worth. The coach's job is to facilitate the client arriving at as objective and realistic a definition as possible.

Some examples of realistic definitions are:

Someone with good intentions but who never really hits the heights.

A helpful person whose desire to help others has held them back.

An idealist who always does the right thing but does not do what they want to do.

A perfectionist who always does things right but not always the right things.

Once the client has a realistic statement of their current definition ask them to re-write the message that they send out to the world, creating their ideal definition.

Then encourage the client to look at what they need to do in order to make those changes for themselves.

Powerful Coaching Question:
How could you increase the meaning of what you are currently doing without a drastic change?

THE INTERVIEW

Eve Jardine-Young

Having a sense of purpose can play an important part in human motivation and can completely change a client's feelings towards 'work'. As the old saying goes, 'If you can find a job you love then you'll never work a day in your life' and this is a goal for which many people strive. There are also those who not only find their own sense of fulfilment but also pro-actively seek to instill a sense of fulfilment in others.

Our interviewee for this chapter, Ms. Eve Jardine-Young, is Principal of Cheltenham Ladies' College - a leading all-girl independent boarding and day school that has just received the highest possible grading in all areas from the Independent Schools Inspectorate.

This interview is a good example of how interwoven our traits often are. You might say that there were elements of perfectionism, Impostor Syndrome, procrastination, people pleasing and performance anxiety sprinkled throughout our chat. However, the trait that came through most strongly of all was that of a desire for fulfilment; not just a desire for her own fulfilment but a desire to guide her students to finding their own sense of fulfilment in life.

Having trained as an engineer, Eve Jardine-Young began her teaching career in 1994 at Radley College, later moving to Epsom College and Blundell's School in Devon before taking up her current position as Principal of Cheltenham Ladies' College. As our interview reveals, changing professions was a big part of Eve's journey to fulfilment and she has since worked hard to incorporate that sense of fulfilment into her day-to-day work.

'Cheltenham Ladies' College prepared me well for a man's world but it didn't prepare me for a woman's world.'

This comment from an alumna strongly resonated with Eve Jardine-Young, the Principal of one of the most prestigious and successful schools not just in the UK but the world.

Cheltenham Ladies' College has a 160 year tradition of preparing girls to break into a traditionally male-dominated world and, with alumnae including Clare Marx, who has recently become the first female to become President of the Royal College of Surgeons, Carolyn Kirby, the first woman to be appointed President of the Law Society, and Rachel Lomax, the first woman Deputy Governor of the Bank of England among others, it must be argued that they have been successful. However, in a rapidly changing world, Eve believes that the school now has both an opportunity and a responsibility to prepare the students for a different world.

'The generation starting out in the workplace now has sometimes been considered work-shy, expecting too much for what they are prepared to put in. The employers we speak to feel differently. If engaged with and managed well, they are just as motivated and driven. On the whole though, they are less materialistic and more often need to be clear about a sense of purpose and meaning to their careers to be fully satisfied and committed to that work in the longer term. The young people I see are idealistic, discriminating and really want to make a difference.'

'When I went through the intense interview process for this job, including being interviewed by a panel of students, I was forced to really think about what my vision was for education.'

Eve explains that there is no point educating people 'to the factory gates' but rather there now needs to be a process of educating them for their whole lives.

'I want us to think *what's the world like, and what's it going to be like*', before deciding what to teach. These girls will probably be working great-grandmothers at age 80 with no pension. They will need to be constantly learning and re-learning throughout their whole life, so they will have to intrinsically enjoy learning.'

She tells me of a conversation with a leadership coach who reports working with professionals in law and finance in their late thirties and early forties, who, despite having all the trappings of success, are not actually happy because they feel a deeper hollowness inside.

'The fact that they have the house, the car and everything else shows that they made good choices at one level but if they aren't at peace with those choices, if they've made them to avoid upsetting other people or 'fitting in' for example, then they are effectively bad choices. My girls will probably live to 100 or 120 and that's a long time to be unhappy. So I see my job as helping them become comfortable with making holistic decisions and valuing the ability to make decisions that are right for them.'

When I ask her why she cares about how hollow these children are when they reach 80 or 100 years old, I can tell that this isn't the practiced spiel that she would give to prospective new parents.

'Well, on their way to 80, they will be 40, 50, 60 and they will be our leaders, influencers and decision-makers of the world. They will be the ones shaping the society that I will become less and less empowered in as I grow old.'

We then diverge into a discussion about how it is all too easy to become disillusioned with society and she worries about the messages that her girls get from the world.

'All of the traditional pillars of society that we thought we could trust are crumbling around us. It started with some disillusionment with the monarchy, then there were paedophiles in the church – and protected by the church. Then politicians were all fiddling their expenses, the ice caps are melting, the polar bears are dying and our TV celebrities are going to jail for abuse.'

Eve tells me that it would be very easy to adopt a bleak sense of nihilism at times and think 'What's the point? Everybody's flawed' but the one thing that continues to inspire her is how the children aren't getting dragged down; they are still inspired to change the world.

'So do the children restore your faith in the world?' I ask.

'Absolutely,' she says, and then tells me how five of her senior students recently set up a charity named *Empower Her Voice*, completely out of their own initiative, campaigning to empower disadvantaged women worldwide. One of the founders, herself originally from Iran, cited her recent visit to Iran as motivation for the beginning of this movement. When she was there she spent time with a girl of similar age who was beaten by her father for daring to apply to study at university.

Have children always been an inspiration to her? Is that why she got into teaching?

'I was an engineer to begin with and I remember sitting in the office all day, scheduling reinforced steel. I was looking at the clock every twenty minutes and wishing the day away. I had little interaction with anyone and remember thinking 'I can't do this every day'.'

She tells me how she had always dismissed the idea of being a teacher due to the stammer that she has had since childhood.

'I thought that the last thing you do if you have a stammer is stand in front of a class of teenagers! But I wanted to test my assumption and so enrolled on a month-long course of Teaching English as a Foreign Language and, as soon as I was in front of a class, I was fluent!'

She tells me how this unblocked the latent anxiety that had previously paralysed her, stopping her from taking a part in the school plays, public speaking and many other things that she could have done at school. Looking back she believes she was fluent in front of a class because, for the first time, she was at peace with herself and was doing something congruent with who she was.

She also quickly realised that she got a buzz from helping others get excited about their potential and that being a teacher gave her a 'sort of vicarious achievement'.

'The spontaneous letters I would receive from students telling me how much I had helped them gave me an immense feeling of fulfilment and I never found myself looking at the clock when I was teaching.'

As her career has developed, I wonder if Eve's sources of fulfilment have evolved too. She talks passionately about developing innovative working practices to help close the gender gap and ensure that there is no disconnect between the messages the school is sending to the students.

'On the one hand, we are telling them 'you can do anything so go out there and take on the world' but on the other hand we aren't yet really leading the way imaginatively enough with family-friendly employment practices that help these girls change society.'

Eve tells me of plans to explore links with local crèches run in line with the school pick up times, greater encouragement of paternity leave, potentially longer maternity leave with more permanent cover and other plans to 'reduce the disconnect' and I can see how seriously she takes her position, not just as a steward of the educational and business facets of the school but also as a role-model for the children.

'I believe if we practice what we preach to the girls then they will grow up to expect and demand these fairer practices; they will make choices to make them happen and they will be not just more successful but happier too. This is how society will change.'

'It's one thing preparing women to go out and take on the world but they also need to be able to have a conversation with their husband or partner about how they will jointly handle the responsibilities of the family, for example.'

So if Eve now gets her fulfilment from being a role model and inspiration to the next generation of world-changers, helping them to be not only successful but also fulfilled, what advice would she give a student who asked her the secret of fulfilment?

'I think it's knowing how to be content and that stems from being aware of how we make decisions and being both emotionally articulate and aware.'

CHAPTER TWELVE

Coping with Loss

'Every one of us is losing something precious to us. Lost opportunities, lost possibilities, feelings we can never get back again. That's part of what it means to be alive.'

HARUKI MURAKAMI

THE CASE STUDY

'I'm not sure I will ever get over this.'

Mary cried for most of the first session. She had phoned me to book an appointment on the recommendation of a friend and I learned that she would be funding the coaching with money she had received from a settlement agreement when she lost her job.

During the session I didn't really do much other than sit with Mary and let her cry. From time to time she managed a few, fairly incoherent, words. I learned that she had worked for the same company for 20 years and was a very conscientious employee. For reasons unknown to Mary they had decided to let her go and came up with a settlement agreement for her. I knew she felt like she was 'finished' and 'on the scrapheap'. I heard that she was approaching 50 and had no idea whether she would ever get another job. She kept asking herself 'Why me?' because she didn't understand what she had done to deserve the redundancy.

I really felt for Mary. She was distraught and bewildered. We agreed to meet again in a couple of weeks, but I doubted whether I had been of any use to her at all. I had said no more than a few words in two hours. As she left, her parting words were 'I'm not sure I'll ever get over this.'

Supervision

I went to my supervisor for guidance about whether this was a case for coaching or for counselling. I also knew that I wanted to rescue Mary, which was my repeating pattern as a coach. I had wanted to start creating a list of action points to move her towards getting a new job, but I also knew that I had successfully resisted this desire and that I had succeeded in giving Mary the gift of time and attention. I really didn't know, however, whether this had made any difference to her.

Through talking with my supervisor I was reminded of the 'Change Curve'.

THE KÜBLER-ROSS CHANGE CURVE

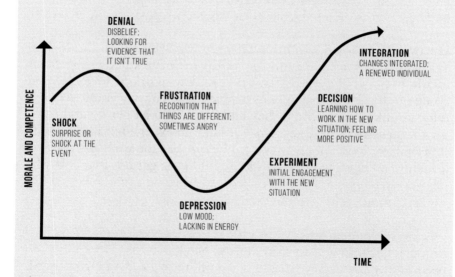

This model was developed by Elisabeth Kübler-Ross in her book *On Death and Dying* [Ref 43], but the results of her work can also be applied to any kind of loss such as redundancy, retirement, or divorce.

There is no prescribed time for someone to stay at any one stage of the Kübler-Ross Change Curve; they will work through the stages at the necessary pace for the individual.

There is no prescribed time for an individual to stay at any one stage of the Kübler-Ross Change Curve; each individual will work through the stages at the pace appropriate for them, and progress is not linear.

My supervisor suggested that it could be useful to share the model with Mary as it might help her to normalise her response.

He also reminded me that there is no point trying to coach someone when they are in 'survival mode'. When a client is stressed and in survival mode, their strong emotions can hijack their thinking and they can find themselves unable to think rationally, objectively or strategically. A coach may wish to encourage their client to reflect, plan, consider options, try to take an objective view of the situation, receive feedback and think ahead. When a coach encounters someone under stress who is operating in survival mode the coach has to help the client back into competency mode before coaching can begin. This can mean one of two things:

- The coach creating a safe space and listening to the client with empathy and unconditional positive regard until the client is ready to start thinking about moving forwards.

- Proposing that the client find a trained counsellor to help them to deal with their loss and return for coaching when the counselling has brought the client to a more resourceful place.

My supervisor and I discussed whether I should refer Mary for counselling or continue working with her myself *[Ref 44]*. He asked me whether I felt competent and comfortable to continue with the sessions. I did and I felt that listening to Mary was the most useful thing I could do in the early stages of her loss.

In Gerard Egan's book *The Skilled Helper [Ref 45]*, he proposes that the first stage of any helping relationship is 'Exploring the Problem'. He suggests that the client will often feel confused and overwhelmed by issues at this stage. The client wants to explore the problem without being judged and they are looking to feel safe in the coaching relationship.

The coach's role involves:

- Listening.
- Empathising.
- Demonstrating understanding.
- Summarising.
- Clarifying.
- Checking.
- Building rapport.

The coach should avoid interpretation, solution finding or goal setting at this stage.

My supervisor raised some concerns about Mary's state of mind and urged me to watch out for persistent signs of depression. These might include:

BEHAVIOURAL SIGNS	CHANGES IN THINKING	FEELINGS
DECREASED ACTIVITY	I CAN'T COPE	DEPRESSED
DECREASED SOCIALISING	THERE'S NO POINT	HOPELESS
DECREASED SELF CARE	I CAN'T STAND IT ANY MORE	HELPLESS
INCREASED RELIANCE ON FOOD, ALCOHOL OR DRUGS	I WISH IT WOULD ALL STOP	EMPTY
DECREASED MEMORY	IT'S POINTLESS	WORTHLESS
DECREASED CONCENTRATION	I CAN'T DO ANYTHING ABOUT IT	ISOLATED
EARLY MORNING WAKING		SCARED

We agreed that if there was no change next time I met Mary, I would offer Mary the alternatives of either being referred to a counsellor or continuing to work with me. My supervisor felt that Mary would probably elect to continue seeing me as she had already invested in our coaching relationship. I was clear, however, that if, at any point, I felt that I was outside my area of competence, I would let both Mary and my supervisor know.

Sessions Two and Three

Session two followed the same lines as the first session, but although Mary cried for the entire session, she stopped from time to time to go over the events that led up to her being 'managed out of the business.'

Reliving the event is an important part of coming to terms with what has happened and realising that life will never be the same as it was before.

I knew that it was usual for a bereaved person to talk repeatedly about the event and the feelings caused by it, so I resisted any temptation to problem solve or even to ask questions for clarification. I simply listened to Mary without interruption. I also reassured myself that being listened to and understood was exactly what Mary needed at this time and that this was the most valuable thing that I could give her.

Attempting to move Mary forward or start planning her next steps would be following my agenda. Mary was not ready to start thinking about rebuilding her life or her career because she needed time to grieve for her loss. It seemed she was using the session for a 'time-limited' expression of her loss because when the session came to an end she stopped crying, thanked me and arranged the next session in a business-like manner.

There was some change in Mary when we met for our third session. She said that she had found our first couple of sessions really helpful. Since she was paying for my time she hadn't felt bad about crying and talking about herself and her situation for two hours.

'I just don't feel like I can do that with anyone else. After all, I have only lost a job – not a loved one or my health – and I think people are running out of patience with me for that reason. I understand that, but it doesn't make any difference to how I feel. This has hit at the very core of me. I feel discarded. I need to keep talking about it but I can see other people starting to roll their eyes when I mention it again. It has been great to be able to speak to you about it, knowing that I am paying you to 'shut up and listen!"

Loss is loss. If we are suddenly separated from something we hold dear and which forms part of our identity this can be an extremely unsettling and disorienting event.

I explained this to Mary and reassured her that she was right not to judge her own feelings on the basis of other peoples' interpretations of her situation.

I encouraged Mary to feel comfortable expressing any thoughts or feelings in our session and then sat back and listened to her some more. In this session Mary talked again about the events that had led up to her job loss. I learned that her company had got a new leadership team and had changed direction.

'Everything was fine until I got a new line manager,' she said ruefully.

Mary told me that soon after being appointed her new line manager had started to suggest things were not working out with Mary. Mary was told she was not a strategic thinker and, after years of positive appraisals, she was no longer seen as having the qualities required to work at her current level. Before long the company had presented Mary with an exit package in the form of a settlement agreement.

'I was dispatched from the business without so much as a thank you.'

I sensed a little more anger and frustration in Mary and wondered if she was moving along the change curve from the 'shock' and 'denial' stages. I decided to take a bit of a chance

'What would you like to say to your line manager?' I asked.

She jumped at the opportunity to tell him exactly what she thought about how he and the whole organisation had mismanaged the situation. She was able to articulate clearly what her employer could have done differently and how that would have helped her. Mary even expressed her views about how the company was moving in the wrong direction and that this would eventually have disastrous consequences for the business.

At the end of the session Mary looked at me and, for the first time since I had met her, gave me a half-smile. 'That felt good,' she said. 'Doing that made me think that I don't want to work for people like that.'

Often when people find themselves reaching the anger stage of the change curve, they look for someone to blame for their loss.

Sometimes they turn that blame on themselves but I was pleased to see that Mary was looking outside herself to apportion blame. This seemed a healthy sign. I was very happy to continue with Mary as a client.

Sessions Four to Six

Before our fourth session, Mary had emailed me to say that she had decided to view this event as a positive experience and wanted to use her time with me to explore other options in her life. I was delighted to receive this email as it was more evidence that Mary was moving in the right direction. By the time our session came around, I was very excited about it.

'Right,' she said, in a very determined way. 'How should we do this?'

I was slightly concerned that this might be too soon and that her apparent determination was merely a fragile façade, but I decided to press on while making a mental note to keep a watchful eye for signs that this might be too much too soon for Mary.

I felt that we had two clear choices as to how to proceed. One was to focus on Mary getting another job, and the other was to look at other aspects of Mary's life. I didn't want to influence Mary's decision too directly but I said to her that, given how dedicated she had been to her work for the last 20 years, I wondered whether there were other areas of her life that might have been neglected a little. Mary thought about it before replying. 'I think I need to live a little. I'm financially stable and so I don't have to jump straight back into the job market. Let's leave talking about work for a bit.'

While I probably couldn't explain why, this felt like the right thing to do at the time. I asked Mary to take a little time and think about the following scenarios in order to come up with a list of things that she liked to do:

• You have come into a small amount of money that you weren't expecting. What do you spend it on?

• What did you previously really enjoy doing that you haven't done for ages?

• You have a completely free weekend, what would you do?

• What has always been on your personal 'to do' list that you've never got round to doing?

• You are snowed in the house but have all the supplies you need. How would you spend your time?

- You have to put one enjoyable thing to do in every day of your calendar for the next week. What would you schedule for yourself?

- You receive four tickets to an event or show of your choice. Who do you take and what do you go to see?

- You can transport yourself to any place in the world. Where would you go?

- You can get together with anybody you've ever met. Who would you choose and what would you do?

- You have access to an expert teacher who is offering to teach you a new skill. What would you like to learn?

Mary seemed to enjoy this exercise and quickly came up with a list of 20 things that she would enjoy doing. I then asked Mary to pick a couple of these things that she would most like to do and to think about how she might make them happen. I asked Mary to analyse in each case how much it would cost Mary, what she would need to do to make it happen, how quickly she could realistically achieve this, and whether there were any risks that she would need to bear in mind or consider.

Mary picked three things to focus on - visiting some old friends, going on a photography course and joining a yoga class. We agreed that we would check on her progress over the next few sessions.

Session Seven

When I remembered the woman who had spent all of the first two sessions crying, Mary now seemed like a completely different person. She was full of energy, zest and self-belief. While this rejuvenation process had been fun for both of us, I felt it could now be the right time to ask Mary about her future work plans. I was fairly sure that Mary was not in a position to retire just yet and I felt we could channel Mary's positive outlook and energy into the potentially difficult process of getting back into the job market.

'You're right. I know I can't live the life of Riley forever. It has been great to rediscover things that I enjoyed and to find new aspects of life that I previously hadn't time for. When I think about it, though, I actually do miss the challenge of work.'

I reminded Mary that, of course, she did not need to make a choice between one or the other, she could have both a working life and a healthy set of interests outside work.

I walked Mary through the Career Time Line exercise *[see Chapter One: Impostor Syndrome]* to look at how she had gone about getting jobs in the past. We then did a personal audit to clarify her strengths and also ran the 50 Values exercise *[see Chapter Eleven: Searching for Fulfilment]* to look at how she would evaluate which jobs and companies might match her values. As a result of all of these exercises, Mary decided that she would like to train to be a counsellor.

'I have always enjoyed helping people and been able to empathise with almost anyone. Now that I have gone through something traumatic I believe these strengths of mine have been enhanced. I like the idea of learning - not just learning new skills but also learning more about myself. I think re-training to become a counsellor would be really rewarding and would give me a positive goal to aim for.'

I was really pleased and I felt that Mary could make a really good counsellor. My job now as coach was to help Mary find the path towards her goal. I asked Mary what resources she needed to make this happen and where she could access these resources. These included the need for Mary to find out what professional training options there were, as well as support Mary to evaluate those options and make decisions.

I asked Mary whether there might be any impact on her family during her training period – in terms of time, money, focus etc. - and the next three sessions were spent fleshing this plan out.

Conclusion

After her tenth session, we decided to cut down the frequency of our sessions to a more ad hoc basis with a different emphasis. As Mary was now looking to become a counsellor, she felt she had more need of guidance from someone willing to share their experience in a helping profession and so asked me to change roles and to be her mentor instead of her coach. I agreed to this.

I often look back to my initial sessions with Mary and remember doubting whether I should have taken her on as a client. I am really glad I made an informed judgement to continue working with Mary. This case always reminds me of the restorative power of listening and that you can never tell where a coaching engagement might lead.

TOOLS AND TECHNIQUES

In the case study Mary had experienced a common form of loss – redundancy. Although Mary felt she had less right to be grieving than someone who had lost a loved one or their health, losing anything that helps define who we are can be devastating and disorienting. For Mary her career was a huge part of her identity and having this taken away left her bereft.

While this is not a trait like the others in this book, coaches will often have clients who need support following some form of loss. Sometimes all that is needed is somebody to listen and empathise, while sometimes the client will need some help in getting back on track or finding a new way forward in their lives.

A Thinking Environment

Listening to your client with rapt attention, warmth and positive regard is a skill that all coaches should practice.

This kind of listening – we sometimes call it *dynamic listening* – means having the ability to listen in silence and with the powerful belief that giving the client the gift of time and interest will be of service to them. It is an art that many people have never really learned.

Dynamic listening is not about listening with the purpose of formulating solutions for your client or to enable the coach to provide advice or information. Instead such listening and attention will give your client the safety and confidence to explore their thoughts and feelings and to come up with their own solutions.

Most clients experience a need to 'tell their story' at the beginning of a coaching relationship. This process helps them communicate their experiences to the coach and make sense of their experiences for themselves. Hearing their own thoughts spoken out loud and being listened to without hurry or judgement is in itself an opportunity for learning and growth.

When a client experiences a loss they often have a need to confide the story of their loss to others. This is a recognised part of the process of recovery which helps the client put back together the pieces of their life. Telling and retelling the story allows the client to make sense of the 'new world' in which they find themselves. Allowing a client to express their emotions without judgement is an important part of the process of recovery from loss.

We advocate the use of a *Thinking Environment* as described in Nancy Kline's book *Time To Think [Ref 46]*. A Thinking Environment is a set of ten components, or behaviours, that enhance people's thinking so that they are able to clearly reflect on their thoughts and become clear about what they want to do. In a Thinking Environment, a coach listens with:

- Attention.

- Equality.

- Ease.

- Appreciation.

- Encouragement.

- Feelings.

- Information.

- Diversity.

- Incisive Questions.

- Place.

'How do I know for sure that what I am about to say will be of more value than what they are about to think?'
Nancy Kline

In a Thinking Environment, sometimes the coach makes no comments, suggestions or verbal interventions but powerfully creates the right environment for the client to think for himself or herself.

When this happens, the client comes up with their own unique solutions to their own unique problems with the coaching intervention largely consisting of dynamic listening and generative attention. This is based on one of Nancy's strongly held beliefs that the mind that generates the problem can also generate the solution.

> **Powerful Coaching Question:**
> I am sorry this has happened to you. Would you like to talk about it?

20 Things I Like To Do

When coping with loss, it can be empowering to reflect on your values, and what has previously given you joy.

This technique can also be used to help with career planning, retirement planning or work-life balance. The objective is to help your client rekindle their interest in activities that previously provided them with joy, relaxation and balance and also to look at activities that they may previously had never found time for.

Start by asking your client to list 20 things that they like to do. These could be as simple as 'taking a walk in the park', as expensive as 'travelling first class to a foreign destination', as creative as 'painting a landscape picture' or as potentially emotional as 'looking at old family photographs and reminiscing'. It's not essential for clients to list 20 items, but the more the client can think of the better so be prepared to give your client plenty of time and perhaps prompt them with questions.

For each activity ask your client to consider some of the following questions:

- How long has it been since you last did this?

- How did you feel when you did this?

- What do you imagine this would be like?

- Does it cost money or is it free?

- If you had to book one of them into your calendar now, which would it be?

- Is this something you would do alone or with someone?

- When is the soonest you could do one of these things?

- Is it fast or slow paced?

- Is it mind or body related?

- Is it job related?

- When would you like to do this next?

Powerful Coaching Question:
How can I help you with this?

Dérive

Getting clients away from their regular environment can open up their thinking and give them fresh perspectives.

Dérive is a technique which originated from the work of psycho-geographer Guy Debord in his *Introduction to a Critique of Urban Geography [Ref 47]*.

The dérive, or drift, was defined as the 'technique of locomotion without a goal', in which 'one or more persons during a certain period drop their usual motives for movement and action, their relations, their work and leisure activities, and let themselves be drawn by the attractions of the terrain and the encounters they find there'.

We have used this in our coaching practice. One beauty of this technique is that it can be used in the outside environment, in the open countryside or in an urban environment – even a shopping mall. This can be particularly useful if you are coaching corporate clients and want to get them away from the building in which they spend most of their time.

The coach begins by walking alongside their client and asking them to 'drift' or wander without a goal. Encourage the client to take in the sights, sounds, sensations and smells around them and invite them to notice which particular things are capturing their attention. Maybe the client is drawn to a tree, or a particular person, or the rubbish in the street, or birds in the sky, or the sound of traffic. Invite the client to be aware of all their senses. When the client's attention is drawn to a particular thing, let them tell you what it is and then begin a coaching discussion about this sight, sound or experience. The coach may explore with the client whether what they have noticed relates to any aspect of their life or thinking. What the client has noticed will often have some metaphorical or symbolic purpose of which the client may not be conscious.

'What we see depends mainly on what we look for.'
John Lubbock

The coaching principle that underpins this is the idea of projection. Freudian psychotherapy suggests that we tend unconsciously to project our own thoughts or feelings onto other people or things. An example we encountered when working with a recently divorced client was that the client noticed a number of birds sitting on a telephone wire and one solitary bird on the end of the wire with no other birds next to it.

This might also be considered in relation to the notion of the Reticular Activating System (RAS) [see chapter five on cynicism]. The RAS will notice things that we believe are important to us at any given time, without our conscious awareness *[Ref 48]*. In the example above, the recently divorced client had separation on his mind and so was more likely to notice examples of separation and isolation.

Powerful Coaching Question:
What have you learned from this experience?

THE INTERVIEW

Steve Cunningham

I met Steve a few years ago when I engaged him as a motivational speaker for an association of coaches. It can be difficult to inspire and motivate an audience of coaches who seek to provide inspiration and motivation to others for a living but I remember the powerful impact Steve had on all of us.

The world's fastest blind man, with multiple world records to his name, Steve Cunningham has been described as the most inspirational man alive. Where he was once offered a life of selling matches on a street corner, he now works with businesses and schools around the UK to help motivate and inspire people of all ages and abilities to reach their own potential.

It was the mid-seventies when Steve lost his sight, aged just twelve. He says that at first he thought that losing his sight was 'a killer' for him. There was very little support, advice or information available for him or his parents. Steve had to try to make sense of what had happened to him on his own.

Steve was a talented schoolboy footballer at Aston Villa and had wanted to turn professional but, when he went blind, this opportunity was cruelly taken away from him. People regularly told him what he couldn't do when he lost his sight. He was denied opportunities and decisions were made for him based purely on his disability rather than his ability.

While Steve recognises that there was no guarantee he would have achieved his dream if he had remained sighted, losing this aspect of his life and his identity could have been crushing for him. However, the story of how he changed his outlook is inspiring.

It was his talent and interest in football that gave Steve the initial break he needed. One of the Aston Villa players, goalkeeper John Burridge, took Steve under his wing and together they developed a way for Steve to continue playing his beloved game by designing an innovative type of football filled with peas, rice and small ball bearings so that players could hear rather than see the football.

Steve says that Burridge was 'like a god' to him.

'He phoned me regularly, visited me, took me to games and practice matches and introduced me to the other players.'

'At the time, I didn't realise the positive effect that this was having on me but eventually I came to realise that I had skills that other people didn't have. I had feet and a brain that worked really well and I had real speed. Football was my thing and it gave me a sense of self-esteem and a 'can do' attitude so I became competitive.'

Steve is a great example of someone who shifted his perspective to focus more on what opportunities he now had rather than dwell too much on what he had lost. It took time but eventually Steve came to view his blindness as merely an inconvenience and turned his thoughts more and more to what he could do.

Steve remembers his Mum saying to him a couple of years after he lost his sight that she thought he had gone blind for a reason. As he reflects on his life to date, Steve admits that he has now come to believe this himself.

'I look at the things I have achieved and believe I have had a far more rewarding life than the one I would have had,' he says.

While football was Steve's natural starting point, it didn't stop there. Steve turned his attention even more to his love of speed and went on to achieve five world speed records, setting the World 100m Junior Sprint Record in 1977 and then the World Blind Land Speed Record in 1999. Not satisfied with land speed records, he set the World Offshore and Inshore Powerboat Records in 2000 before setting the World Record for a blind person circumnavigating the UK in a light aircraft in 2004.

Steve is clear that he didn't go out to break these records for personal gain but rather to show people that it is possible to break barriers. He is a warm, humorous and compassionate man who, throughout the conversation, shows genuine interest in me and takes time to ask me about myself.

One strong theme that comes across is that Steve is passionately committed to changing attitudes towards blindness and other 'disabilities'. The fact that people were all too ready to point out what he couldn't do still sits heavily with him and he has taken it upon himself to inspire the rest of us to see that we can help ourselves and others to do more than we think we can.

'If you give people confidence, then the right mental attitude will get them to the next level' he says.

'What is the right mental attitude though?'

'There is a difference between seeing and looking, just as there is between listening and hearing and it is more about your attitude and your abilities than your disabilities.'

Steve once applied for a job and sent two CVs that were exactly the same except that one mentioned his blindness while the other, sent under a pseudonym, did not. Only the latter resulted in an invitation to interview. Steve is still very frustrated by the ignorance of others and society towards blindness and disability.

Steve comes across as a man on a mission and this mission has not only served him well but many others as well. He has used the power of reframing to his advantage by focusing on the opportunities that became available to him as a result of his loss. He has also been driven to reframe the perceptions of society as well.

At the end of our time together, Steve had once again inspired me with his response to the loss of his sight and I had taken away some clear messages for dealing with setbacks. He had challenged my perceptions of disability and ability and motivated me to focus on my strengths and what I have got going for me in my life. He had inspired me to set myself more challenging goals and, above all, to celebrate life. Not bad going for a 45-minute interview.

'Blindness is a state of mind,' Steve insists. 'I am not a blind man. I am a man who can't see. It amazes me now how many people think that blindness is an illness. It isn't – it's a condition which you learn to manage and to live with.'

TECHNIQUE MATRIX

In each of the chapters of the book we have selected three techniques that you may find helpful when coaching somebody with that trait. Many of the techniques in this book are applicable in many situations though and so, below is a matrix that maps which techniques can be useful for each of the traits. You can also use this matrix as a reference to locate specific techniques within the book.

TRAIT

TECHNIQUE	Coping With Loss	Cynicism	Driven By Fear	Fierce Independence	Going To Excess	Impostor Syndrome	Ostrich Syndrome	People Pleasing	Perfectionism	Performance Anxiety	Procrastination	Searching For Fulfilment
20 Things I Like To Do	p.350	•	•	•	•			•				•
360° Feedback		•		•	•	•	p.206	•	•	•	•	
5-5-5		•		•		p.24	•	•		•		
50 Values		•	•		•			•				p.323
Anchoring	•	•		•	•	•				p.295	•	
Assertiveness Practice							•	p.55		•	•	
A Thinking Environment	p.348	•								•		•
Attribute Shopping		•		•	p.80	•		•	•		•	
Career Timeline	•	•	•	•	•	•	p.22			•	•	•
Coach The System	•	•	p.108	•	•	•	•	•	•	•	•	•
Creative Goal-Setting		p.172							•	•	•	•
Define Perfection							•		p.235	•		
Dependency Check				p.110				•				
Dérive	p.352	•								•		•
Dream Journaling		•		•	•	•	p.204			•	•	•
Emotional Positions	•	p.139	•							•		•
Energy Investment Model		p.129						•				
Good Boss, Bad Boss		p.141		•	•	•	•			•		
Human Givens Audit		•	•	•	p.71			•				•

TRAIT

TECHNIQUE

TECHNIQUE	Coping With Loss	Cynicism	Driven By Fear	Fierce Independence	Going To Excess	Impostor Syndrome	Ostrich Syndrome	People Pleasing	Perfectionism	Performance Anxiety	Procrastination	Searching For Fulfilment
Identity-Based Goals		•		•	•	•		•	•	•	p.266	•
Inner Boardroom				•	•	•	•	•	p.237	•		
Johari Window		•		•	•		•	p.191		•		
Know How		•	p.168	•	•	•	•	•	•		•	•
Leadership Styles		•		•	•				•	p.221		
Locus of Control	•	•										p.317
Low Frustration Tolerance		•		•	•						p.255	
Magazine Interview			•	•	•	p.27					•	•
Miracle Question			p.101									
Mindfulness	•	•		•	p.82	•	•		•	•		•
Modelling Internal Strategies		•	•	p.84		•			•	•	•	
Nirvana Letter	•	•	•								•	p.321
Perceptual Positions	•	•		•	•	•	•	p.53	•	•		
Performance Impact Exposure		•	p.96						•	•		
Positive Psychology	•	p.142	•			•			•	•		•
Power Pose		•				•				p.292		
Prepare and Practice						•				p.293		
Present Moment Focus	•									•	p.282	•
Push Me Pull You		•	p.170	•	•						•	•
Relationships Audit	•	•		•	•			p.56				
Shrink It Down	•	•				•			•	•	p.268	
Step Up & Speak Up			•	•	•	•					p.264	•
Stretch Zone	•	•		•	•		•			•	p.286	•
The Caterpillar Question			•				•		•			p.325
Try Something New	•	•					p.202					
Walk A Mile		•	p.107			•			•	•	•	•
Wheel Of Life		•		•	•	•			•	p.239	•	

REFERENCES & FURTHER READING

IMPOSTOR SYNDROME

1. Clance, P & Imes, S, (1978). The Imposter Phenomenon in High Achieving Women: Dynamics and Therapeutic Intervention. Psychotherapy Theory, Research and Practice. 15 (3)
2. Margie Warrell (2014). Afraid Of Being 'Found Out?' How to Overcome Impostor Syndrome. [Online] Available At: http://www.Forbes.Com/Sites/Margiewarrell/2014/04/03/Impostor-Syndrome/
3. Berne, E, (1964). Games People Play: The Psychology Of Human Relationships. 1st Ed. USA: Grove Press, Inc.
4. Mezirow, J, (2002). Transformative Learning: Theory to Practice. New Directions for Adult and Continuing Education. 1997 (74), pp.5-12

PEOPLE PLEASING

5. Karpman, S, (2014). A Game Free Life: The Definitive Book on the Drama Triangle and Compassion Triangle by the Originator and Author. 1st Ed. USA: Drama Triangle Publications.
6. Berne, E (1999). Transactional Analysis. [Online] Available At: http://www.ericberne.com/Transactional-Analysis

GOING TO EXCESS

7. The Human Givens Institute (2002). Human Givens & Your Needs. [Online] Available At: http://www.hgi.org.uk/archive/human-givens.htm#. vluxb4qswoy.
8. Schön, D, (1987). Educating The Reflective Practitioner: Toward A New Design For Teaching And Learning In The Professions. 1st Ed. USA: Jossey-Bass Inc.
9. Hall, L, (2013). Mindful Coaching. London, UK: Kegan Page.
10. Bandler, R, Roberti, A & Fitzpatrick, O, (2013). The Ultimate Introduction to NLP: How to Build a Successful Life. 1st Ed. London, England: Harper Collins.

FIERCE INDEPENDENCE

11. Coleman, H, (2010). Empowering Yourself: The Organizational Game Revealed. 2nd Ed. USA: Author House.
12. De Shazer, S & Dolan, Y, (2007). More than Miracles: The State Of The Art of Solution-Focused Brief Therapy (Haworth Brief Therapy). 1st Ed. USA: The Haworth Press Inc.

CYNICISM
13. Felps, W, Mitchell, T & Byington, E, (2006). How, When, And Why Bad Apples Spoil The Barrel: Negative Group Members And Dysfunctional Groups. Research in Organizational Behaviour. 27 Pp.175-222
14. Jane McGonigal (2012). The Game That Can Give You 10 Extra Years of Life. [Online] Available At: https://www.ted.com/Talks/Jane_Mcgonigal_The_Game_That_Can_Give_You_10_Extra_Years_Of_Life?Language=En.
15. Dweck, C, (2007). Mindset: How You Can Fulfil Your Potential. 1st Ed. USA: The Random House Publishing Group.
16. Freud, S, (1912). The Dynamics of Transference. Standard Edition. 12, pp.97-108
17. Vector Group (2010). Model: Energy Investment. [Online] Available At: http://www.vectorgroupinc.com/Documents/Vectorgroup_Energyinvestmentmodel.pdf.
18. Magoun, H.W., (1952). An Ascending Reticular Activating System in the Brain Stem. AMA Archives of Neurology and Psychiatry. 67 (2), pp.145-154
19. Boniwell, I, (2006). Positive Psychology in a Nutshell: A Balanced Introduction to the Science of Optimal Functioning. 1st Ed. UK: PWBC.
20. Seligman, M, (2011). Flourish: A New Understanding Of Happiness And Well-Being - And How To Achieve Them. 1st Ed. USA: Free Press.

DRIVEN BY FEAR
21. Freud, S, (1914). Psychopathology of Everyday Life; Trans. By A. A. Brill. 1st Ed. USA: The MacMillan Company.
22. Preston, T, (2009). Coach Yourself To Success. 1st Ed. UK: Management Books 2000.

OSTRICH
23. Cannon, W.B., (1927). Bodily Changes in Pain, Hunger, Fear, and Rage. 1st Ed. USA: D. Appleton And Company.
24. Luft, J, & Ingham, H, (1961). The Johari Window: A Graphic Model of Awareness in Interpersonal Relations. Human Relations Training News, 5(9), pp.6-7.
25. Kruger, J., & Dunning, D. (1999). Unskilled And Unaware Of It: How Difficulties In Recognizing One's Own Incompetence Lead To Inflated Self-Assessments. Journal of Personality and Social Psychology, 77(6), 1121.
26. Farrelly, F, Brandsma, J. M., & McMahon, I, (1974). Provocative Therapy. Capitola, CA: Meta Publications.
27. Robinson, W. L., (1974). Conscious Competency – The Mark of a Competent Instructor. The Personnel Journal. 53, pp.538-539.

PERFECTIONISM
28. Goleman, D. (2000). Leadership That Gets Results. Harvard Business Review, 78(2), 78-93.

29. Enns, M. W., Cox, B. J., Sareen, J., & Freeman, P. (2001). Adaptive and Maladaptive Perfectionism in Medical Students: A Longitudinal Investigation. Medical Education, 35(11), 1034-1042.

PROCRASTINATION
30. Jung, C. G. (1966). Psychology and Religion. Yale University Press.
31. Ellis, A. (1978). Conquering Low Frustration Tolerance. Institute for Rational Living.
32. Epstein, J (2002). Think You Have A Book In You? Think Again. [Online] Available At: http://www.nytimes.com/2002/09/28/Opinion/Think-You-Have-A-Book-In-You-Think-Again.Html.
33. Danziger, S, Levav, J, & Avnaim-Pesso, L, (2011). Extraneous Factors in Judicial Decisions. Proceedings of the National Academy of Sciences, 108(17), pp.6889-6892.

PERFORMANCE ANXIETY
34. Cannon, W.B., (1927). Bodily Changes in Pain, Hunger, Fear, and Rage. 1st Ed. USA: D. Appleton And Company.
35. Tracy, J. L., & Robins, R. W. (2004). Putting the Self into Self-Conscious Emotions: A Theoretical Model. Psychological Inquiry, 15(2), pp.103-125.
36. Carney, D. R., Cuddy, A. J., & Yap, A. J. (2010). Power Posing. Brief Nonverbal Displays Affect Neuroendocrine Levels and Risk Tolerance. Psychological Science, 21(10), pp.1363-1368.
37. Amy Cuddy (2012). Your body language shapes who you are. [ONLINE] Available at: http://www.ted.com/talks/amy_cuddy_your_body_language_shapes_who_you_are?language=en.
38. Bandler, R, Roberti, A & Fitzpatrick, O, (2013). The Ultimate Introduction to NLP: How to Build a Successful Life. 1st Ed. London, England: Harper Collins.

SEARCHING FOR FULFILMENT
39. Ellis, A. (1997). Must Musturbation And Demandingness Lead To Emotional Disorders? Psychotherapy: Theory, Research, Practice, Training, 34(1), 95.
40. Pink, D. H. (2011). Drive: The Surprising Truth about What Motivates Us. Penguin.
41. Rotter, J. B. (1966). Generalized Expectancies for Internal Versus External Control of Reinforcement: Psychological Monographs: General & Applied 80(1) 1966, pp.1-28.
42. Preston, T, (2009). Coach Yourself To Success. 1st Ed. UK: Management Books 2000.

COPING WITH LOSS
43. Kübler-Ross, E. (1997). On Death and Dying. Simon and Schuster.

44. Schön, D, (1987). Educating The Reflective Practitioner: Toward A New Design For Teaching And Learning In The Professions. 1st Ed. USA: Jossey-Bass Inc.
45. Egan, G. (2013). The Skilled Helper: A Problem-Management and Opportunity-Development Approach to Helping. Cengage Learning.
46. Kline, N. (1999). Time to Think. Hachette UK.
47. Debord, G. (1955). Introduction to a Critique of Urban Geography. Critical Geographies A Collection of Readings.
48. Magoun, H.W., (1952). An Ascending Reticular Activating System in the Brain Stem. AMA Archives of Neurology and Psychiatry. 67 (2), pp.145-154

ACKNOWLEDGEMENTS

A lot of people contributed to this book in a variety of ways. We couldn't have done it without you all.

Thank you to:

Our team of reviewers for giving up their valuable time to review our work and for their honest feedback which allowed us to re-shape the book to better effect. The people in this group didn't know one other and all provided different perspectives. Thank you to: Alex Runciman, Andrea Tomasini, Cait Clucas, Dave Perrin, Julie Starr, Marion Scott, Paul Goddard, Pete Freeman, Rebecca Traeger, Roger Malvern, Sam Laing and Sophie Goldsworthy.

Simon Machin should be in the list above but we want to reserve special thanks for him. He has gone above and beyond in his role as reviewer, carving out time where we thought none could be carved and still coming back for more!

All our coaching clients over the years who have inspired us and who have given us our belief in our clients' infinite potential and the transformative power of coaching.

Our interviewees. We have been privileged to interview a number of highly successful people who have generously donated their time, reflections and insights for the benefit of our readers. We learned something from each of them and are greatly indebted to them for their generosity and openness.

Our design team of Ole Størksen and Saira Aspinall who have combined to take our somewhat brief brief and run with it to produce something that looks even better than we could have imagined. Thank you.

Our two editors, Xanthe Wells and subsequently Robin Bradshaw, for their contributions to the editing process and for coping with the interesting challenges of working with two authors.

Our friends and families
Thank you to everyone who has encouraged me over the years to write a book based on my coaching work and to all of you who have supported me during the writing process.

Kim

For my part I can't thank my family enough for supporting me on this project especially so soon after the last one! I will remember Cody's words of 'why do you have to write so much Daddy?' for a long time but he has, along with his sister Freya and my wife Alison, been very patient and understanding of my 'writing time'. Thank you, and I love you.

Geoff